Couples in Conflict

Couples in Conflict

A Family Systems Approach to Marriage Counseling

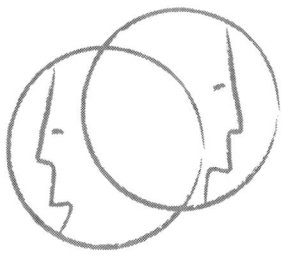

RONALD W. RICHARDSON

Fortress Press
Minneapolis

COUPLES IN CONFLICT
A Family Systems Approach to Marriage Counseling

Copyright © 2010 Fortress Press, an imprint of Augsburg Fortress. All rights reserved. Except for brief quotations in critical articles or reviews, no part of this book may be reproduced in any manner without prior written permission from the publisher. Visit http://www.augsburgfortress.org/copyrights/ or write to Permissions, Augsburg Fortress, Box 1209, Minneapolis, MN 55440.

Unless otherwise noted, Scripture quotations are taken from the *New Revised Standard Bible*, copyright © 1989 by the Division of Christian Education of the National Council of Churches of Christ in the USA. Used by permission. All rights reserved.

Cover art: © Images.com/Corbis/Jami Jennings
Cover designed by Laurie Ingram
Book designed by Zan Ceeley, Trio Bookworks

Library of Congress Cataloging-in-Publication Data

Richardson, Ronald W. (Ronald Wayne), 1939-
 Couples in conflict : a family systems approach to marriage counseling / Ronald W. Richardson.
   p. cm.
 Includes bibliographical references (p. 241) and index.
 ISBN 978-0-8006-9628-3 (alk. paper)
 1. Pastoral counseling. 2. Marriage counseling. 3. Systemic therapy (Family therapy) I. Title.
 BV4012.27.R53 2010
 253.5'2—dc22
                    2010023035

The paper used in this publication meets the minimum requirements of American National Standard for Information Sciences — Permanence of Paper for Printed Library Materials, ANSI Z329.48-1984.
Manufactured in the U.S.A.

Contents

Preface   xi
   A Unique Approach   xi
   A Particular Audience   xii
   A Pastoral Perspective on the Counseling Relationship   xv
   Notes to the Reader   xvi
   Acknowledgments   xvi

Part 1
Family Systems Theory and Marital Conflict

1. A New Way of Caring   3
   The Importance of Theory   4
   A Brief History of Bowen Family Systems Theory   6
   The Family as an Emotional Unit   7
   Thinking about People in Their Emotional Context   8
   Systems Thinking, Theology, Causation,
      and the Counselor's Role   11

2. Emotional Systems   15
   The Idea of a System   15
   Emotion, Thinking, and Feeling in the Bowen Theory   17
   The Life Forces: Togetherness and Individuality   21

3. **Anxiety and the Emotional System**   25
    Two Kinds of Anxiety   26
    Anxiety and Fusion   27
    Anxiety and the Two Life Forces   29

4. **Differentiation of Self**   33
    Fusion and Closeness
        (Or, Two "I's" Do Not Make a "We")   34
    My Definition of Closeness   35
    What Is Differentiation of Self?   36
    The Differentiation Continuum   39

5. **Triangles**   45
    Some Examples of Triangles   46
    The Close/Distant Dance and the Origin of
        Triangles   48
    Fluid and Fixed Triangles   53
    Dealing with Triangles: Neutrality   58

6. **The Emotional Development of a Couple and a Family**   61
    The Marital Contract and the Emergence of
        Counseling   61
    The Two Become One?   63
    Faith and Marriage   64
    The Family Life Cycle   65
    Sibling Position   66

7. **Symptomatic Mechanisms**   69
    Emotional Distance   70
    Marital Conflict   72
    Over- and Underfunctioning Reciprocity and
        Personal Dysfunction   74
    Projection of Anxiety to a Child   77
    The Triangular Relationship   78

Part 2
Family Systems Theory in Counseling

8. **The Counseling Relationship in the Bowen Theory**   85
    The Counseling Relationship as Cure?   85
    Bowen Theory, Counseling, and "Individual Problems"   86
    Emotional Latitude and Differentiation   87
    The Counselor's Family History   89
    The Counseling Relationship in a Larger Perspective   90
    The Assumed and Assigned Importance of a
        Significant Other   91
    Bowen's Different Approach   93
    The Expression of Feelings in Counseling   94
    Counseling as Coaching   95
    Neutrality and Pastoral Caring   96

9. **Getting Started and Assessing the Couple**   99
    The First Contact   99
    Avoiding Secrets   101
    Dual Relationships   102
    Doing Assessments   103
    Assessment Criteria for Moderate and Severe
        Marital Conflict   111
    Assessing for Physical Abuse and Fighting   114

10. **Goals for the Counseling Process**   119
    Reducing Anxiety   119
    Altering the Emotional Climate   122
    Being in Charge of Process   123
    Tracking the Relational Process   126
    First Counseling Session with George and Martha:
        Exploring Reactivity   127
    Interruptions and Being in Charge of the In-Office
        Process   132
    Increasing Self-Focus   133
    Engaging Both Partners and "Resistance"   134

Shifting the Relationship Process   135
Thinking about Family   137

11. Addressing the Triangles in Counseling   141
Defining and Managing Self in the Counseling Triangle   142
Working with the Couple's Triangles   144
Some Examples of Marital Triangles   146
Triangles and Change   149
The Affair Triangle   151
Opening Communication   155

12. The Counseling Process: Beginning Phase   157
Working for Self-Focus   157
The Essence of Change   160
A Verbatim Example: Starting to Develop Self-Focus   161

13. The Transition to Middle-Phase Counseling   173
Markers of the Middle Phase   173
Looking at Martha's Hurt   174
Working with Martha's Bitterness   178
The Next Session and Martha's Emptiness   181
A Turning Point with Martha and "Old Family History"   183
Some Specific Aspects of the Transition Phase   186
A Spiritual Crisis   188
The Move Toward Family and Unresolved Emotional Attachment   191

14. The Counseling Process: Middle Phase   195
Unresolved Emotional Attachment   195
Getting Ready for Family-of-Origin Work   197
Coaching George on His Family Work   198
Martha Goes Further into Her Emotional Cutoff   203

15. Coaching Family-of-Origin Work   211
Reentering the Family as a Researcher   212
Developing a Multigenerational Family Diagram   215

Differentiation and Triangles 216
Special Points of Concern for Coaching 218

16. The Counseling Process: The Termination Phase 223
Premature or Early Termination 223
Termination in Later Phases of the Work 225
Ending with George and Martha 227
Rethinking Beliefs and Values 228

Afterword: On Character 231
Appendix 1: Family Diagram Symbols 237
Appendix 2: Training Programs in
   Bowen Family Systems Theory 239
Selected Bibliography 241
Index 243

Preface

All couples have conflicts. This is normal. Conflicted couples are those who regularly fight over issues without arriving at a mutually acceptable resolution. Unable to successfully negotiate the emotional difficulties of their relationships, conflicted couples experience unhappiness in their marriages, often for many years. Some couples divorce, which creates significant personal and social disruption for all involved. But individuals who choose to stay together unhappily rather than divorce can also develop problems that may not appear as marital conflict. Such problems may manifest in physical, emotional, or social dysfunction in one of the partners (for example, depression or alcoholism) or in issues with their children. The inability to manage marital conflict can have an impact on a couple's immediate and extended family, their congregational relationships, their life of faith, and, cumulatively, on the whole of society.

A Unique Approach

This book is a guide for trained pastors, laypersons, and pastoral counselors in the theory and practice of counseling couples experiencing severe marital conflict. The uniqueness of this book lies in its use of a family systems theory developed by American psychiatrist Murray Bowen as a way of understanding marital conflict and what it means to function pastorally with conflicted couples. What I present is based on Bowen's seminal text *Family Therapy in Clinical Practice* (New York:

Jason Aronson, 1978) and my many years of experience employing Bowen's system in my own practice.

The approach to working with conflicted couples I present does not involve getting partners to experience and express their feelings to one another, although this will happen. It does not involve the pastoral counselor being deeply empathetic and expressing warmth and support for the couple in their struggles, although couples may experience this. It does not involve teaching couples a variety of communication skills and other problem-solving strategies for running a successful relationship, although a couple's skills will undoubtedly improve in these areas. Nor does it involve directly teaching them what our faith says about marriage and the good life, although I believe the couple will become clearer about these things.

The counseling approach offered here is not a simple, quick fix for marital discord. It is about creating an atmosphere in the counseling situation where people can think more clearly for themselves how they want to be in relationship with one another, based on their personal beliefs, values, and commitments. A counselor who acquires the skills described in this book will discover them to be useful not only in counseling situations but in the whole of pastoral ministry.

Although based on Bowen theory, what I present here is not necessarily how Dr. Bowen would have functioned. Rather, it represents my best effort to understand the practical applications of his theory within a framework of pastoral counseling. The outline of this book is simple. Part 1 looks at what Bowen theory says about the context and nature of marital conflict, the various ways it manifests in families, and how Bowen theory concepts apply to the emotional process involved. Following an overview of the counseling relationship, part 2 addresses the practical application of the theory to conflicted couples, with verbatims recounting my work with one couple. Part 2 will make little sense without first understanding part 1. Indeed, without a proper understanding of the theory the practice would be impossible to implement.

A Particular Audience

This is a book about providing pastoral counsel to couples in emotional conflict. I am speaking primarily about married couples, and I am referring primarily to marital conflict, but the principles are applicable to helping any two people (or more) who are experiencing conflict within a close emotional relationship. Although I speak of two people, a dyad, this is really a book about the powerful networks of close interconnections known as emotional systems within which all of us live—often unaware of the pervasive and powerful influence of these connections.

The counseling approach I present includes respecting the individuals we counsel and their concerns, but also the people with whom they are closely connected and the quality of their relationships with those people. This book is about honoring and being respectful of and concerned about the well-being of whole families or the whole system in which the partners of the couple are embedded. When we respect their families, we show the ultimate respect for the counselees.

By "pastoral counselors," I refer primarily to ordained pastors and priests. But I do not mean exclusively ordained clergy. Many laypeople provide pastoral care and counsel to others. As I use it here, pastoral refers to a theologically informed attitude or intent in counseling rather than the counselor's professional designation, qualifications, and type of training. Marriage and family therapists, social workers, psychologists, psychiatrists, as well as the neighbor next door can be pastoral.

There is, however, a difference between pastors who do counseling and pastoral counseling as a profession. I regard someone trained and certified by the American Association of Pastoral Counselors (AAPC) as the ultimate example of a pastoral counselor. Ongoing supervision is essential to being a consistently good counselor. Simply being a good pastor or a caring person is not enough. Certification within a professional organization like the AAPC means recognition by other professionals of one's level of expertise, offers a more objective evaluation of one's gifts, and indicates the growing edges in one's efforts to help others. It is irresponsible and unethical not to have training and supervision in place if pastors want to provide regular counseling to their parishioners. It may make them legally vulnerable as well.

In a nutshell, effective couple counseling requires a practitioner who:

- has a good theoretical grasp of how emotional systems function;
- sees the complex systemic whole and not just the individual parts;

- brings a lower level of anxiety to the conflictual situation;
- defines a self by maintaining his or her own thinking about system functioning, without needing to teach or convince others of its truth;
- maintains a level of differentiation and remains neutral within the normal counseling triangles that will exist;
- is not swayed by the individually oriented diagnosing and analyzing around him or her, that goes with the human condition;
- does not change that way of thinking when under pressure from others; and
- still connects emotionally with all the other parties involved.

Most pastors do not have a lot of time for counseling and must limit the number of counseling sessions they offer a couple. Furthermore, most pastors lack advanced training in counseling, which means that they cannot take on the more difficult and complicated cases. This is especially a problem in rural areas where pastors are often the only resource available to persons in need of counseling.

The Bowen family systems theory can be helpful to pastors with limited time and training in working with moderately conflicted couples on a short-term basis (up to ten sessions). Even a single session with a person trained in Bowen theory will be helpful to many counselees. People presenting with much more difficult and intense conflict will need to be referred to a professional counselor for reasons of time if not expertise (except of course in settings where the pastor is the only resource available).

People who have had some training in the Bowen theory will be able to make the best use of this book. For those who do not have training, I strongly encourage them to seek out a postgraduate training center where they can receive more didactic and practical training in the theory. Many such centers work with a distance-training model, so one does not have to be physically close to a center to get the training, and phone supervision is usually available. I especially recommend this additional training for full-time pastoral counselors. Pastors who work in a setting where financial resources are limited may be able to get denominational money to help with training and support. I give a list of training centers in the Bowen theory in appendix 2. Full-time pastoral counselors and pastors who have more time to give to counseling will be able to make use of the approach described here on an in-depth, longer-term basis.

Based on the idea that there is nothing more practical than a good theory, the goal of this book is to provide a consistent and comprehensive way of understanding human emotional functioning, including our own functioning and acts of caring. It is my hope that this book will provide pastors with a way of thinking and an ability to offer effective counsel to others even when they find themselves in highly unusual marital circumstances—as we often do.

A Pastoral Perspective on the Counseling Relationship

As Christian pastors, we are interested in spreading the gospel message. We see this as a primary calling in life. We also have a calling to care for others. Clergy of other faiths have some similar concerns within their faith framework. There are many ways available to us for communicating the gospel and expressing care. There is a scale of communication of Christian content in which variation depends on the degree of pastor-focused initiative around the message versus a person focus:

1. *Preaching* is very pastor/message centered.
2. *Teaching* is somewhat more interactive.
3. *Pastoral care* tends to be more of a listening office for the pastor.
4. *Pastoral Counseling* is even more person or family centered.

There is a form of counseling that is more focused on communicating the content of faith. I would call it "Christian counseling" rather than pastoral counseling. It sees counseling as an opportunity to evangelize and preach or teach the gospel. In its crudest form it tends to say, "Jesus is the answer to all of your life problems." It can be much more sophisticated than this but the message will be the same in this type of counseling. Counselees tend to be seen as getting better or not based on how accepting they are of the message. I once had a person come to see me who had been to a Christian counselor. I do not know what the counselor actually said to her, but the message she got was, "You won't get better until you eat and drink of the body and blood of our Lord." She did not think that helped.

The kind of counseling I am talking about is not seen as an opportunity to verbally proclaim the gospel or even to teach it. I hope that I am living the gospel in how I relate to counselees, but that is usually as far as I go. I do not normally use faith words to interpret my behavior. This is generally how pastoral counselors, as defined by the AAPC, see their activity. It is counselee focused and works in relation to their concerns. While we clearly see the theological dimensions of what we do, we do not have a specific verbal message to proclaim. It is a form of caring that is based on action and not verbal message.

Notes to the Reader

Although I am retired from pastoral counseling, I write about my work in the present tense. This is simply to provide a greater sense of immediacy and less cumbersome sentences involving the past tense. At points throughout the text I use the word *we* when I could just as easily be talking about counselees. I do this whenever I think the information pertains to us as fellow human beings who may also share in the issue being discussed.

The case histories are all composites of various counseling situations and the identities of counselees are protected; however, they represent what actually happens in counseling and are, in this sense, true.

Acknowledgments

My deepest appreciation goes to those who gave of their time and interest to read and comment on this manuscript: Douglas Anderson, Randy Frost, and Michael Fogel. Their comments and suggestions were most useful in making this a more intelligible and useful book. I also thank Susan Johnson and her editorial staff at Fortress Press for their hard work in making this book more accessible to readers. Of course, any shortcomings are totally my own.

I also wish to thank all of those couples who were willing to open up their lives to me and engage with me in learning about how marital conflict functions in their relationships. They demonstrated a level of courage and commitment to their own development that was admirable.

PART 1

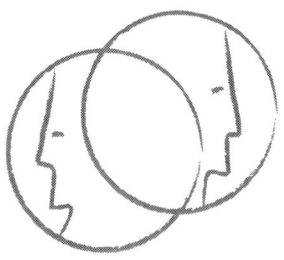

FAMILY SYSTEMS THEORY AND MARITAL CONFLICT

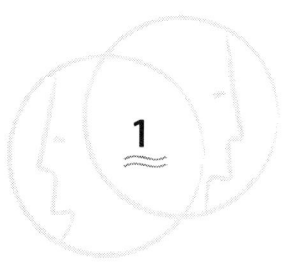

1

A New Way of Caring

George and Martha came into my pastoral counseling office for our first meeting. After some preliminaries, I asked, "What brings you in?" George said, "After over twenty-six years of marriage and fighting nearly every day, we are thinking of splitting. Our grown-up son thinks we should, too. A friend of mine said you might be able to help us." Martha, with a much angrier tone, filled in some of the details as to what they fought about. More important to her than the issues themselves ("All my friends say they fight about these things with their husbands") was the intensity of the anger she felt. She was so resentful of what George had said and done over the years, and what he had failed to do, that she did not think she could ever forgive him, let alone have warm feelings for him again. George was more optimistic but he appeared rather clueless as to why she was so upset. He claimed to have none of these feelings himself. I will trace my work with this couple through the rest of this book.

The number of things couples can argue and fight about is unlimited. There are the standard issues like money, sex, love (as in "Do you love me?"), affairs, children, relatives, work schedules, roles in and out of the house, reliability and trustworthiness, vacations, beliefs, politics, and so forth. Each couple has its own creative way of discovering twists and turns in these issues. George and Martha fought over all of these. In addition, George had had a couple of one-night stands at conventions he attended.

So what do we do when couples in conflict present us with their unique stories of warring with one another, wanting our help? How do we proceed? How do we provide pastoral counsel? What will be truly helpful? I want to introduce you to a new way of caring for people in emotional difficulty.

A mature, experienced minister had a reputation for being of help to couples in difficulty. He had a young seminarian working with him who had heard about his reputation and asked if he could sit in on a counseling session. The minister said, "Sure. As a matter of fact, a couple is coming in right now and you can join us." So the couple came in and the minister asked them what the problem was. The husband started with a long list of complaints about his wife and all the ways she was wrong and behaved badly. At the end of his complaints, the minister responded to the husband, "You know, you are exactly right." Then he turned to the wife and asked her how she saw things. She launched into a similar list of complaints about her husband, how wrong he was and how fed up she was. Then the minister said to her, "You know, you are exactly right." The seminarian, staring at the minister in disbelief, blurted out, "But Reverend, you just told each of them they are right. They can't both be right." The minister then said to him, "You know, you are exactly right."

This is not a postmodern book about the relativity of perspectives, or a book that claims there is no ultimate good or bad, or right or wrong in the world. As its author, I am more of a positivist than that. I believe in facts, I believe in values, and I believe there are better and worse ways to accomplish our goals. Part of the point of this story has to do with how we think about all of these things. And that is where I want to start this book: How do we think about human beings and the difficulties we get ourselves into in our close, intimate relationships? Moreover, what is a good way to get through it all and get on with doing the good things life and marriage can be about?

The Importance of Theory

Our assessment of the nature of human difficulties stems out of the theory with which we are working. Whoever we are and however we proceed to try to be of help, we will be operating out of some kind of theory about human functioning that assumes some answers to the questions above, whether we have consciously thought about the theory or not. This is inescapable.

What "works" in counseling is a theoretical issue. If we are serious about being of help to others, on a consistent basis, it behooves us to look at the issue of theory. Does the theory fit with our identity as pastoral counselors? Does the theory's idea of a good outcome fit with our own beliefs and values about marriage?

Dr. Murray Bowen taught psychiatry at the Jesuit-governed Georgetown University in Washington, D.C. He would not have spoken about his work as pastoral care, but there was plenty of caring in his work with his patients. He had a decent dialogue with theologians at the university and a number of them were able to claim Dr. Bowen's ideas as consistent with (though certainly not the same as) their own beliefs about human beings. This was one of my attractions to Bowen as well. This book is a challenge to look at your own beliefs and to figure out where you stand theoretically. I make the challenge by telling you where I stand.

Theory, as I use the term here, does not mean an idea or a hunch as it often does in popular use, as when people say, "I have a theory about that." Bowen used the term as a scientist would, as a formal statement of how things work. It is based on observation of behavior, forming hypotheses, developing experimental protocols as a way to test the observations, and then confirmation through being able to predict behavior using the hypothesis or theoretical concept. Does the hypothesis fit what is happening? Does it allow prediction as to what will happen next? And does it offer useful explanations for the observed relationship patterns and what to do about them?

Dr. Bowen pointed out that people had long been looking at old fossilized bones embedded in sedimentary rock, of creatures that lived many thousands of years before us. No one knew quite what to make of the bones, especially since many of the creatures were not known to exist anywhere on the planet. Then along came Charles Darwin who offered a theory that could help make sense of what was being observed. As Bowen said, without Darwin's theory we had a kind of "observational blindness;" we were unable to account for what was right in front of our eyes. This is what a good theory does for us. It provides a way of seeing what has always been in front of us.

Whatever you arrive at theoretically for yourself will have tremendous practical significance. All action is based on some sort of presumption about the nature of reality, of what constitutes human nature, and what it means to be effective in our acts of helping. We cannot function without a theory, whether it is examined or not.

A Brief History of Bowen Family Systems Theory

Dr. Murray Bowen worked with a huge variety of deeply troubled individuals, couples, and families. His truly pioneering work in developing family-systems-based psychotherapy, starting in the early 1950s, is equivalent to the kind of revolution wrought by Sigmund Freud. He won a National Institute of Mental Health (NIMH) grant to hospitalize not only his severely impaired schizophrenic patients but also their mothers. Quickly discovering that the emotional issues were much larger than just between the patient and the mother, he got another NIMH grant in 1954 to hospitalize whole families.

He put together a team of researchers to observe, as objectively as possible, family interactions. This was not primarily a treatment program. He wanted to understand the functioning of these families and what sort of family processes might, for example, lead to a schizophrenic break for "the patient." Whole families lived in cottages on the NIMH grounds as they led normal lives. The father went off to work and the "normal" siblings of the patient went to school. The researchers observed each family member on a round-the-clock basis. They watched the family as it "ate, played, and worked together through periods of success, failure, crisis, and physical illness," for up to two-and-a-half years.

The prevailing theory at the time was that the schizophrenic child's problems were a result of a dominating mother and a passive father. However, the mother was seen as the real problem. She was called the schizophrenogenic mother. Bowen wanted to see whether any of this was so, and how things worked in these families. Eventually, he began to see that the psychotic breaks of the patient were, in fact, the symptom of an emotional process at work in the whole family.

Bowen, who enjoyed watching football, said that his research was like observing families from the top of the stadium, rather than being down on the sidelines and having a more limited, partial view of the action. From up high, with a wider angle of view, he could see the whole process of interaction, what each person was doing and how they were moving within the family.

By 1960, he decided that most children's problems were connected with difficulties between the parents. He stopped treating the children who bore the symptoms and who appeared to be "the problem" in the family. Parents who bought the idea that the issue was theirs and that they needed to modify their relationship discovered that their child's symptoms disappeared. He began to use his theory exclusively with all of his patients, including those in his private practice, and it lead to good treatment outcomes.

Then he made a huge, unprecedented jump: he began to apply his concepts to himself and his own family. Thus began a twelve-year effort to study his own family of origin and his part in the emotional process there. He discovered a consistency of emotional process through all of the families he worked with, including his own. The primary difference between them was in the intensity of the emotionality, with the most symptomatic families being the most intense.

In addition, his psychiatry residents at Georgetown tried out his ideas in their own families as well as with their patients. He noted that the students who worked on relationships with their own family members were also doing the best in their clinical work. They were working out their own personal and relational issues with the use of his theory, and presenting themselves less often for therapy.

The Family as an Emotional Unit

Bowen developed the idea of the family, rather than the individual, as the primary unit for understanding human functioning. He thought trying to understand problems from the individual point of view gave only limited information. Individuals' problems (and strengths) are strongly connected to their interactions with others. Individuals contain only a part of the problem. They are not "*the* problem." A good understanding of any one individual is accomplished only by seeing that person as part of a larger whole.

This perspective is not the same as seeing the family as a group. The group concept is still about a collection of individuals who have "group interactions." His approach conceives of the family as a single emotional organism, not simply as a group of individuals who have somewhat closer emotional ties. Even though the forces may be invisible, the governing power of the emotional system over the individual can totally affect the trajectory of a person's life.

Bowen's thinking about families went against the prevailing theoretical and therapeutic ideas of his day. Nearly all of psychology and psychoanalysis focused on the individual and the deep inner processes of the psyche. In couple conflicts, for example, the difficulties might be because an obsessive personality had married a hysteric personality. This was a typical diagnostic formulation. Each person needed psychotherapy in order to get past their impasse. I used this model when I began doing counseling after graduate school. I did not just use it with counselees. I could also diagnose my wife's problems, or anyone else with whom I had conflicts. Conveniently, the individual model allowed me to leave myself out of these diagnostic formulations.

One small, nontherapeutic example of the usefulness of the perspective of family as the primary emotional unit is when I do consultation with various kinds of staff groups. As part of my work with them, I often ask them to do a presentation of their family of origin to the group. As each staff member presents his or her family, the others express some variation of enlightenment like, "Ah, now I get it. I can see how you got to be the person you are with us here on this staff." The person's staff behavior is put in a larger perspective. It is as if they are seeing a person whole, as part of a larger unity that they knew nothing about before; they are now getting the complete picture and the person makes more sense to them. Staff groups find this helps them stop personalizing their problematic interactions with one another.

Thinking about People in Their Emotional Context

Seeing the family as a single emotional organism requires a major shift in our own thinking. From infancy, not just in graduate school, we are taught to see problems as a result of processes within individual people and their personalities ("You are a bad little boy"; "You are a good little girl"). This goes all the way back to the garden of Eden. When God asks Adam about eating the fruit of the tree of the knowledge of good and evil, Adam blames Eve. She was the problem, not him. Then she blames the serpent, attempting to excuse herself. Neither one included him- or herself as a part of the problem. The more anxious we are, whether as participants in an emotional difficulty, or as helpers, the more likely we are to fall back on the individual model—"The difficulty in this relationship is you. You need to change and things will be better."

George and Martha each perceived themselves as a victim of the other who was the oppressor. We as helpers can easily take on the expected role of rescuer, siding with one individual against the other. This is a standard triangle. It is automatic. All families do a version of it around many different issues. Being a fluid process, the role of each family member can change. Family is where we learn our specific ways of acting out the pattern. Then we can play it out in any social grouping as adults: in a congregation, in our workplace, with friends, and even at a societal level between groups of people.

George and Martha had been to another counselor many years before coming to see me. George had the clear sense that the counselor sided with Martha and saw him as "the bad guy." George said, "I know I did a lot of bad stuff, but I don't think it was all just me." After just a few sessions with that counselor, George refused to continue so the marital counseling stopped. Martha continued for a few more sessions and said she enjoyed the counselor's support but eventually decided it was not doing any good if George was not involved.

Bowen's research team, in those early days, also could fall into this typical triangular way of thinking. In families where there is psychosis and anxiety is very high, it is a powerful temptation. His team members tended to identify with whomever they thought was the victim (they did not always agree on who this was); they would applaud the rescuing hero in the family, and be angry with the oppressive villain or persecutor. Bowen had to keep pulling them back from this individual good/bad orientation that required finding who was the bad guy that needed to change.

Slowly the team became more able to take the focus off the problematic behavior of a particular individual and his or her inner motivations and watch the overall process within the family, and even within themselves. They could stick with speaking in simple terms about the consistent patterns of family interactions, and how these fluctuated as the emotional intensity of the family went up and down. They learned to speak of function and stopped using the language of motivation and defenses that went with the individual model. They began to see the family as an emotional unit.

In our role as pastoral caregivers, even if we are not committed to the individual model, the more dramatic the parishioner's story (say it involves incredible acting out with wild drinking behavior, or homicidal or suicidal behavior, or physical abuse) the more we as helpers are likely to become anxious. The higher our anxiety level the more we feel the expectation to rescue particular individuals in difficulty. Those who can stay calmer and think systemically have a better chance of maintaining a unitary view and acting on it. The normal forces of emotional systems will want to drag us back into the individual model. It may "feel right" to do so.

Bowen described the difficulty his research team had with understanding families in the early days of his work:

> A nonparticipant observer might aspire to scientific objectivity, but, in the emotional tension that surrounds these families, he begins to participate emotionally in the family drama just as surely as he inwardly cheers the hero and hates the villain when he attends the theater. Clinical staff members have been able to gain workable objectivity by detaching themselves emotionally from the family problem. When it is possible to attain a workable level of interested detachment, it is then possible to defocus the individual and to focus on the entire family at once. (Bowen 1978:50)

In this book I show how finding the "workable level of interested detachment," what is also called neutrality, is the best way we can help people with emotional conflicts and difficulties. It is not easy to put this approach into practice. Apart from the intellectual challenges of understanding the theory, our own personal family functioning plays a major role in utilizing the theory. By becoming better observers of people in difficulty and reducing our level of emotional reactivity when in contact with them, we will get beyond blame and provide a better resource for them to deal with their difficulties.

Family-of-origin work is the best way I know to bring together theory and practice in our own lives. When we can achieve this way of thinking, and act on it, while in the midst of emotional processes in our own family, we will do a much better job with those we counsel.

Systems Thinking, Theology, Causation, and the Counselor's Role

Our main theological traditions, being the product of more individualistic philosophies, do not reveal much in the way of systems thinking (in spite of our term *systematic theology*). Causation is an issue that can interest both scientists and theologians, but they come at it from very different angles and with different assumptions. Biblical and theological thinkers are concerned mostly with ultimate causes. They try to answer "why" questions. When human beings behave unlovingly toward one another, we say that it is because of sin. Sin becomes the ultimate explanation for all of our bad behavior.

Science does not deal with ultimate causes. It cannot answer questions like why do we exist? or why are we sinful? It is interested in proximate causes. Scientists ask questions that have to do with *who, what, where, when,* and *how*. It is the same with Bowen theory and therapy. As Bowen theory practitioners, we do not ask why. Other forms of psychotherapy can spend a lot of time on why questions. This makes them more philosophical than scientific. Often their answers become elaborate and convoluted. This is in part why the psychology section on bookshelves is right next to the religion section.

Once we get started down the "why" road, it becomes a never-ending journey. Each "why" leads to a new one, and we sink deeper into the primordial ooze of causation, more and more losing any sense of what to do about it all. By restricting ourselves to the proximate causation questions, we counselors can deal with the observable facts of human functioning. None of us understands our own motivations, let alone those of others.

George and Martha had frequent arguments over "why" each was the way they were. When I told them that trying to discover the answers to those kinds of questions was not going to get us far, they agreed. As they learned to focus on the more proximate questions they gradually got out of the "why" thinking orientation. A focus on the functional facts is a way to understand complicated emotional systems.

I am even tempted to say that "why" questions help us to avoid taking responsibility for our actions. In the garden of Eden God did not ask Adam and Eve "why" they ate the fruit of the tree. God simply asked about the fact of eating. Did they do it? But they responded with "why" answers. They would have loved to debate the "whys" with God and, ultimately, they might even have been able to argue it was God's fault that they went against the command not to eat the fruit. Debating "why" can let us off the hook.

I am not arguing there is no such thing as evil in the world. What I am saying is that when we eliminate ourselves from some sort of involvement in the problems we face, this is itself, in fact, a kind of evil. It can be, metaphorically speaking, the work of the devil to eliminate our own responsibility in our difficulties. Theologically, if we take the doctrine of the fall seriously, we cannot escape partial responsibility for the sins of the world. The good thing about this is we can be part of the solution as we focus on our part in it all.

In terms of traditional theological categories, I am talking about the doctrine of humanity, or theological anthropology. To go down this theological road is not the subject of this book. Who we are as human beings and how we factually function in relation to one another, at what times and in what ways, is where Bowen theory and our theology meet. We come at it from different angles and we use different language systems to talk about it. But the phenomenology of the action is the same.

In my role as counselor, I do not think of myself as an evangelist. I see myself as like John the Baptist, preparing the way for the Lord. In a sense, I am calling people to repentance, asking them to look at their behavior with each other and change it. I do not use biblical language to describe this to them. Functionally, I am asking them to think about their beliefs and values within the context of their marriage and family life, and decide how they could better live whatever faith they profess.

I see my work within the traditional theological category of sanctification—that we will grow toward becoming better, healthier, and more mature human beings. Bowen's concept of differentiation of self—maintaining who we are as individuals, while in relationship with others—is a primary goal of the counseling. Working on this goal is not a matter of salvation or works righteousness. We are justified before God whether we are better functioning human beings or not. However, working on our level of differentiation could be viewed in theological terms as growing into the human beings we are called to be.

As a pastoral counselor I regard myself, conceptually, as living on a bridge that connects two countries. At one end of the bridge is the land of science and Bowen theory and the concepts it uses. At the other end is the land of theology and its understanding of the purpose of human beings. They each have their own language and frame of reference, but both refer to the same human phenomenon. I never try to merge the two into one coherent way of thinking or language, but I can go back and forth, from one country or language system to another, and have commerce with both sides. If anything, I am the connection between them. I am the unity between the two in my own beliefs and opinions.

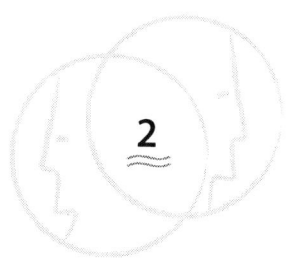

2

Emotional Systems

When George and Martha walked into my office, they were not just two individual people locked in conflict. They brought with them the emotional forces within which they were embedded. I think of these forces as an emotional aura, unseen but very powerful. Family systems theory helps us to sort out the influences resident both inside and outside of each partner and to decide where to focus our attention.

Of the eight primary concepts in Bowen family systems theory, three are about the overall characteristics of a system: (1) the nuclear family emotional system; (2) differentiation of self; and (3) triangles. The next four concepts deal with more specific emotional process characteristics: (4) sibling position; (5) projection to a child; (6) multigenerational projection process; and (7) emotional cutoff. Societal emotional process, the eighth concept, is about the application of these concepts to organizational and social groups. These concepts are about observable processes in a family and when they are described, people typically say, "Oh yes, of course. That fits with my experience."

The Idea of a System

My favorite image to describe a system is a hanging mobile. Each piece connects with the other pieces in a delicate balance. The movement of any one piece affects all of the others. If a piece disappears (death or divorce), or is added (birth or marriage), or changes weight (promotion or retirement), the balance of the whole is affected, and each part must adjust to create a new equilibrium.

Human family systems are like this except they are more complicated and the members are more deeply interconnected. As living organic systems, families change, grow, and shrink on their own. Their life is in constant flux. There are periods of stability and instability. People are content during times of stability and upset when instability strikes, as it inevitably will. Some upsets are major, requiring significant rebalancing, and life will never be the same for that family again.

For example, when the last child is grown and moves out, this leaves just the husband and wife together. They may not have experienced this situation for twenty to thirty years or more. The adult children who move out are also dealing with change and imbalance. This was the case with George and Martha. They came in to see me within four months of their twenty-two-year-old son leaving home. After managing, with some significant difficulty, so many other changes, this is what brought them into counseling.

I was immediately curious about the nature of the systemic attachments that influenced George and Martha. I began to see the strings that attached them to others in their family. As I began to inquire about these strings, they also became more aware of them. I am not suggesting they were puppets, but these influences affected the way they functioned, not unlike a classic *New Yorker* cartoon, which shows a couple with puppet strings attached to each of them. They are handing the control bars to each other and the wife says, "Free will is overrated." We are not completely autonomous in our relationships.

What happens in a family, for example, when one central member dies? Emotional shock waves can reverberate through a system with the loss of a key person. This person may have been the emotional fulcrum of the family's life. The more problematic or fused the family emotional process is, the more likely the shock wave will have profound consequences. Ideally, as families move through their normal life-cycle changes, the process is one in which all members are able to adapt flexibly without much difficulty.

As counselors, we see people connected to each other in powerful ways, even though the connections may not always be obvious. One high-level executive was apparently the model of the independent, self-made man. He had a wife and children, but he also had multiple affairs over the course of his twenty-three years of marriage. He did not think he could enjoy life without these affairs. Incredibly, his wife, with her own issues, had no suspicions of his affairs. She thought of him as a workaholic and that was why he was gone from home so much.

This man had little to do with his family of origin. He had not visited his eighty-plus-year-old parents for over twenty years. He said they did not figure in his life anymore. When, later in counseling, I suggested he might fly the two thousand miles that separated them to pay his parents a visit, he visibly shuddered. "Why would I want to do that?" he asked. It took this man, who was tough as nails in a boardroom encounter, a long time to find "the courage" to make this trip and spend a few days with his parents. When he was with them during the visit, his basic feeling was fear. This ignored connection with them was still very powerful, in spite of the passage of time and distance. In counseling, it became clear they were highly relevant to the way he managed his family life and his extramarital affairs.

George and Martha had strengths as well as difficulties. They managed to survive some major challenges and kept their family on track. They had enough flexibility to keep things in balance. Their grown son was doing okay in life and had now established some independence. He was launched successfully. George had gone to work each day in a tough, competitive environment, and Martha was a good homemaker. They also maintained an active social life.

I try to point out early in counseling the strengths every couple displays in their lives. When they come for counseling they often feel like failures. I make sure they know that I see the ways they are competent in life. This helps them put their difficulties in a larger perspective.

Emotion, Thinking, and Feeling in the Bowen Theory

It can be difficult to distinguish the way the Bowen theory uses terms like feeling, emotion, and thinking, so I am going to describe those here. The *emotional system* is much more than those powerful, conscious, affective experiences we call feelings like anger, sadness, fear, and joy. We are all deeply emotional creatures. It is part of being a living, breathing human being. Our word *emotion* has two linguistic sources: it comes most directly from the French word *emouvoir*, which usually means "to stir up," and from the Latin combination of *ex* ("from") plus *movere* ("to move"), often translated as "to move away" and sometimes "to disturb." When we are stirred up, as when angry, we distance ourselves emotionally. Emotionality is a disturbance of our normally calmer, more tranquil selves. As I use the term, however, we can still appear to be rational, calm, apparently unfeeling and unruffled—as many people, mostly males, are trained to be—and still be acting out of our emotionality. Frequently in counseling, one partner describes the other as unemotional. That partner can indeed behave like a computer or be machinelike in his or her way of functioning, and yet we can understand this as an aspect of his or her emotionality. This is different from whether or not they experience or express their feelings. Emotionality is like the nine-tenths of an iceberg that is below the surface, unseen but hugely powerful and dangerous if disturbed. It can be dangerous even for us clergy. I once knew a minister who responded to an emergency call from a wife who was fighting with her husband. He went to their house and when he tried to intervene the husband shot and nearly killed him.

Emotionality includes our instinctual behaviors. These are so basic to our being that they are observed in all human communities. These include the various types of processes related to the gathering of food and eating, reproduction, nurturing the young, sleep cycles, and so forth. Emotionality includes our physiological, cognitive, and behavioral processes. It includes the autonomic nervous system that keeps our bodies in functional balance without our conscious participation. Quite clearly related to the issue of marital conflict, it includes the universal fight/flight reactions. It includes our subjective feeling states (like fear, sadness, anger, joy) that we may or may not be aware of and that can influence our physiology. A great deal of our daily life is governed by our emotionality.

To speak of an emotional *system* recognizes that our relational processes are interconnected. I feel affected by what you do, in a close relationship with you, and you feel affected by how I react in response. In addition, it is not just you and I who are involved, but all the other people to whom we are connected. They impinge on our relationship with each other. They all make up our emotional system.

The mechanisms at work in our relationships are like automatic reflexes. They are as predictable, as Dr. Bowen said, as the life force that causes sunflowers to keep their face toward the sun. If we can accept that we are a part of these powerful emotional systems then we have a better chance of managing ourselves within them, of being different in our relationships, and of developing some degree of mastery over our automatic emotionality.

I mention one important side note here. There is a tendency to reify systems, to turn a systemic process into a thing. Systems do not exist as things. We cannot say "the system" thinks, feels, acts, and so forth. We do not even diagnose or provide counsel to systems. A term like "nuclear family emotional system" simply means the collective, deeply interconnected relational processes of the people involved as they go through their life together. A term like "the system" is shorthand for this emotional process.

The *intellectual system* refers to our ability to think, reason, and be more objective and less subjective about life and relationships. Subjectivity means the tendency to make ourselves the subject of whatever happens. Little children are subjective when, for example, they come into a room and find their mother crying; they think automatically that it is about them or something they did. We tend to put ourselves at the center of our emotional universe. Bette Midler has a great line in the movie *Beaches* when she says to her date, "Well, that is enough about me. Let's talk about you. What do you think of me?" As the saying goes, "It's not all about you." Subjectivity leads us to think it is.

No one is ever totally objective but some are more than others. To be more objective is to get outside of our own skin. It is the ability to see others and ourselves in context, to understand the larger processes at work and not "personalize" everything. In the work with George and Martha, they slowly became more objective. For example, their automatic emotional system led them to counterattack whenever one said something in anger that the other found insulting. As they became more objective, they were more able to interrupt this automatic reaction, and wonder, "What has him/her so stirred up? Is it really me, or something else? If it is me, what was going on when I did or said that? How are we going to slow this down and sort it out? What do I need to do right now to get something different happening?"

People have both emotionality and an ability to think and be rational. These are not totally discreet and separate processes in our brains. One is not better than the other. Generally, however, people who are more satisfied in their lives and relationships have a greater ability to separate the two and know when they are working more out of one mode or the other. There is a significant range of variability between people around this ability. The ability to be more thoughtful and rational when in the midst of emotional turmoil is a sign of more mature functioning.

What we call *feelings* are a result of the emotional and thinking systems combined. They are the more rationalized part of our emotionality; they are the part we can label as personal conscious experience. Subjectively, they are experienced either physically, or as an emotional state. They include our opinions that we "feel" strongly about. Often, when stating an opinion, we say, "I feel that . . ." We can hold our beliefs in this way. They can be part of our feeling experience and it can be difficult to have them as dispassionate intellectual experiences.

As we grow up in our families, we learn to label certain emotionally stirring experiences in particular ways with feeling words. Not all families and not all cultures label the same experiences in the same way. Here is a simple example. I am a certified ski instructor. If I take five neophyte skiers up to a steep mountaintop and say, "We are going down here," each of the five might have different feelings in reaction to the same event. One might be terror stricken, unable to move or even voice opposition. One might be fearful but trusting and say, "Whatever you say. You are the expert and you know best." One might be angry at me and say, "What kind of a sadist are you? Why are you making me do this? Are you trying to kill me?" One might have images of broken bones in a fall, but still feel sad that he cannot do what I say should be done. He knows it is his own fault because of his inadequacy and it will be another notch in his depressive lifestyle. Another person might say, "Oh boy, let's go. I can't wait to rip down this mountain. No more baby hills for me. Thanks for bringing us up here, Ron."

Each of these people has chemical reactions going on in their brains that represent the stirring up of their emotional system. They have each developed, over their years of growing up, different ways of interpreting and reacting to challenging situations, related partly to their temperament and partly to their contextual perceptions of themselves and others. As part of the intellectual system, they apply feeling words to the deeper, emotionally based subjective experience. None of the feelings are more right or wrong. It is just their personal feeling experience, developed over many years of living within their varied emotional contexts.

2 — Emotional Systems

The Life Forces:
Togetherness and Individuality

There are two powerful life forces at work in all of us: the force for togetherness and the force for individuality. We want to be together with others, and we want to be our own person. There is a universal human desire to be closely connected with other people, to have their approval and support and to live in harmony with them. We also want to pursue our own goals and be autonomous around what seems important to us. We do not want others always to tell us what to do, or how to be in life.

In relationship systems, when things are calm and there is a relatively low level of anxiety, both of these forces can be seen as compatible. Individuality is not in conflict with togetherness. As anxiety increases in an emotional system, however, the two forces can be perceived as opposites, pulling in different directions. Then, the togetherness force becomes more potent and individual thinking is discouraged. This can be an absolute advantage for survival. In times of physical crisis (like with floods, fires, earthquakes), it is normal to see people come together, to try to save others and work together to overcome the challenge.

This same dynamic can be observed in times of emotional crisis as well. The language of unity and teamwork will begin to dominate the discussion. People are encouraged to "get on the same page," and to think the same way. Anyone who wants to exercise their individuality, who does not think the same way, who wants to head in a different direction is considered selfish, uncaring for others, and maybe even traitorous. Just weeks after 9/11, one magazine invited twenty well-known authors to give their thoughts about the event. Susan Sontag, in her essay, did not see the United States as a totally innocent victim. She suggested that U.S. foreign policy shared responsibility in creating the conditions that led to this event. Some people immediately called her a traitor. Her life was even threatened. Apart from whether she was right or wrong, it was a clear example of how individual thinking was strongly criticized in that time of anxiety and crisis. If she had written these sentiments before 9/11, the reaction likely would not have been as strong.

In families, when the level of anxiety increases, the togetherness force becomes more powerful. For example, take a family of parents and three teenage children. One of the children may get in trouble with the law and be headed for "a delinquent life." It is common for the other four family members, in their anxiety, to focus on him and say that he is the problem in the family. They will pressure him to shape up. Perhaps the mother does not see it quite the same way. She speaks up for being "more understanding." Then the mother and father begin to have arguments in which each blames the other for the boy's behavior. They may fight with some version of the standard parental argument, where she says, "You are too strict!" and he says, "No, you are too lenient!" Then the other two children get more anxious as they watch their mother and father argue, and they lean on their brother even more, wanting him to shape up because he might cause their mother and father to divorce. He then says to them, "Look, I'm just living my own life. I can do what I want. Leave me alone." This demonstrates the togetherness and individuality forces as work.

George and Martha, like most conflicted couples, could not agree on many issues. Just as people can feel anxious and threatened in times of crisis and insist on a unified stance, and feel more anxious if unity is not achieved, so there can be an anxiety based on the threat of being swallowed up by the forced unity of togetherness. The threat is that self can be lost. Nearly everyone has struggled with their parents around this very issue. Having a sense of who we are, of our own unique individual identity, is basic to being a human being. We each want to be our own person. So the desired state of closeness that we want in marriage carries with it a potential threat. As a popular song asks, "If the two become one, which one will they become?" That is the dilemma every couple faces; how to be together while each partner remains a unique self. How to balance individuality and togetherness.

Often, without conscious thought, couples will divide responsibilities for this balance with one in charge of the closeness (this person is called the *emotional pursuer*) and the other in charge of the distance and getting some space for self (this person is called the *emotional distancer*). Pursuing and distancing, in overt or subtle ways, is a dance performed in nearly every close relationship in an attempt to deal with the two life forces of togetherness and individuality.

Sometimes these relational strategies get confused with the personality of a person. For example, a wife said of her husband, "Oh, he is a big distancer. He doesn't want to be close." I asked in response,

"Tell me what he was like when you were courting? How did the two of you manage to get together?" Then she said, "Well, that is the interesting thing. Back then I was pretty uncertain about wanting to be with him. I was actually kind of cool toward him and he totally chased me. He wanted to be with me all of the time. It bugged me. But he eventually won me over." Then I said to her something like, "Isn't that interesting—this guy who doesn't seem to want to be close to you now, back then wanted closeness more than you did. What do you think changed?"

Questions like this begin to challenge the idea that issues of closeness and distance are simply about personalities rather than about relational processes. When people can hear a question like this and begin to think about it, then a shift begins to happen between the partners. They will see the interactive quality of the relationship and how each person plays out a different part of the process.

The togetherness force brings us together in marriage, to create families, and to join other social groupings. Human beings are the most social species on the planet. We enjoy watching a dance group or hearing an orchestra perform. Even as each person plays his or her own individual part, together they form a team. We enjoy being part of a cheering crowd rooting for our favorite team or politician, or singing together as a congregation. We enjoy the closeness of sex, one of the most intimate forms of togetherness. The togetherness experience is highly rewarding. In so many ways, the intimate connection with our partner, or our team, just feels good.

That close connection works well until we find ourselves rooting for a different team or a different politician than everyone else in our group. Then, depending on the level of anxiety in the group, we may be singled out with negative adjectives attached to our difference. Pressure may be put on us to conform to the group, to go along with others, to stop causing dissension and upsetting others, and to give up our own unique, or "weird" way of thinking and behaving. The force for individuality is often admired in people during calmer times; but it will be attacked in anxious times.

Relationship systems always work with these two life forces. We try to find, often beyond awareness, just like the homeostatic processes in our bodies, a proper balance between them. All couples struggle with this. Most satisfied couples find some way for each partner to be uniquely his or her own autonomous self, and do not feel threatened by the other's differentness or try to change them, and they still work together toward some common goals, however broadly defined.

3

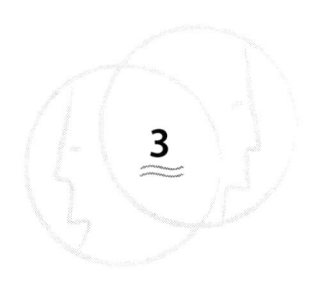

Anxiety and the Emotional System

Two primary variables exist in parallel within an individual person: the degree of chronic anxiety and the degree of differentiation of self. The more differentiation of self there is, the less chronic anxiety there is. Differentiation of self is the principal goal of the counseling effort, and learning better to manage and lower one's own anxiety level is a part of the process for getting there.

Bowen defined anxiety as "the experience of threat, real or imagined." People vary in their sense of threat. Take, for example, the experience of anger. George and Martha both were highly sensitive to expressions of anger in each other. They came into their marriage with this sensitivity in place. Each one experienced the other person's anger as threatening, and they each typically responded in kind. In addition, each might imagine that the other was angry and become reactive to that, even when this was not the case.

Better-differentiated people do not experience that much threat in their partner's anger and have no need to defend with a counterattack. They are curious about what got the person angry and ask, "Hey, what's going on? Tell me about it." They listen to the person's complaint without being defensive, and then gradually work toward some resolution of the situation. They are not threatened by their partner's anger.

We can measure anxiety physiologically. One method is biofeedback. The various kinds of feedback machines include: a GSR (galvanic skin response) that measures the electrical conductivity of the skin through the minute presence of sweat; a simple finger-temperature machine; and a machine that measures heart rhythms, or breathing, or brain waves. Each has its own way of showing the physiological presence of anxiety. One researcher, John Gottman, has attached couples to machines like these while they discuss some difficult issue and has been able to see how their anxiety affects their interaction biologically.

When we are anxious, our bodies release certain hormones like adrenaline. In the early days of human history, these hormones helped humans to cope with the physical challenge of a threatening situation, such as the attack of a vicious saber-toothed tiger. In most modern-day stress, it is less reasonable for us to respond physically (running from or striking out at an angry boss is generally not an option). Therefore, as these hormones build up in our body, we simply become "stressed." Cortisol is one of these hormones that researchers have been able to measure in saliva as it builds during marital upsets.

Two Kinds of Anxiety

There are two kinds of anxiety: *acute* and *chronic*. They differ in both intensity and duration. Most of us can adapt to the challenges of acute anxiety. We feel it in actual threatening situations, like when a mugger confronts us on the street or in some sort of catastrophe like a flood, a fire, an earthquake, or a car accident. It can result from the loss of someone close to us (as in death or divorce), or a change in a major important relationship (our partner has a stroke and is no longer fully functional). Most people would feel some level of threat to their normal life, or be upset in these situations stemming out of some degree of acute anxiety.

Acute anxiety has a time-limited quality to it and usually we develop the ability to adjust or cope more effectively to the new challenging situation. Our automatic physical and emotional reactions, including the hormonal responses of the fight/flight reaction, are designed to deal with the immediate, real situation, and then, eventually, we get on with what life requires of us in the new circumstances.

Chronic anxiety interferes with our ability to cope with real situations. It can be unrelated to any clear, immediate threat and it may even be beyond our conscious awareness. Chronic anxiety is like a constant sense of being on edge, being alert to any possible sense of threat, and even tending to see threat when it is not there; it is imagined. This can be so ever-present that it feels normal and we do not "feel" anxious.

3 — Anxiety and the Emotional System

Chronic anxiety increases our sensitivity to any potential threat in our environment. Cognitively, we narrow our focus and take in less information—we become single-minded—and thus make poorer decisions. Behaviorally, we go on "autopilot" and react instinctively. As our level of threat goes up so does the intensity of these responses and they impair our ability to relate effectively to others. We monitor other's behavior for signs that they are being emotionally threatening, and we go "on guard." This becomes part of our emotional atmosphere and conflict can flare up instantaneously.

Chronic anxiety is like the tilt mechanism in a pinball machine. Part of how a player influences the direction of the ball is to give the machine a nudge or a push. However, if we push too hard the machine says, "Tilt" and the game is over. We do not get to play the rest of our balls. Every pinball machine has a different sensitivity as to how much pushing it will take. Some are very sensitive and will easily tilt. Others can take a great deal of shoving before they stop the game. We each carry around in us our own level of tilt. Better-differentiated people can take a lot more "shoving" before they hit tilt.

Chronic anxiety is a major issue in how we manage our relationships. George and Martha could both arrive at tilt easily. They were highly sensitive to any sense of threat from the other and would typically react with anger. When I described this kind of process to them they both said, "Yes, that's what it's like. I don't like being pushed and I will push back. Then we fight."

When the stir-up of chronic anxiety happens, we each have developed specific responses based on the learned reactions we had while growing up. Every family has its own average level of chronic anxiety—based primarily on the level of anxiety in the parental system—and each of the children will develop their own levels, with some variation from sibling to sibling. In some families, the discrepancy between levels of chronic anxiety between any two siblings can be quite significant depending on the projection process and the normal sibling birth-order characteristics.

Anxiety and Fusion

Chronic anxiety feeds emotional fusion, which is the opposite of differentiation. Both processes have a personal internal component and a parallel interpersonal component. Individually, fusion is the merging of our intellectual and emotional systems so that emotionality dominates. Flooding the intellectual system with emotionality makes it difficult for us to separate thinking and feeling as we face life and relationship difficulties. The sense of threat dominates our thinking. Eventually this leads to paranoia. We become more subjective. Interpersonally, we are unclear about what is self, about what is and is not our personal responsibility, and where we end and the other person begins. This is the issue of boundaries.

Fusion also represents a merging of the selves of the people in an emotional system; the functioning of each is tied into that of others. They are more reactive to one another. It is harder to think and act for self. The more there is fusion within self and between people the more likely the life course of people will be difficult and symptoms will arise. The greater the fusion, the greater the intensity of the problems. There was a sense for both George and Martha that the other was in charge of self. They were less capable of autonomous action. They could not get emotionally unhooked from each other.

Although he later dropped the phrase, Bowen initially referred to fusion as the "undifferentiated family ego mass." There is a graphic quality to this description. I have worked with some families with a number of grown children where it is difficult for any one member of the family to make an independent decision, or to say, in effect, "I will do this . . ." One family of adults said, "We are kind of amoeba-like. None of us seems able to move on our own or to take a position. We each wait for someone else to decide; but no one does. We are just stuck together and unable to move in a direction of our own the way we see other people do."

One family, consisting of a mother and eight adult children, had a large project, started and developed by their deceased husband and father, that consumed much of their physical and emotional life. His dream was that they would all be together around this project and be a happy family as they worked on it. When the family was younger, everyone seemed to enjoy working on it. Now it was problematic because it demanded a lot of work for each of the siblings who also had their own careers and families. The second son was the most caught up emotionally in his father's dream and pushed the others to do their portion of the work and get together on a regular basis.

This family, composed of likeable, intelligent, and otherwise very competent people was stuck with father's dream. They could not pursue their own dreams. A sticky emotional amalgam fused them all together. If anyone suggested dropping the project, other family members treated him or her like a traitor. After I worked with this family for a little while, the oldest son said to the others, "That's it. I'm done. This was Dad's dream, not mine. Dad is dead. Mom, I know you will be unhappy that we don't all still get together like Dad wanted, but I have to get on with my life and family. I won't keep working on this project. I love all of you, but I'm out."

There was a general sense of panic in the family. The second brother who pushed the dream felt betrayed and angrily accused his brother of disloyalty to their dad and to them all. However, the oldest son's decision to define himself and not be a part of this project any longer provoked others to think for themselves and to consider where they wanted to put their life energy. After some turmoil, at a later meeting of the family, others began to declare themselves, saying they had wanted out for a long time. Together, they developed a way for the second brother to take over the project as his own and they would each have voting shares in it, but not do the work. There developed a general sense of relief in the family, including for mom, and eventually they all thanked the oldest son for making his decision. When I asked him to review for them what he went through in making the decision, he said he had to think beyond his anxiety and the powerful emotionality involved—whether he was in fact betraying his dad and the family—and to think through what was best for him and his own family. This was differentiation in action.

Anxiety and the Two Life Forces

The two life forces of individuality and togetherness can be lived out or expressed in more differentiated ways or in more fused ways. We could imagine a vertical line with total fusion at 0 (zero) on the bottom, and total differentiation at 100 on the top (neither of these positions exists in reality), and then a horizontal line with the togetherness force on the left side and the individuality force on the right side. The two lines would intersect at some point, like moveable crosshairs in a telescope. Where they intersect differs with each of us depending upon our level of differentiation, and what is going on in our lives at a particular time. Functionally, our level of differentiation/fusion will vary, as we balance out the togetherness and individuality forces in each circumstance.

When chronic anxiety activates us, behaviorally we tend to move down the scale toward greater fusion. Most of us push for greater togetherness, like the second son in the example above. Some of us, when anxious, move away from others, isolate ourselves, and want nothing to do with others. In fact, the oldest sister in this family tended to be this way. She was so phobic to the togetherness that physical and emotional distance was the only way she could feel like a self. This was not the case with the oldest son. He moved more toward individuality, but up the scale of differentiation. This meant he did not cut off from the others. He defined himself more clearly, but continued to relate to them, nonreactively, while they were upset with him. Differentiation leads to a better emotional connection with others rather than isolation from them.

When times get tough and anxiety goes up, we either push to be together with important others or we push away from them and go off on our own. As we better differentiate a self, we can do both togetherness (as connected to others) and individuality (as comfort with being alone when necessary, as did the oldest brother in the decision he made) in a more balanced way. We can look after our own concerns while also being attentive to the concerns of others. The oldest brother was sensitive to the concerns of others but he was not going to be governed by them.

When I started seeing this family, it was stuck in a more fused togetherness. As the oldest brother was able to work at his own level of differentiation (both internally and relationally), the fused togetherness force in the family first tightened, condemning him, and then, as he maintained his stance, began to loosen. Initially, the second brother tried to enforce the togetherness. The older brother stayed on course with his more differentiated individuality without getting defensive or angry or attacking the others. Nor did he try to coerce them into accepting his position or ask for their permission. He did not cut off from them saying he wanted nothing more to do with them. Nor did he have to distance from them to get more autonomy.

As tension increases in a system, people attempt all sorts of manipulative efforts to get others to join into the togetherness. These behaviors include pleading, crying, demanding, arguing, attacking, criticizing, being authoritative and dictatorial, seducing, bribing, and invoking authorities who will take our side.

All families have some degree of fusion. None of us escapes it and we can each feel its power. It does not always show in symptomatic ways, but in tense times, when life challenges the family in some way, the fusion will be easily seen or felt. A simple example would be a young couple at Christmastime trying to decide which set of parents to celebrate with or whether to avoid them both.

Most marriages, like that between George and Martha, have to clarify what their emotional intimacy looks like. The more fused the marriage, the more the closeness will feel, at least for one partner if not both, like being trapped. This gives rise to the many "ball and chain"-type jokes that men often make about marriage. Women have their own versions of feeling trapped in a marriage. The overall sense for both partners will be decreased satisfaction in the marriage.

4

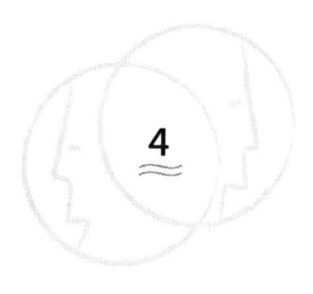

Differentiation of Self

Every relationship has to negotiate the differences that inevitably occur between the partners. Marriages that prosper have figured out how to do this successfully. Those that founder have not. George and Martha had a list of things they differed on and repeatedly fought over, but they had stayed together. I asked them how they had managed to do this with so many differences. They did not expect this question, but they took it seriously. It challenged the picture they had of themselves. One could think of them as a terrible twosome that loved nothing more than a good fight. They said their son and a few close friends thought of them this way. I demurred, saying that did not quite make sense to me. They struck me as passionate people with strong feelings for each other. They quickly confirmed this and talked about the passion they felt in their courtship. This put them back in touch with some of the warmth they had for each other.

Early in our counseling sessions, we began discussing the central, critical issue for every relationship: how to be a self with our own thoughts, feelings, beliefs, values, opinions, commitments, and ways of dealing with life while also being closely connected to, loving, and caring for a person who differs significantly from us on these things. They were intrigued with this question and we wandered in and around it throughout the whole of our counseling work together.

This is the territory of differentiation of self. Bowen considered this concept the cornerstone of his theory. It is the focus of our counseling, whether with individuals, couples, or families. As people work on this key personal and relationship challenge, their lives will improve.

Fusion and Closeness (Or, Two "I's" Do Not Make a "We")

Typically, conflicted couples talk about how they are not close. I sometimes say, "That's odd. You strike me as very close." Once they get over trying to figure out if I am crazy, I ask them to define what they mean by closeness. This is nearly always some version of having no differences, walking hand in hand through life into the sunset, never arguing. I say that such people may exist but I have never met them and that picture does not fit with my own experience of marriage. My wife and I differ a lot and sometimes fight over these differences. I cannot imagine us not having differences, and in fact, such a life sounds rather boring to me. Besides, how could we ever learn anything if we did not encounter each other with our differences?

Fusion defines closeness as sameness. Many, if not most couples, especially conflicted ones, enter into a lifelong project of trying to change the other to be "just like me" or "just like how I want you to be for me." For example, when we tell each other what the other "should" or "should not" do, this is what we are doing. This is at the heart of our passionate struggles with one another. Bowen called this definition of closeness a "we-ness." This we-ness almost automatically leads to conflict.

Listen to couples talk. To what extent do they use the word *we* versus *I*. Here is a simple example. A wife may say, "We never take beach holidays. We don't like the beach." I might say, "Well, that is interesting. You are both the same on this? Which one of you likes the beach least and which one likes the beach more?" She may say, "Well, Michael doesn't like the sand. He finds it dirty. And he doesn't like the glare of the sun. I suppose I kind of find the beach relaxing." Then I say, "So you are not really the same on this? You have decided to go along with Michael's wishes on this. Tell me how that happened. How did the two of you both decide 'we' don't like the beach when that is not really the case?"

Couples often make it their project to create sameness. Part of what I am about in my counseling is clarifying their differences (rather than minimizing them) and that they are two "I's" trying to become a "we." When they come in for counseling, couples often think I am going to help them get over their differences and be together by being the same, that I will help them meet their fusion-based goals.

My Definition of Closeness

By definition, intimacy is what occurs between two different people. If they are the same it is not intimacy; it is symbiosis or, more accurately, the fusion of two people into one personality. Whatever the words of Genesis mean, that "the two shall become one," I am sure it does not mean obliteration of the personalities of the two people in relationship.

What many people call closeness is a fused version of togetherness. A more differentiated version of togetherness, of intimacy based on openness between two different partners, might be described like this: I can tell you who I am, what I think, feel, believe, want to do, and have done, without getting anxious or worrying about what you may think about what I have told you, even if I believe you disagree with me and disapprove. You would reciprocate with the same kind of openness, and I could listen to you and not feel the need to change you to be more like how I want you to be.

Neither of us has the need to change the other even though there might be an effort to be persuasive around the important things we talk about. The self of one partner does not feel impinged upon or intimidated by the other partner, even if the other does want to change us. In fact, the more differentiated we are, this desire to change the other is much less urgent. Our own level of well-being is not based on the other's intent or way of being with us (as in, "You must accept me for who I am in order for me to feel okay"). In fusion, we rely on the other to give us permission to be the self we want to be.

Better-differentiated couples make accommodations to each other. They make compromises if they cannot find a way to satisfy both persons' wants. However, this accommodation is not made at the expense of one person losing self to the other. Here is a simple example of accommodation from my own marriage. Early in our life together, Lois discovered that she shared with me a love of the outdoors. She had not hiked much or camped at all before our marriage. After marriage we did a number of long-distance backpacking trips. Up to that time I had only hiked with other guys and we all moved along at a pretty good clip. At first, Lois tried to match my pace, but this wore her out. Finally, she said she would not go that fast anymore. I was upset. I wanted to cover ground and get to the destination and she wanted to go more slowly, rest more, and enjoy the trip. This is a typical issue for couples. We move through the world at different speeds.

I understood that the experience was different for her and, rather than spend a lot of time being upset or trying to argue her into going faster like me, I began to think how I could make going slower more interesting to me and not feel like a loss. I decided I would start taking photographs along the way and soon discovered that I quite enjoyed this. I often wanted to stop when I found a scene I would like to record or play with visually. She got her rest and sometimes would complain to me that we were not moving fast enough! And I developed what has become a long-lasting interest in photography.

What Is Differentiation of Self?

Bowen said, "Differentiation is the degree to which one self fuses or merges into another self in a close emotional relationship" (Bowen 1978: 200). He had biology in mind when he chose the term. Starting out at conception, as one cell divides first into an amorphous mass of undifferentiated cells, they continue to divide, and gradually differentiate into well-defined different parts of the organism. They take on specific functions as they stay connected to one another. Differentiation does not mean separating from and being unconnected with the rest of the organism; it means each part stays true to its own identity and function while remaining connected to the whole. Differentiation would not exist without the connection.

Better-differentiated people develop a more solid and less fused self. The solid self can remain true to its own self-chosen beliefs and principles for living and is not swayed by the emotional system to change those positions. Bowen referred to the part of a person that can be swayed by others as the pseudo-self. I remember in my early days in the church changing my beliefs to fit with those whose approval I wanted. My beliefs were not truly my own. I also adopted certain life principles from them that I had not really thought through in order to gain acceptance. Others were happier with me if I adopted their beliefs or principles as my own. This is a powerful emotional reality in most churches, as well as in families, and it does not help people define a more solid self. As they begin to think for self, people may drop out of church (or family) simply because they think they cannot be who they are in that community.

Differentiation within a person is the opposite of fusion. Internally, differentiation is about knowing the difference between functioning out of emotionality and feelings, and operating out of rationality and intellect. Knowing the difference between these two guidance systems within themselves, people then are freer to choose which one they will go with at any particular moment. Fused people have less choice. They are reactive to and governed by the emotionality within and around them.

The more we are governed by emotionality the poorer are many (not all) of our life decisions. We react to the immediate situation, imagining threat where there may be none, and perhaps miss more significant real threats. For George and Martha, being so sensitive to each other, just a look or a slightly angry tone of voice from one of them could get the other to react in kind; then there was a reaction to the reaction, and it became very difficult for them to step out of this reactive circle.

They had come to regard this way of functioning with each other as almost normal, if not happy. They could not see an alternative. Emotionality blinded them to any other way of being. It was so automatic and immediate they could not stop it or step back and do the proverbial "count to ten before responding." Each one focused on the other and that determined how his or her self would be. Each one put the other in charge of self.

This was the first and most productive thing counseling did for them. I interrupted the reactive cycle by being in charge of the emotional process in the counseling room and not letting them run away with it. I did not let them rehearse their usual arguments in front of me. I provided them with a different way of being with each other when they differed and got upset. They appreciated this. I did not instruct them or tell them how they "should" be. I modeled it in my calmer, more curious presence. My being in charge of the emotional process, and slowing it down, helped them to get clearer about self. They valued this experience. This is what kept bringing them back each week.

I was interested in how the emotional process worked for each of them: what one had to do for the other to react as they did, and then what one had to do internally to get reactivity stirred up in his or her self, and then react back, and so forth. My curiosity and interested questions about their internal and interpersonal processes helped each of them attempt to be more thoughtful about the whole process. They developed a better sense of when their own anxiety was stirred up and how to calm it down.

They also began to let go of some of their simplistic ideas about who was right and wrong in the relationship. They began to realize they had a choice about how to be, and what sort of behavior might benefit each of them, personally and together. For example, Martha had always perceived George's distancing from her as a rejection of her, as a contemptuous not caring about her. She could easily slip into this perception, feel negatively attacked, threatened by the fear that he would divorce her, and then feel hurt and resentful of him and go on the counterattack.

As we talked, an alternative explanation began to dawn on her that his withdrawal was about his own emotionality and high level of sensitivity to her, rather than about his insensitivity. She began to see his reduced eye contact, his physical distance and not touching her, his brief verbal responses and bristliness, and his unwillingness generally to talk with her as really about his heightened sensitivity to her. He began to get a better sense of this as well. He got more interested in his sensitivity and reactivity and felt less guilty and conflicted about it.

Over time, it began to feel better to both of them to think things through, to challenge their automatic explanations, to clarify what was and was not threatening, and then decide how to be in response. Their more rational side was growing up and assuming its proper role. It was giving them more choice and they liked that. They could already be logical and rational about things that did not involve them personally. It was a new idea that this could apply to their interpersonal experience as well.

The differentiated use of the intellect within our emotional experience of life is not the same as intellectuality, which is a classic defense mechanism against threatening, underlying emotional issues. People can use their intellect to argue for irrational causes. Both George and Martha used their intellect in this way in their arguments. They used it to build their emotionally based cases against the other. People in the manic phase of their bipolar disorder, or paranoid people, can display amazing feats of pure intellect in service of their deep, emotionally based irrationality.

Differentiation is appealing to us. It is a part of our normal developmental growth process. All of us—even those who are more fused than the general population—differentiate a self to some extent. We would not survive into adulthood without doing that. It is not a technique, or something created by Murray Bowen. He just identified how we normally do the process and what interrupts and sidetracks this normal process as we develop within our families.

The Differentiation Continuum

We all exist on a continuum of differentiation. The continuum offers us a way to think theoretically about how we vary from one another. Bowen called this the "scale" of differentiation but later regretted this term because it implies there is a paper-and-pencil test we can take to discover our level. He assigned theoretical numbers to the various levels; his scale went from 0 to 100.

The scale is useful in counseling for assessing people and knowing how to gauge our expectations for their improvement. Those people with much less emotional intensity around the concerns they present, and who are comfortable with and more tolerant of differences between them, are likely higher on the continuum. They can listen to each other around an emotionally charged issue, ask questions of one another, and explore each other's thinking in an open way. These are relatively easy people to work with and their counseling will go more quickly and smoothly. The further down on the scale, the more difficult the counseling will be and the longer it will take.

There is no such thing as "normal" on the continuum. There is also a problem with terminology like higher/lower and better/worse levels of differentiation. These words (which I use) are only about variation and imply nothing about a moral good/bad idea. They simply describe our level of functioning and degree of self. We all struggle with the same kinds of emotional issues and the only difference between us is one of degree. By accident of birth, some of us come out of better-differentiated families and some of us out of less well-differentiated families. This has a major impact on the quality of our lives and our general life course, and that is just the way it is. While it may be fortunate or unfortunate in terms of our life course, our level of differentiation is not good or bad.

No one has achieved full differentiation at 100 on the scale, and no one is at zero, existing in total fusion. However, the great majority of us function below 50. Being below 50 means that our emotional system is more influential in our lives than is our intellectual system. This is not about intelligence. I find it relatively easy to write a book like this, but much more difficult to manage myself well in close relationships. The lower we are on the continuum the more fused we are, and the more vulnerable we are to stress and anxiety. Given less stress in our lives, most of us will look higher on the continuum than we are. Given very high levels of stress, those who are actually higher can function less competently, but they will also bounce back more quickly.

Those with the Most Fusion and Least Differentiation (0–25)

Characteristically, persons at 0 to 25 on the continuum live in a world dominated by emotionality. They are extremely sensitive to the feelings of others and can easily "be made" to feel badly or be reactive to the feelings or behavior of others. Their decision making is less planned and thought through and tends to be more impulsive. They are generally oriented to getting love, acceptance, and approval from others, and can be destroyed (or hostile and very angry) by not getting it. Very little of their life energy goes into responsible, self-focused goals for directing their lives. If such goals do exist, the ability to maintain a focus on them is easily lost as the emotional currents of relationships will distract and sidetrack them.

This group will have the highest percentage of life problems, physically, emotionally, or socially. They will have more severe psychological problems like character disorders, significant depressions, and neurotic issues. They may regularly be in trouble with the law, or at a minimum behave unethically, or abuse various addictive substances that help them with their anxiety. Being unable to delay gratification, they will be impulsive and irresponsible. At the very lowest levels of this quartile are people who have great difficulty functioning independently in life.

These are people with the least amount of solid self. They are multiproblem people who have many life challenges and are unable to get their lives launched, or, if launched, are vulnerable to having it all fall apart on them under stress. They are relationship oriented in that the relationships in their lives are the most important thing, even more than their life goals. How they are in life is nearly totally dependent on how important others behave with them. They are happy when others are happy with them. They seek comfort in their relationships over anything else, like, for example, maintaining a life of thought-through goals and principled behavior. It they do not get this acceptance, they may withdraw from others, or engage in intense fights to get it, attacking those who do not give it. Some, in reaction, become hermit-like and withdraw from society.

In terms of beliefs and principles, there will usually be either little consistency from one issue to another, or they will rigidly hold to a set of beliefs in a highly dogmatic way. They may make devoted disciples and, since they lack self, rely almost exclusively on what some authority has asserted. The authority could be of any sort like a scientist, a theologian, a health guru, or whatever. They can be smart and academically accomplished. A good example could be a professor who really knows his field, but in department committee meetings is always in conflict with others. Or he could have chaotic or abusive relationships with his students.

Rebels and those who are regularly in conflict with others can be just as relationship oriented as those who are devout disciples. Whether there is conflict or not does not say much about the degree of self in a person. Each of them focuses on others, whether they want to emulate and please the others or fight and defeat them. Like couples who stay focused on their polarized conflict with the other, change does not happen.

It is very difficult for people at the lowest end of the continuum (20 and below) to improve their functional level of differentiation. This requires the kind of focus that they normally do not have the competence to maintain. Those who want to help them (friends or counselors) will have to provide a great deal of support and be willing to put up with significant amounts of turmoil in the relationship. They need environments where there will be few challenges to raise anxiety and where a consistent, routine life is offered to them. In this sort of environment, they may be able to do well.

Those Who Are Somewhat Higher on the Continuum (25–50)

Most of us exist in the range between 25 and 50 on the continuum. As we move up the continuum toward 50 there is a greater ability to differentiate a self. The emotional system will still dominate our lives but if we get ourselves calm enough and can shut down the anxiety, we can do better at staying goal focused. A goal focus is about how we want to be in our life and to what purposes we will devote our life energy. It is about clarifying the principles we will live by and then being able to stay true to those principles.

A goal focus is the opposite of a relationship focus, but it is not anti-relationship. It can be about how we want to be in our relationships. However, a relationship focus is about how we want others to be with us (or, vice versa, how we have to be with them to get their approval) and what happens to us when they (or we) are not that way. In a goal focus, how others are is less of an issue; we are much less willing to give up self just for the sake of approval and acceptance. The question is, Are we being the kind of person we want to be with them? And in life generally, are we living up to our own standards and beliefs?

In this quartile, we will still be reactive to important relationships and feel "great" or "terrible" depending on how happy important people are with us. The closer to 50 we are on the continuum, the more solid our self, and therefore our relationships will be less problematic than those of people who are lower on the continuum. We have increasing abilities to be responsible for self, think our way through our difficulties, decide on a plan of action for ourselves, and then pursue it with consistency. But issues of loving and being loved can still intrude in such a way that we can lose our focus, with our self-esteem still being somewhat dependent on what others think of us. I placed George and Martha at somewhere around 30 on the scale.

Those at the Higher Levels of Differentiation (50–75)
Bowen considered levels above 75 to be theoretical, indicating where humans might someday arrive. Even people in the 50 to 75 range are relatively rare. As we move above 50, there is a more solid self. People have thought through their life principles much more clearly, hold to them with greater consistency, and can act on them in even highly emotional situations. They are probably more intelligent simply because they are able to think well, but they are not necessarily well educated. They are capable of more easily relating to anxious others and therefore they have generally good relationships. In difficult circumstances they can look at the overall, larger picture, consider the

many influences involved in the context, and sort out priorities more easily than most people can.

They will rely much less on what any authority says they "must" believe, and they will arrive at their own self-determined beliefs and opinions based on what makes sense to them. Others may be troubled by the questions they raise and by their refusal to accept readily what an authority says they should. For this reason they could be deemed as "troublemakers" by other, more fused people in the emotional system.

They are used to thinking for themselves and began doing this within their own families while growing up. They most likely lived within families that encouraged this and had parents who modeled it. Since they are not dogmatic, they can always rethink their beliefs. They are open to new information and willing to change their position if the facts warrant it.

Not being at the level of 100, they are still capable of giving in to the pressures of the emotional system, conforming to the beliefs of others, and compromising their principles. There is enough sensitivity to the results of emotional disharmony that they would prefer to not go through it, and this is more often a conscious decision.

I am always impressed and a bit awestruck when I discover people at a much higher level since I would put myself only in the high 30s. On a couple of occasions, I have had such people in counseling. With them I do as much as I can to stay out of their way and just ask the best questions I can. They will typically come into counseling in times of very high stress and they need to have someone with some degree of objectivity listen to them as they sort their way through it all.

I remember one couple who lost their oldest boy (about five years of age) to an accidental death in which each had some involvement. Many couples do not survive such events and within a year or two they will have divorced. This couple did not divorce but still they had to sort through the loss for themselves. It was a privilege to watch them do this. They thought I helped but I think they did it themselves and I was a simple catalyst. Another couple executed one of the best thought through divorces I have ever witnessed, and managed to be good friends and good parents together as they got on with their separate lives.

People at these levels know how to enjoy the intense and pleasurable parts of being close—like having good sex—easily joining in with the togetherness experience. They are still capable of allowing the emotional system to run major parts of their lives, enjoying what it has to offer, trusting to those sensitivities as an important part of life and relationships, but they are also capable of stepping out of that way of functioning when stress builds and situations become difficult.

These are the people we often most appreciate as church members and as leaders. Even people who are above 40 on the scale make good leaders. They are able to be more objective and thoughtful, less reactive to the emotionality of others, and move deliberately with self-discipline, even in anxious circumstances. Their emotional and intellectual systems function more like a cooperative team. As Bowen says: "They are able to live more freely and to have more satisfying emotional lives within the emotional system. They can participate fully in emotional events knowing they can extricate themselves with logical reasoning when the need arises" (Bowen 1978: 369). In marriage and other close relationships, they function more like true partners, allowing themselves the joys of closeness with less loss of self. Both partners can function in autonomous ways as well as join in with the togetherness. This sort of relational competence carries over to their parenting as well. Later, Bowen says:

> Spouses who are more differentiated can permit their children to grow and develop their own autonomous selfs [sic] without undue anxiety or without trying to fashion their kids in their own images. The spouses and the children are each more responsible for themselves, and do not blame others for failures or credit anyone else for their successes. (Bowen 1978: 370)

Obviously, a major goal in marital counseling is to work for the greater differentiation of the partners. This requires us as counselors to work on our own functional level of differentiation. Counselors with less differentiation will uphold more fused ways of being together as the ideal. While this can be on the side of some of the pleasurable aspects of togetherness, it will also guarantee continued difficulties and problems for the couple.

5

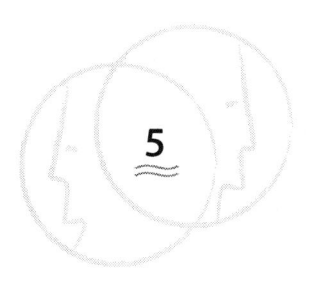

Triangles

To be effective counselors, we must learn about and recognize triangles and know how to manage ourselves within them. Bowen called the triangle the basic molecule of emotional systems. If individual people are the atoms, then the grouping of three people around some relational issue is the molecule. More than three people, as in a family or a workplace or a congregation, is a system of interlocking triangles.

Once they have learned how triangles work, people begin to see them everywhere. Our relational life is filled with triangles. They are the primary way social systems function. We are involved in many ongoing triangles every day. Right now, you may be so preoccupied with a triangle that it is difficult to focus on this page. Triangles are pervasive and powerful and occupy much of our emotional life.

Triangles are activated by the build-up of anxiety within an emotional system. Anxious people begin to look for others who will support them or take their side when some conflict emerges with someone else. Structurally, triangles have two close insiders (individuals or groups) and one person (or group) on the outside. As anxiety intensifies, this process also grows and intensifies. The close twosome can act like they are in agreement on most everything; they act in concert against the outsider, who is somehow wrong, bad, sick, ignorant, or whatever. Think of two parents who appear to be in total agreement presenting a united front against a problem child.

Counseling is aimed at identifying and modifying the triangular emotional process within a system. There are two primary ways of working with triangles in counseling. The first way deals with the anxious counselees' quite normal efforts to triangulate the counselor into their emotional process. By staying emotionally connected to them and yet not participating in that process, the counselor is able to modify the triangle in the counseling session.

The second way involves identifying one member of the family who can function differently within the family triangles outside of the counseling sessions. When one motivated family member learns about triangles and changes the part that self plays in a primary family triangle, the whole system will be affected, and change will begin to happen.

Some Examples of Triangles

Some of us, at the mention of the word *triangle*, may think of the common, classic use of the term as in husband, wife, and mistress. We regularly hear of actors or politicians who are involved in such triangles. These kinds of relationships and the public interest in them have probably been going on since the beginning of human life. I can imagine early cave people gossiping about the clan chieftain and who he is sleeping with now.

The Bible is full of triangular stories. In fact, it is hard to think of any that don't involve triangles. The story of David and Bathsheba is a famous one and similar to that of some of our political leaders today. The story of the woman taken in adultery and brought before Jesus is full of triangles. Most triangles, in and out of the Bible, are not of such salacious interest.

One common triangle that also involves marital conflict is when a couple focuses on the problems of one of their children and begins to see the child as "the problem" in the family. This is projection of anxiety to a child. The couple may fight—or not—over the management of the child, but as the two close insiders they ignore their own underlying anxiety, fusion, and differences. The perceived problems in the child—the outsider—help to reduce the anxiety and level of felt tension the parents have with each other.

Another common triangle involves one of the partners developing some kind of physical, emotional, or social dysfunction. In their over- and underfunctioning reciprocity, one partner becomes "the problem" and the other partner is the "healthy," "good," or "sane" one. Other family and nonfamily members may be recruited to focus on or fix the problem partner. For example, a husband may lose his job because of poor work performance. He does little to look for another job or to participate in the running of the household. A psychiatrist decides he is depressed and offers medication. However, his life situation does not improve. His wife is functioning well but resents his lack of initiative, his refusal to take over household tasks, and focuses on him, along with the psychiatrist, as "the problem." Whether she decides to help him and support him, or to attack him and threaten divorce, he will be the focus.

We have a triangle going on right now as I address you, the reader, about Murray Bowen's theory. What I am presenting to you is my understanding of the Bowen theory. I could act as if what I say about the theory is exactly what Bowen said; he and I are the close twosome. And yet this cannot be. Nobody can speak with Bowen's mind. Bowen recognized that people would attempt to do this after he died, that people like me could misinterpret his theory when he was no longer around to clarify what he meant. He used to wonder out loud, "How do you differentiate a self when you are dead?"

Triangles are easier to do when one of the two insiders is dead. Then they cannot speak for themselves. In the church we frequently engage in this sort of process with Jesus, or passages from the Bible. We quote Jesus or Paul as if they are saying the same thing we are saying, as if they back us up. In a debate about some theological issue we say, for example, "Jesus said . . . ," and use him as our authority. He is on our side. His words, as we use them, make us right. We are the close twosome making "our" point to the others. Notice the fused "we-ness." A parishioner may think he has a closer walk with Jesus and quote other words of Jesus back to us, showing how Jesus is on his side. Couples may also do this in their fights with one another. It is common, if they are related to a church, for at least one of them to use Scripture or the pastor's words to justify their position in an argument and "prove" they are right.

When people in the church start telling you a negative story about someone else in the church, then you are in a more problematic gossip triangle. They are treating you as if you agree with them. You are the close twosome. If you agree with this person in any way, whether you say so or not, then the two of you will probably keep telling each other negative stories about this third person, building a case against him or her, offering each other further proof of how wrong the other person is.

If you do not agree and say so, the person telling you the negative story may well pull away and go to someone else with their story. Not agreeing with them does not end the triangling process. You will just be in the outside position along with the other person being talked about. You will become one of "them" (the outside position of the triangle) instead of one of "us" (the inside position). Our triangular options in the church are endless. Who is "in" and who is "out" will vary from situation to situation, relationship to relationship, and from time to time.

The Close/Distant Dance and the Origin of Triangles

The triangle begins with one person distancing from the other out of anxiety. The two-person dyadic relationship is unstable. As long as things are calm between us, the two of us can get along well and maintain a stable one-on-one relationship without using a triangle. As soon as there is some stress or anxiety, it will become more difficult to maintain the one-on-one relationship where we can openly discuss the issue as in what I think, what you think, how we relate around it, and what we will do. We stop exploring the thinking of the other and being open about our own. Early in counseling, George and Martha were too anxious to be open and too sensitive to be vulnerable with each other.

We each have variable comfort zones around closeness and distance with the people who are emotionally important to us, when we do not feel too vulnerable in either direction. Say you are an important person in my life, like my partner or my mother, and I reveal to you some important information about myself. If you then start getting "too close," wanting to know more than I feel uncomfortable talking about, because I might feel judged by you, I will distance myself from you. If you start telling me what I "should" think or feel or do, like a parent may do, then I will start backing away out of fear of getting absorbed by you. As I back away you may pursue me, still trying to convince me. This will then become the typical emotional pursue/distance pattern that is common in relationships.

There is implicit (if not explicit) pressure for me to become like you, to see life and run my life the way you want me to. In the fusion, my individuality may feel threatened. This is, for example, a typical parent/adolescent conflictual experience. In a particular situation, a parent says what the child should think, feel, or do, and the adolescent backs away, saying, "I am my own person. You can't tell me what to think (or feel or do)."

We have many ways of creating emotional distance but one of the most common is inwardly pulling a shade down over our eyes and figuratively covering our ears, while outwardly smiling and nodding our head as if we agree. This is the "Yes, dear" approach. We are keeping the peace while not really agreeing to engage on the issue. Preachers of Sunday morning sermons can recognize this reaction in the pews.

Distancers are not the only ones who engage in this process. Anxiety inspires pursuers as well as distancers. If I, as the pursuer, am saying things about how you ought to be, then I am feeling anxious about your difference from me. As the pursuer, I help to set up the reactivity in you so you feel the need to distance. I do not make you this way; I am not responsible for you; but I will be a part of the overall emotional process. If I want to connect with you, I have to find a way to talk that invites you in rather than inspires anxiety and the need to distance yourself and/or get reactive by attacking me. This is what an effective counselor does.

Attacking the other, as in a couple's argument, is one form of distancing. Then, when attacked, the other partner counterattacks, saying, in essence, "Me!? You think I'm wrong? Well what about you? You always . . ." And it is off to the races with both partners throwing their accusations at one another. Arguing is a peculiar way of staying somewhat connected (neither has walked out the door), but with significant distance. Neither is being open and vulnerable about self.

Both partners are involved, but at this point I will focus just on the emotional distancing. It is a universal human phenomenon. We all keep that adolescent bit of self well into adulthood. I can still get those feelings when I see a particular look in my partner's eyes, or that posture, or hear that tone of voice, and emotionally, if not physically, I am inclined to back away. I may nod my head in assent but inwardly I am going "blah, blah, blah." I have stopped connecting. I may disappear in silent resentment, show outright defensive anger, go on an angry counterattack, or just walk out of the room, but these are all methods of emotional distancing.

Here is a typical dyadic interaction between a husband and wife with anxiety emerging.

1. They start in a *calm, stable,* one-on-one relationship. There is very little stress and neither partner is anxious. They are somewhat able to be a self and be open with the other.

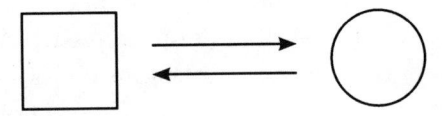

2. *Pursuit-distance*: Then, out of some anxiety of her own, the wife begins the pursuit around a topic or relationship issue that the husband finds uncomfortable, so he distances. He may have learned to handle his anxiety by staying late at the office, reading the paper, watching TV, being involved in a hobby, taking care of a child, or whatever.

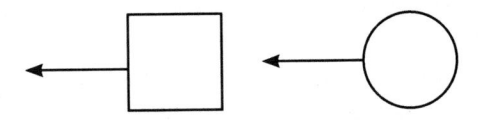

3. *Reactive distance*: After some period of time of pursuing, feeling as if she has run into a stone wall, the wife gives up her pursuit, saying she cannot get through the wall. (Remember you pursuers, a distancer can always outdistance a pursuer.) So the wife, after enough experiences of this sort, in a mix of despair and anger, reactively distances.

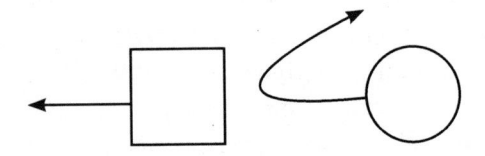

4. *Reactive-pursuit*: Eventually, after enough repetitions of this experience, she may have fantasies of leaving the marriage, or make actual plans to do so. When that happens, the husband will sense it and begin to feel anxious about her distance. He will begin to fear, if she moves too far away, that he might be abandoned and left alone. He then begins to pursue his wife (while she is reactively distancing), saying to her, "I'm sorry. I'll do better. Please don't leave."

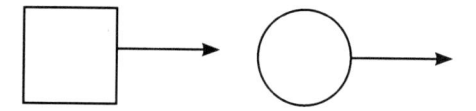

If she has not become too bitter, she may respond to this overture and equilibrium between them will be reestablished. At some point later, however, the process will repeat again.

At one time in my relationship with my wife, Lois, I was the distancer and she was the pursuer. I would get labeled negatively for it and be called a "typical, uncommunicative man." Then, once I learned about this phenomenon in the theory, I, just for the fun of it, became an emotional pursuer and watched her distance from me. We both learned then that it wasn't as simple as men are distancers and women are pursuers. These movement patterns are each aspects of a relationship and any one person can do either side, depending on who has what sort of anxiety. In about 25 percent of the marital cases I have seen, the man is the usual emotional pursuer and the woman is the regular distancer.

In one case, the woman's first husband died. She loved him but her big complaint was that he never talked, especially about his feelings. She would pursue and pursue and he would always out-distance her. When she was ready to remarry, the number-one quality she wanted in a man was someone who was warm, sensitive, talkative, and so forth, and she found one. However, it was not long after marriage that she was trying to get away from him. She said, "All he wants to do is talk, about all of my feelings and everything. I can't stand it. He is so intrusive. He needs me too much. I need time on my own." She sounded like a lot of men and said, "Now I see how my first husband felt." She saw the irony.

This close/distant dance is the start of triangulation. Anxiety is what moves us either to distance from or to pursue one another. It is anxiety over fear of engulfment or incorporation into the other (in the case of distancing), or abandonment by the other (in the case of pursuing). It is about being "too close" or "too far apart."

When I distance, however, I do not just distance from you. I also move toward someone or something else. For some people this may be their job, but it could be a high level of involvement with the children, a group of friends, a particular friend, a hobby, TV, or a sport like golf. In one case, the husband set up a huge, elaborate model railroad in their bedroom and spent nearly all of his free time playing with it.

There is some debate in Bowen theory circles as to whether a thing can be part of a triangle. Strictly speaking, if the triangle is an emotional process then each corner needs to be capable of emotionality and be capable of agency in some sense. My own resolution to this is to say that things can play an emotional role for the other two people. The husband found comfort, contentment, and a sense of competence in playing with his model train. The wife was angered by his withdrawal from her and his involvement with the train. She focused on it as the problem. The dynamic could be similar if he just spent time talking with a good friend who also was involved with model trains.

When the woman in the example above began distancing from her new husband, she decided to become an artist and did very well with it. Now her art was the "good" reason she had no time to sit and talk with him. He came to resent her art a bit because it took her away from him. So distancers move toward someone or something else, where they usually feel more comfortable, perhaps more competent, less anxious, and that creates the third corner in a triangle. She began to spend a lot of time with her female artist friends.

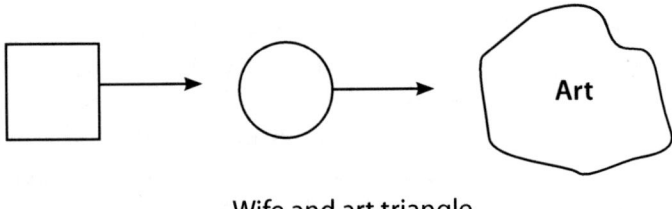

Wife and art triangle

When pursuers are not getting what they want from the object of their pursuit, they may recruit a third person to help them. This could be a friend, a therapist, or a pastor. Perhaps the distancing husband has an okay relationship with the pastor, and the wife pursues the pastor with the hope that she can get the pastor's help to pull the husband back into a closer relationship with her. So the wife pursues the pastor to form a triangle, in order that they both, as the close twosome, can focus on and fix the husband.

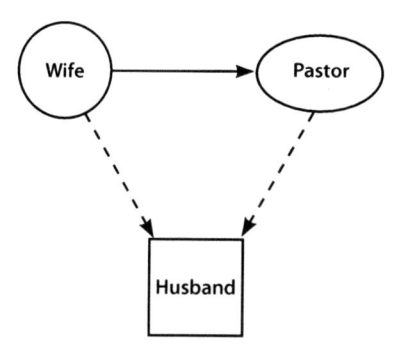

Wife and pastor triangle

I often have pursuing wives dragging distancing husbands into marital counseling and their implicit, assumed contract with me is, "Let's you and I fix him to be more like how he should be." Of course the pursuers (and it is not always wives) learn early on that I do not work that way. Because of the way I work with the pursuers (explained in part 2), the distancers find that counseling is a relatively comfortable and safe place to be.

Fluid and Fixed Triangles

We are each born into a primary triangle in our families, and we grow up living constantly within it. "Mom, dad, and me" is the first, and usually the most powerful, triangle in our lives. We are probably never out of that one. Then there are triangles involving the other siblings who came either before or after us. Then there are all the other relatives, and then our friends and enemies, and our coworkers. And on it goes.

Triangles come in two basic types: fluid or fixed. The basic *fluid triangle* involves two people who appear to be close, like Bill and Jane, who are married, relating to each other around a third person, Jerry, a close friend who appears at the time to be the more distant outsider. In fluid triangles, who is the close twosome and who is the distant outsider shifts around. Bill and Jane could talk about Jerry and what his problem is. It does not have to be malicious talk; they could just be concerned about him.

Then Bill gets together with Jerry and they talk about Jane and act as if they agree about what her problem is. However, Bill does not say to Jerry what he said to Jane about Jerry. Nor does Bill say to Jane what he tells Jerry about what he thinks of her. They get their apparent closeness by talking about her, and then she is in the outside position.

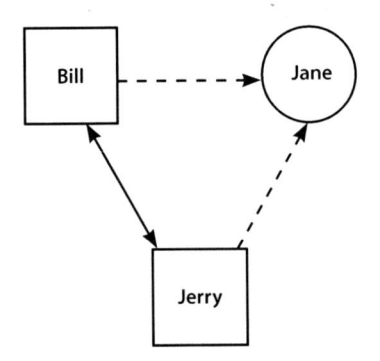

Then Jerry and Jane get together and they talk about Bill. Neither of them says to each other what they have said to Bill about the other, but they act as if they are close through their mutual evaluation of Bill. If Bill walks up while Jerry and Jane are talking about him, they immediately change the subject to the weather or something else and he may find himself feeling funny and wondering what is going on.

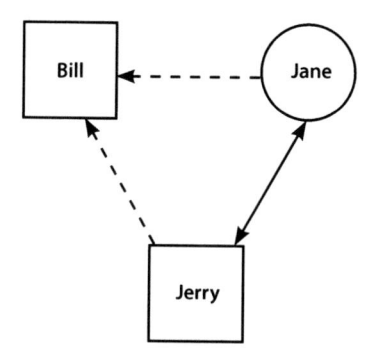

5 — Triangles

[Diagram: Bill (square) ← - - - Jane (circle); both connected to Jerry (square) below with arrows pointing up to Bill and Jane]

In triangles like this, one never knows where they stand with others. Rarely is anything said directly between the two people involved. There is general confusion about what is going on in a relationship. The three dyadic relationships are not functioning well. They are not direct, open, personal relationships for the three people involved with each other.

Here are two principles to remember about triangles: (1) *If you feel frequently confused in a relationship, then think triangles.* Whenever I feel confused about what is going on in counseling, I am curious about what triangle I am missing. Once I discover it, then I learn about the missing link in the story and things begin to make sense. (2) *If someone talks* with you *in this triangular way about someone else, then they will talk* about you with others *in the same way.* I can almost guarantee this.

There are *fixed triangles* where the close twosome and the person in the outside position remain the same over time. This triangle will often have a stabilizing effect for the system. This could be, for example, a parent and a teenage child focused on another problem parent who drinks heavily.

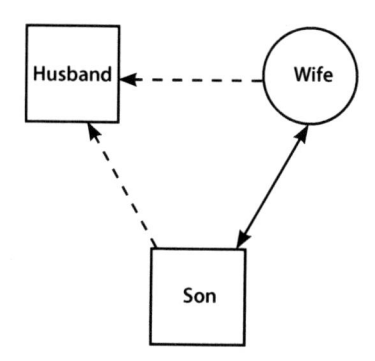

[Diagram: Husband (square) ← - - - Wife (circle); both connected to Son (square) below with arrows pointing up to Husband and Wife]

Feeling "Caught" in the Fixed Triangle

In fixed triangles there can be a sense of being "caught" in something that we do not want. Everyone involved can have this uncomfortable sense. Here is an example from one of my counselees:

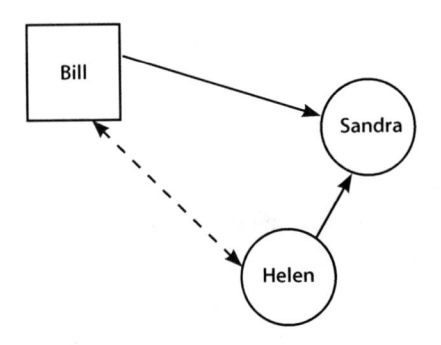

Sandra came to me for a variety of reasons, but one was work related. In her own agency, where she was a counselor, she was Helen's supervisor. Sandra's boss, Pete, had problems with Helen and would regularly talk to Sandra about what he wanted her to do in relation to supervising Helen. Sandra had her own concerns around how Helen functioned as a counselor but she thought Pete, who was the executive director of the agency at the time, should address his issues with Helen himself. Sandra often suggested this to Pete. She said she could not speak for Pete. Then he would say, "Oh, Helen won't listen to me. I think it would be better for this message to come from her supervisor, especially since you are a woman."

Helen would also complain to Sandra about Pete. She was confused about the messages she got from him and would say, "He seems to have some problem with me, but he denies it." When Sandra would encourage Helen to talk to Pete, she would say, "He says he has no problem with me and just walks away when I try to talk with him." Both Pete and Helen were each pursuing Sandra to be on their side and she felt caught.

Sandra began to learn about Bowen theory from me and was doing her own reading. She started to get the concept of triangles. At the time, her agency clinical staff met once a month with a psychologist who led them in a staff process group. The point was to look at how they were doing with each other as a staff and to talk out any difficulties they had. They had a kind of encounter-group ethic.

5 ⁓ Triangles

One day in the staff process group Helen said to Pete, "Pete, I think you have some kind of problem with me that you won't talk with me about." Just that morning, before anyone else arrived at the office, Pete had been complaining heavily to Sandra about Helen. But when confronted by her now in the group he said, "No, Helen, I don't have any problem with you." Sandra was surprised but thought this was her moment of decision for dealing with this newly perceived thing called a triangle. She took a big risk and said, "Pete, that's not what you said to me this morning."

Bang! Now Pete was caught. And Sandra didn't feel so caught anymore. Her repositioning in the triangle changed the feelings of all involved. To his credit, Pete fessed up and laid it all out to Helen. He said directly to Helen what he had been saying to Sandra about Helen. The rest of the session focused on the two of them, and Sandra felt generally relieved, although she was somewhat worried about what she had done in her relationship with Pete.

As it turned out, because she had become a kind of favorite daughter to Pete on staff, she got away with what she did. He did not retaliate in any way, and life actually got much better around staff relationships generally. It seemed to her that all of the staff triangles she knew of just went dormant. The interlocking triangles calmed right down. A couple of weeks later, one of the other staff said to her, "Sandra, things really seemed to have calmed down around here since you did that thing with Pete."

After about two months, because they had never talked about it, Sandra said to Pete, "Pete, what was it like for you when in the process group I said that you had issues with Helen?" He said, "Well, at the time I thought to myself, 'You bitch,' but, as it turned out, Sandra, that was the best thing you could have done. Helen and I are getting along really well right now and I can talk with her whenever I feel the need. I guess I learned something. But," he said, "don't ever do that again!"

So it all turned out okay. Sandra got away with what easily could be considered an unethical act only because of her favorable position in the system, and because of Pete's generally high level of maturity. Let me be clear in giving this example that I do not recommend this way of dealing with triangles in the work setting. It could easily get you fired. However, the story illustrates how people in fixed triangles can each feel trapped and unable to move. When someone decides to move differently and not be governed by the triangle, things can open up.

Dealing with Triangles: Neutrality

It is critical as helpers that first we understand triangles, and then have a sense of how to position ourselves. We have to assume a position of emotional neutrality. This is also called *detriangling*. This was critical in the work with couples like George and Martha, which I will discuss further in part 2.

I see neutrality as an essentially pastoral stance. In neutrality, we can see both sides and we can avoid judging either side. When people tell us their stories about their life and relationships, if we see them as either victims or victimizers, or one as more right and the other more wrong, then we are likely to be in the triangular roles of oppressor or rescuer. If they bombard us with stories about how awful someone else is, asking us to go along with the story, it is our job to keep defining self and not take up a function within the triangle.

Here is the basic principle. We want to find a way to push the triangling person back toward the person with whom they are having the problem. This is what Sandra did with Pete and Helen. If we feel overly sympathetic, guilty, responsible, angry, frustrated in hearing someone's story, or feel sorry for them, then we are in the triangle and we will not be of help. We will be part of the problem, even though the person we are listening to may thank us for our warm, caring understanding and support.

The key as a neutral helper is to stay connected with both sides of a triangle without taking sides. Staying connected involves:

- having curiosity about each person's experience;
- asking questions about the self of each;
- hearing the feeling expressions without focusing on them;
- getting facts about actions and events clarified;
- getting the thinking that is behind a person's behavior; and
- looking for signs of our own triangulation.

5 — Triangles

Repositioning ourselves to a more neutral place within triangles is easy if we can see how they work. However, it does require being a better-differentiated person. It does not help to say to people, "I don't do triangles. Don't ask me to take a side here," or "Hey, that's a triangle; you shouldn't do that." This reactive stance judges and puts down people, and it puts us in an over-against position.

Detriangling is not really a technique. It is about how we think about relationships and how we relate to others within an emotional system. Defining ourselves is a part of detriangling. Doing so, we are more emotionally autonomous and neutral when in contact with counselees. For example, say you are sitting with a couple and the wife is complaining at length about how much her husband is critical of her. He may or may not be present. She presumes that you, the counselor, will see it the way she sees it, see how her husband is wrong and she is the poor victim of a harsh man, and that you, as rescuer and supporter of the wronged, will agree with her about how tough she has it, and how unreasonable he is. If you say nothing, or simply nod your head with an empathic look as she tells her story, or say something about his behavior that is negative, then you are in a triangular position.

A self-defining statement that reveals that you are in a different position than she assumes would be to say something like, "You don't seem to appreciate how important you are to your husband." She will most likely be taken aback; her assumed agreement between the two of you ("We are together against him") is not there. She may say, "What do you mean?" You could say, "Well, he puts so much energy into you; you must be very important to him. Otherwise he wouldn't take note of how you are. Have you ever considered in what ways you might be important to him?"

The point here is not really to interpret what is going on with the husband and what he thinks of her. That is a common counselor move that involves being in the triangle, essentially taking his side. It is to communicate a different than assumed position for you. It may also broaden her framework for thinking about the relationship with him. The husband will also get the message about where you are in the triangle, and he also may have a new thought to consider about the source of his criticisms.

Being neutral in an emotional system while keeping meaningful emotional contact with people in it, or working to remain emotionally objective within an intense emotional field, has many applications outside of counseling. The skill of managing self within triangles is often what will make the difference in relational success or failure as a pastor or a counselor. I will demonstrate this self-definition in several ways in later chapters.

6

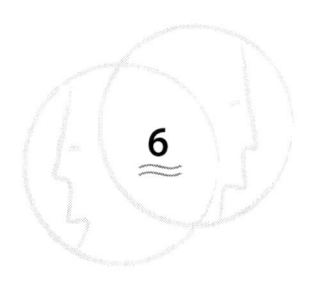

The Emotional Development of a Couple and a Family

The Marital Contract and the Emergence of Counseling

All marriages begin with an understanding of what each partner will give and receive in the relationship. These expectations are not always verbalized; they are often assumed. They may be held unconsciously, only to be discovered after the wedding. Whether or not the expectations are fulfilled is central to whether the marriage is experienced as "good."

The nature of the marital contract, and specifically who is involved, has varied over the centuries. Historically, three general types of contracts have existed. The *family contract* involves the two families of the partners. Marriage is a coming together of two families and perhaps the merging of their wealth and/or power. The families often arrange the marriage. The *religious contract* involves God and the representatives of God, like the church and its ministers. In the Christian church, pastors often pronounce the marriage as final when we say something like, "Whom God has joined together, let no man put asunder." In past centuries, pastors had total power over who would marry, and they did not allow divorce.

The *companionate contract* is the primary model in modern life. Today, we think that a marriage is simply between two people who love each other. It is not essential that God/church or their families be involved in their coming together. The partners may involve one or both of these, but many people do not consider them central to the marriage. Their consent is no longer sought, except perhaps as a formality.

In this modern contract, the essential element is the level of satisfaction of the two partners. Do they fulfill each other's hopes and expectations as life companions? If they do not, then there are "problems" in the marriage. If they do not overcome them because of "irreconcilable differences," they may choose to end the marriage. In the previous two forms of marital contracts, these differences were so routine and unremarkable that people had little hope of resolving them. Most often, any marital difficulties were addressed by either the family or the pastor telling the wife to submit to the husband.

The companionate model has increased the role of marital counseling. Given that people are now so mobile, taking jobs that are thousands of miles away from their parental homes, their families are rarely directly involved in their daily marital life and strife. In addition, since fewer people are active in a church, the direct influence of this sphere on a couple has declined. Counselors have entered the triangular gap. They are, in some ways, the modern third party to the marriage.

If the troubled couple sees a pastoral counselor for help, there may be some lingering sense in their minds (and in that of the counselor) of the church as part of the marital contract. They may either want or fear some faith-based moral pronouncement about how to manage the marriage. All counselors, whether connected to a faith group or not, have to decide what they believe about the marital contract and just how this affects their approach to marriage and divorce in counseling. It is inevitable that we will have opinions or beliefs about these issues that could influence our work, and it is best that these are consciously known to us.

It is also important to discover the two partners' beliefs around who else is important to the continuance, or the ending, of their marriage. The two people are the ones deciding legally whether the marriage will continue or not, but this is not always the case emotionally. Partners, for example, may decide not to divorce simply because of either their faith, or their family. George's mother had opposed his marriage to Martha. While, on the one hand, he continued to desire his mother's approval in many areas, he struggled with feeling controlled by this. He did not want to admit to his mother that the marriage was not working. Paradoxically, this kept him in the marriage. To divorce would mean he had to endure his mother saying, "I told you so."

The Two Become One?

Apart from what the Genesis author may have had in mind, when people come together in marriage and start a family, they create a new emotional unit. When the two people feel that powerful attraction that eventually leads to marriage, they rather quickly develop an emotional relationship where each is increasingly attuned to the other. The way two people manage the development of this emotional process is one of the first insights we can gain into their level of differentiation as a couple.

Typically, as courtship proceeds to engagement and then marriage, they begin the fusion process of giving up some of self and merging more and more into a common self; the two individuals start becoming a "we." Courtship can be a blissful time of mutual harmony and cooperation. People think that this is what "being in love" means and things will always be this way. As they move toward the marriage event itself, however, issues will begin to emerge and decisions will need to be made that are indicative of what is to come. It can be useful for a counselor to hear about these and how they were managed at the time.

Some of the most conflicted couples I have worked with say something like, "I was deeply, head over heels in love during courtship. He/she seemed perfect, and only after marriage did I discover who he/she really was." Those who are most romantically in love to start with, with the development of major conflict, are often the most hostile to each other in married life, and have some of the bitterest divorces. The same powerful passion they began with remains; it simply changes from positive to negative valence. They did not get to know each other during courtship and each, in a fused way, hung on to the romantic images they had of what marriage itself, as well as what their partner personally, would do for them in their implicit marital contract. They are deeply disappointed. Their more fused romantic expectations stem from their unresolved emotional attachments to their families of origin.

As a way to manage the fusion experience within marriage, part of what the partners do is focus on their differences. This helps them with the experience of being absorbed into the fusion. By highlighting their differences, by saying, "I am not like you," they attempt to keep some distance. At the same time, battles emerge around who is going to change the other to be more like the one wants. The two pseudo-selves form a fused "we-ness" and this becomes the terrain over which they fight. Who is going to define "we?"

Faith and Marriage

While having a personal faith can definitely contribute to a positive experience in marriage, it is not the essential element. Research has shown repeatedly that people of faith (regardless of the specific faith) generally live better, happier, and longer lives. However, atheists can have very good relationships and live long, satisfying lives; and people of faith can have very poor relationships. The key variable for all people is their level of differentiation. This is what decides how well people can live their faith within their relationships.

Better-differentiated people can do a better job of consistently living up to their stated beliefs and principles, even under trying circumstances. What people profess to believe is one thing; how well they actually live those beliefs is another. I am not saying that people are intentionally hypocritical. It is just that it takes emotional maturity to be able to live according to what we say we believe. There is a difference between professed faith, sincerely held, and what I call functional faith—how we actually behave.

For the less well-differentiated, life together can be highly problematic, chaotic, emotionally damaging, and even dangerous if violence is involved. For the better-differentiated, in spite of facing many similar kinds of problems, life together can be loving, respectful, affirming, and supportive of personal development for both partners. They will get through the normal challenges with less emotional drama or damage to either partner.

There are many books about what makes for a good relationship. The amount of advice available to a couple about how to be more loving and how they should relate is overwhelming. If only advice and telling people how to live worked, then there would be nothing but good people and good marriages. Occasionally, people have difficulty in life because of simple ignorance about what to do and how to be. In these cases, advice helps. More often they may know what to do but be incapable of carrying it off emotionally. This is about their level of differentiation. Our job as counselors is usually not about giving advice; it is about helping them to work on their level of functional differentiation so that they can implement the good, thoughtful advice that is available to them.

The Family Life Cycle

An important area to be aware of in the emotional development of a couple and family is people's stages in the family life cycle. The stages include:

- the unattached young adult in transition;
- courtship and marriage;
- birth of the first child and the family with young children;
- first child beginning school;
- adolescence of the children;
- children leaving home for college, work life, or marriage;
- divorce;
- remarriage, forming "blended" families;
- the parental couple alone together;
- aging and the related physical and emotional needs of the parents, including who/whether the children will be available for help; and
- the death of the parents and their siblings.

Each stage will present new situational challenges to the parental couple and other family members. Each stage inspires some degree of acute anxiety. Think of the shifting of the balance in the family mobile. These challenges are not just around the physical rearrangement of each person's life, but also the emotional rearrangements that must take place. Family members will each have different emotional expectations for how to deal with the stage.

For example, a new husband and wife may do just fine with each other in their companionate-style marriage until the birth of their first child. Then the husband could feel displaced as a priority of attention and affection from the wife, and jealous of the attention she gives to the infant. To deal with this, he may withdraw from them and invest himself more in his work or in a hobby. At the same time, the wife may want more help and support from him in her new challenges as a parent just when he is becoming less available. Greater ease in being flexible around these changes, and not feeling threatened by them, is one indicator of the higher level of differentiation of the partners. The changes involved in each stage challenge all couples. The less well-differentiated couple will have more difficulty moving through them and the better-differentiated couples will do better.

In George and Martha's case, although they had conflict right through the marriage, it came to a head for them after their son had left home. Neither one was sure they could or wanted to face life together when it was just the two of them. They had, they said, "stayed together for him." I told them that obviously they had not heard of the ninety-year-old couple standing in front of a judge and asking for a divorce. The judge asked them why, at this point in life, they wanted to divorce. They said, "We wanted to wait until our children were dead." Somehow, I knew they would both laugh at this. It also demonstrated a lightness in my own approach that they appreciated.

When looking at life-cycle issues, one area to pay attention to is the impact of what Bowen called emotional shock waves. For example, not all deaths are the same in an emotional system. Some will have more impact on a system depending how central the person is to the emotional functioning of the system. Someone who always emotionally relied on his or her mother may become more anxious and symptomatic with her death. The issue here is not so much going through "the stages of grief" as much as opening the system to talk about the impact of the loss, and how family members adjust in response. Open emotional systems will automatically do a better job of dealing with loss and grief.

Sibling Position

One other concept in the Bowen theory relates directly to marital development. It is the sibling position of each partner. This is the only concept that Bowen incorporated from someone else. Bowen frequently said, "No single piece of data is more important than knowing the sibling position of people." The only change he made to Dr. Walter Toman's research was to say that the level of differentiation and the effect of the projection process could dramatically modify the sibling characteristics.

Toman first did research in the early 1960s, in Germany, to show the impact of sibling positions on the course of a marriage. At the time, the divorce rate in Germany was 5 percent. It was the same for his non-clinical sample of 2,300 couples. He described what he called complementary and noncomplementary sibling relationships in marriage. A *noncomplementary relationship* was an older brother of brothers married to an older sister of sisters. They had both a rank conflict, as two oldests, and a sex conflict, in that neither grew up with direct peer experience of the opposite sex. The divorce rate for this group was 16 percent—well above the national average.

A *complementary couple* was an oldest brother of sisters married to a youngest sister of brothers. Their divorce rate was 0 percent. They had neither a rank nor a sex conflict. They grew up having a good knowledge of how the other sex functioned in life and they had worked out with their siblings a way of functioning around their different issues. Their marriage repeated this arrangement. In addition, these couples tended to have more children and they went to "Child Guidance" clinics less often for parenting help. If they did, it was usually for more minor problems with a child. Toman repeated this research in Massachusetts in the early 1970s with the same results.

Toman describes ten basic sibling positions: older brother of brothers, oldest brother of sisters, oldest sister of sisters, oldest sister of brothers, youngest brother of brothers, youngest brother of sisters, youngest sister of sisters, youngest sister of brothers, only children, and twins. Middle children have a mix of one or more of these positions depending on a number of factors, like who they were the closest to when growing up. Each of these ten positions has particular personality characteristics related to their position in the family that affect their social life as adults.

I have found this information to be quite helpful in understanding my counselees and in helping them to understand each other better. For example, it helps to depersonalize some of the behavior of each to say that how they are behaving goes with their sibling position. There is less need to say he or she is this way because he or she "does not love me." This has been quite enlightening information for couples, and it introduces a bit more objectivity into thinking about their relationship.

I worked with two gay men who were both pastors. They lived together and they were out in their different congregations. They were loved by their churches and functioned well as pastors. One of them, Jeff, had come in for personal work around his frequent moderate depressions, and I asked to see him with his partner, Mark, who came in willingly. What emerged was a pattern of Jeff giving up self to Mark and always going along with his ideas in their life together, rarely arguing for his own position. This mystified me a bit since they were both oldests and I would have expected Jeff to be more forceful in the relationship and for them to have more open conflict. I looked at their parents' sibling relationships and saw that Jeff's father was a youngest. Mark's father was an oldest. As we talked, it became clear that each had adopted some of the characteristics of his same-sex parent, which is normal, and that Jeff had seen his youngest-sibling father give in to his mother a great deal. His father also had wrestled with depression.

All of the sibling positions have their beneficial aspects and their difficulties. Bowen pointed out that the better differentiated people are, the more they can make use of their positive sibling traits, and the less well-differentiated they are, the more they will heighten their negative traits. He also showed how the projection process would greatly modify a person's sibling position characteristics. This was true with both Martha and George.

I do not have the room in this book to go into all of the ramifications of the impact of sibling position on marriage, parenting, friendships, careers, and how we function within them. It is important, however, that we as counselors acquaint ourselves with this information on sibling position as it will be helpful in our marital counseling, as well as in our own marriages. Nearly all of the couples I have worked with have found it quite useful. Because the information was so useful to us personally, my wife, Lois, and I wrote a book called *Birth Order and You* (Richardson and Richardson 1990).

7

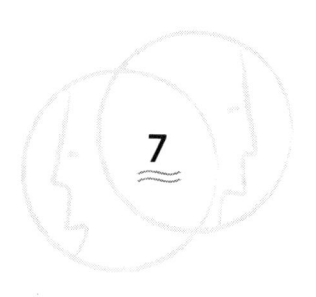

Symptomatic Mechanisms

As the fusion in a marriage intensifies, couples make use of four common emotional mechanisms for attempting to deal with it. Nearly every counseling situation involves one or more of these symptomatic mechanisms: (1) emotional distance; (2) marital conflict; (3) physical, emotional, or social dysfunction in one partner; and (4) projection of anxiety to a child.

When things are calm in a family and there is less emotional tension and symptoms may be reduced or absent. The family members may look and feel "normal." However, their chronic anxiety can easily activate, with the addition of acute anxiety, and symptoms can return or intensify. Since anxiety is infectious, it can move about from person to person within and between systems. One relationship may cool down and another one will heat up. As parents focus more on a problem child, their marital conflict may subside. If one of them is facing a critical health issue, marital conflict may also then recede.

Counselors often focus just on the presenting symptoms and through various therapeutic techniques perhaps get an improvement in the symptoms. This is the approach of most short-term counseling techniques. They are symptom focused. However, what may also happen in these cases is that with improvement in the presenting symptom, the anxiety begins to move into one of the other mechanisms and, over time, new symptoms erupt.

Good pastoral counseling, just like the best medical practice, involves going beyond symptoms. In the Bowen theory, these symptoms are understood to be a product of the family emotional system.

They result from people's efforts to deal with the anxiety and fusion they experience within their relationship system. In most cases, rather than having a symptom focus, Bowen theory counseling aims at reducing the level of anxiety and fusion, and increasing the functional level of differentiation in a family. When this is achieved the cause of the symptoms is reduced if not eliminated. Physical violence might be a case where the symptom is focused on first.

Family anxiety does not necessarily go into only one of these mechanisms; it may spread out among all four, though the mechanism of emotional distance is always present. A common example that combines all four mechanisms for dealing with fusion is the pattern of heavy drinking. Socially, people who drink heavily can get themselves into serious difficulties with the legal system. As alcohol lowers the normal inhibitions, social acting out of various sorts can result. Medical and emotional problems are also part of the drinker's life. Drinking also contributes significantly to marital and other relationship conflicts. Much physical abuse involves alcohol as a part of the emotional process.

In assessing a couple for marital conflict, we have to ascertain what other mechanisms may be present. In this book, I focus only on emotional distance and marital conflict, but I will briefly describe all four mechanisms in this chapter.

Emotional Distance

Emotional distance is a central component of each of the other three mechanisms. All people use this mechanism to deal with the fusion experience. Distance does not end the fusion; it just helps us feel more comfortable. This is something we all learned to do in our families to some degree. We did not say to our parents everything we thought, felt, did, or wanted to do. To let ourselves be known fully to them (with most parents anyway) was to invite them into telling us how to run our lives. So, to some extent, we kept our distance in order not to feel controlled by them. We said to ourselves, "What they don't know won't hurt them," but we also meant by this, "Then they can't interfere in my life." We use the distance mechanism to some extent in all of our relationships and especially in our marriages.

7 — Symptomatic Mechanisms

We can distance from our partners physically by leaving the room, or emotionally by not listening to them. Doing this, we try to regain a sense of being in charge of self and not being directed by the other when he or she wants to tell us what to do or how to be. For instance, when we feel we have given up too much self in the closeness and adapted too much to the other, then we push for greater separateness saying, "I need more alone time," or "I need my space," or "I need a project of my own without you being involved."

Better-differentiated couples can understand and accept the separate desires for either greater closeness or distance. They will feel less threatened by movement in either direction. When this level of comfort is not present then the emotional dynamic of pursuing and distancing begins to prevail.

When used on a regular and consistent basis, with a certain level of intensity over time, emotional distance in a marriage becomes an emotional divorce. This is a more or less permanent distance that is difficult to come back from. It is similar to the phenomenon of emotional cutoff. Bowen, who made cutoff a separate concept in his theory, intended this term to be used for various degrees of emotional distance between people of different generations, as between a parent and a child. Martha would be a good example. She had cut off with her mother and had an emotional divorce with her husband.

To get to this place of emotional divorce, expectations have been significantly unfulfilled. Usually there has been a great deal of hurt experienced by one or both partners. Things have been said and done that feel unforgiveable. Hurt is an important topic of discussion with people in counseling. It tends to be resolved only as people can move from fusion toward differentiation. I will demonstrate this process in part 2.

In the more severe forms of marital conflict, as with George and Martha, the partners have experienced a great deal of emotional damage. They become unwilling to trust in the good intentions of their partners, possibly forever. They say, and mean, "I can never forgive you for saying/doing that." These situations typically move to a legal divorce, but if they try to bring about a reconciliation the process will be long and difficult. These people are not candidates for short-term work; more often, years are involved in improving their relationship.

Marital Conflict

The basic pattern in marital conflict occurs when neither partner is able to give in to the other and adapt to the wishes of the other in a way that is comfortable and that requires no loss of self. Any vital relationship between two thinking and feeling people will include some kind of struggle over differences. It can be done kindly, with mutual respect and civility, or even with passion and strong words. In better-differentiated couples, these passionate arguments will not include the vituperation that happens in more severe marital conflicts. The conflicts may even involve some periods of emotional distance, but eventually, in healthier couples, they will find ways to reconnect, arrive at some mutual decision about how to proceed, and get on with their lives.

Couples in significant conflict fight over either big or small issues, but even if the issue is a small one, it will always feel like it is "a federal case." What is often not recognized about their apparently petty fights is that the threatened sense of self is the so-called federal issue. This is a big deal for both of them. When they do compromise, it is often with a sense of resentment; the one who gives in is waiting for something to go wrong in order to blame the other.

Marital conflict can be a cold war as well as a hot war; however, it is usually those who are engaged in open battle that come in to see a counselor. The cold warriors have made their separate peace and may be content to live with it until something dramatic happens to disturb their arrangement, like the discovery of an affair. They may even be civil and relatively decent with one another but with little sense of real passion, warmth, and caring. This situation may develop because one partner is dependent on the other for financial reasons and may not want to give up his or her material lifestyle.

Fusion and Responsibility

Each partner will have a strong focus on the other and how the other is behaving, feeling, or thinking. These perceived elements in the other become the basis of feelings in self. This is fusion. How self is depends on the perception of how the other is. There is a constant monitoring as to whether the other is being what the one partner wants.

When they have focused all of their undifferentiation on their partner, this will then allow them to have relatively good relationships elsewhere. So each partner may think, "I can get along with everybody else in my life, why can't I get along with him (or her)? It must be his (or her) fault, not mine." When the marriage ends and the partner is out of the picture, then another close relationship in their life becomes problematic. The fusion shifts to a new focus. This is very frequent in cases involving affairs where the affair is experienced as a "good" relationship until there is a divorce. Then, when the first partner is out of the picture, the fusion focuses on this now different relationship. Their former good relationship depended on the presence of the first marital partner in the triangle.

Not all couples openly say the other partner is the problem. In their efforts to be fair when they come in to see a counselor, they may say something like, "Our relationships is in difficulty." They say, "The relationship is the problem," not the partner. However, relationships are not things. They do not have properties that (as in the common parlance) can be "worked on" or fixed. A focus on "the relationship" is a triangular way of avoiding responsibility for self in relating to another. The relationship is only the process that happens between them and they each, separately, contribute to that process.

Fusion and Triangles
Triangular attachments to others, like an affair, have a stabilizing quality, but if something happens to change the relationship, then things may heat up in the marriage. For example, a close friend or a relative may move away, or become very sick, or even die. Having no one else to share his or her anxiety with, a person may become more reactive in the marriage. When doing assessments of a couple, it is important to know who each partner talks to about his or her life and marital issues, and what advice is given. It is also important to know if there has been a change in any of these relationships.

Sometimes these others (family or friends) may say, in effect, "Don't try to involve me in this. This is between you and your partner." The third person wants to stay in the outside position of the triangle and not be "dragged in" to take a side. The complainer might experience this as rejection or lack of caring. The person may go to someone else to complain and no longer feel so friendly toward the person who did not want to be involved. If pastors take this position, and it is part of their way of functioning, this story will feed the interlocking triangles against them.

In recognizing that the general direction of conflicted couples is to become more closed, and that they will get in greater difficulty as this happens, the counselor is interested in developing greater openness. However, I do not teach people how to communicate, or even insist that they do it. My intent in counseling is to create an atmosphere of safety, with a lowered level of threat, where people feel less anxiety. As this happens, they will reveal more of self, be more open, and communicate better.

The only exception I make to this statement is in the case of significant physical abuse. While abusive behavior can be a part of the emotional process between partners, a process for which each person is responsible, the abused person is never responsible for being hit or physically hurt by their partner, no matter how provocative is their own behavior. In more significant cases of physical abuse, I do not work with them together simply because it is impossible to establish the required level of safety for openness to develop. After a session the abusive person will punish the other for what was said in the counseling session.

To attempt to provide counseling in this context is irresponsible and the counselor could be complicit in the abused person being further abused, damaged, and maybe killed. Instead, I refer them to special programs designed for them. I may encourage people who experience significant abuse to involve the police, if they have not yet done so, and to resort to a place of safety. Research indicates that this is one of the most effective interventions for stopping the attacks. I regard major abusive behavior as assault, not simply the result of marital arguments.

Over- and Underfunctioning Reciprocity and Personal Dysfunction

The development of physical, emotional, or social symptoms in one partner can begin with the couple generating an over- and underfunctioning pattern between them. Very often in a marriage, one partner looks more mature and functionally competent in managing the various tasks of family, work, and social life than the other. The Bowen theory understands this discrepancy as one way the couple manages their fusion with each other.

7 — Symptomatic Mechanisms

Over- and underfunctioning reciprocity is present to some extent in all marriages, but the pattern is more intense and consistent with these symptomatic couples. The patterns were probably already established in their separate families of origin and the couple simply continue them in marriage. A person who was a caretaker (or the one needing care) in his or her family may perform the same function in marriage. The marriage is just a continuation of life as they have known it.

At the nonsymptomatic level, for example, it is normal when one partner is ill that the other partner may step in temporarily to do whatever the ill partner normally does in the family routines. Another traditional over- and underfunctioning pattern involves the wife taking most of the responsibility for household management and the children, and the husband being in charge of providing income, doing household repairs, looking after cars, and other mechanical things. Modern couples have been challenging the sex-role stereotypes related to this division of labor but in essence the process is the same; only the content of who does what is different. The more mature the couple the greater their flexibility in adapting to new challenges and in being able to decide who will do what.

The over- and underfunctioning reciprocity means one partner becomes more dominant and the other more submissive in one or more areas of life. The overfunctioner appears to be in charge of the relationship but it may seem to that person, as well as to some observers, that things often go the way the underfunctioner wants. In fact, each partner gains something in the reciprocity as well as losing something. Typically, overfunctioners become highly competent people who work very hard. Eventually, however, since they have difficulty setting limits on the demands made on them, they may have a breakdown as the only means of letting go of their load of responsibility.

Neither partner is solely responsible for this reciprocal pattern (both help to create it), and the overfunctioners may say they have no choice but to act as they do. They "have to" compensate for the other partner's underfunctioning, and the underfunctioner may say that they "have to" adapt to the desires of the overfunctioner. The overfunctioner, either male or female, may be dominating, authoritative, and demanding. In the face of this, the other partner crumbles into compliance and weak submission.

The under- and overfunctioning reciprocity can become emotionally ingrained in a relationship and over time, with enough intensity, it may lead to symptoms in one partner. As a part of the related fusion process, it is a way to avoid conflict around dealing with differences. There are many forms of depression, but one that often shows up in my office is when one partner is depressed and the other appears to function normally. They do not live a normal relational life because of the depression.

When such a person presents for help, I often ask myself, after assessing some of the history of the depression, "Who is this person giving up self to?" Even though theirs is an individually focused symptom, I always make a point of getting the person's spouse (or other relevant family members) in for a visit early in the process, with the assumption that as the depression begins to lift the marriage will start to show some difficulties. This is nearly always true and by having established a positive relationship with the spouse early on—before change happens—they are usually more comfortable with coming in as a part of marital counseling.

The underfunctioner is usually seen as "the problem" in the family. Counselors may be recruited into a triangle with the overfunctioner to join in "fixing" the underfunctioner. Instead, counselors need to see the fusion in the marriage as the focus of intervention. The more the overfunctioner overfunctions, then the more the underfunctioner underfunctions. They go hand in hand. As this process continues over time, the underfunctioner appears more and more symptomatic.

Often, rather than working with the "problem person," I choose to work with the overfunctioner with the goal of getting him or her to lower their level of overfunctioning and to withdraw energy from doing for the partner what the partner could do for self. This is not easy to achieve, but when they do, the underfunctioners will (eventually, not immediately) raise their level of functioning. This has worked for me in some cases where I rarely worked with the underfunctioning person.

Underfunctioners may appear to be compliant, saying, "Whatever you want, dear," and then manage to screw things up somehow while all along pleading innocence and good intentions. George could do this pattern well. Individual-model therapists call this "passive aggressiveness," but that diagnosis ignores the interactive, reciprocal process at work. George originally developed this pattern in his family of origin. Some people assume these patterns are about individual personality characteristics. They say things like, "She is a major overfunctioner," but this way of talking obscures the reciprocal quality of the couple's functioning. One must always see them as interconnected.

Projection of Anxiety to a Child

The projection of anxiety to a child is universal and nearly all families with children have it to some degree. Projection is a way of reducing anxiety in the parental generation and loading it on to one or more children. Parents project their own lack of differentiation onto a child, who then becomes less responsible for his or her own life. As parental differentiation decreases in a family, the potential for more intense projection increases. The child begins to underfunction (physically, emotionally, or socially) and becomes "the problem."

Children impaired by the projection process will do less well in life generally and may have lifelong difficulties in functioning. They will have lower levels of differentiation than their siblings. Through marriage to a partner at their level of differentiation, they can be part of an ongoing multigenerational projection process, producing increasingly impaired children. When this process repeats over several generations, it can result in severely impaired children.

North America tends to be a significantly child-focused society and this reinforces the projection process. The number of books, articles, workshops, and media stories on problem children and parenting, in order not to raise problem children, or to fix problem children, is immense. As a result of this intense child focus, paradoxically, our children tend to be more anxious, more problematic, and less responsible.

Quite often in this process, the parents are educated, intelligent people who want the best for their children. They have researched the literature on their child's problem and become semi-expert in it. The early strategies for dealing with the problem often involve being more loving and caring parents. Some children learn to take advantage of this and the more loving and forgiving the parents are, the more the child (usually at adolescence) will accuse them of not really caring.

This child will feel deprived, and the parents will be described as inadequate.

The emotional process tends to focus around whoever is the principal caretaker of the children, usually the mother. We have to be clear that the caretaking parent is not the cause of the problem. Because of the biological givens of childbirth and the way family life is constructed in most societies, mothers tend to be central in the relationship with children. Indeed, family life tends to revolve around mothers. Any anxiety in the family focused on the children will tend to be funneled through the mothers, but they are not the cause.

The projection process involves parents who are more focused on their children than each other. Their focus determines whether symptoms will present as projection to a child or as marital conflict. Fathers play a significant role. They may, in response to the anxiety shown by mothers, support the mother's focus on the child. They may note, consciously or not, that she becomes calmer as she focuses on the child and this is fine, especially if it calms down her relationship with him.

Often the parents' child focus begins very early, with the birth of the child or even before. One or both parents may have hopes and fantasies about what their child will accomplish or will be for them. As a result, the attachment between the parent and that child becomes more intense. Normally, this attachment appears as a positive relationship while the child is young, but the valence often goes negative as the child approaches the normal, more independent life of adolescence.

The Triangular Relationship

If the child becomes involved with authorities outside of the family (such as pastors; teachers; school counselors; the medical, psychiatric, or psychological community; police; and the court system), this serves to intensify the process even more, especially if the child being focused on gets a diagnosis of some sort from an outside authority. It is rare that any of these outside systems will be a resource to the parents in their own differentiation issues. More likely, they will join in with an intense focus on the problem child. These authorities may also blame the parents for the child's problems. Bowen says,

7 — Symptomatic Mechanisms

> [It is] a triangular emotional process through which two powerful people in the triangle reduce their own anxiety and insecurity by picking a defect in the third person, diagnosing and confirming the defect as pitiful and in need of benevolent attention, and then ministering to the pitiful helpless one, which results in the weak becoming weaker and the strong becoming stronger. It is present in all people to some degree, and by over-compassion in poorly integrated, over-emotional people, powered by benevolent over-helpfulness that benefits the stronger one more than the recipient, and is justified in the name of goodness and self-sacrificing righteousness. (Bowen 1978: 434)

These negative statements about the do-gooder quality of those who want to help the child were not aimed specifically at the church but it easily could fit there. The good intentions of others to fix the child feed into the triangular process by helping the parents ignore their own lack of differentiation and focus their anxiety on the child. It would be easy for pastors and people in the church to see the parents as good and the child, in some sense, because of his or her acting out, as bad.

Blaming is a central part of this triangular process. The question all parties tend to ask is, "Who is at fault here?" Parents blame the child, as well as each other, and the child blames one or both parents. This blaming approach exists at many levels of society and these social patterns reinforce the family pattern. Finding who is at fault and labeling them as the problem that needs to be fixed or changed is a common way of dealing with difficulties. Often parents blame the schools for their child's problems and, of course, the schools and teachers blame the parents. Neither one gets anywhere in relation to the child. No one is willing to take responsibility for their part in the process and just focus on self and what self will or will not do. Siblings and other members of the extended family may join in with the triangular blaming and side-taking process.

This projection process does not result from either a liberal, more permissive parenting style, or a stricter, disciplinarian one. Many parents shift back and forth between trying to be more lenient or trying to be stricter. The issue is the degree to which the parents tend to focus their fusion on the child and try to help or control or manage the child. Instead, they need to be more responsible for themselves and control themselves better.

Both George and Martha had been a focus of the projection process in their families and while in both cases it was equally intense, it played out in opposite ways. As a mature man, George could act more grown up and function relatively well at work and in his social life. However, his mother continued to infantilize him and he played his part. Moves toward greater emotional independence on his part caused anxiety in her, and this stimulated his own anxiety. He would quickly move to reassure her that he still cared about her, and her growing calmness helped him feel less anxious. He never had enough self free of her to fully invest emotionally in the relationship with his wife and, comparing her to his mother, she never came off as caring in the way his mother did. Mom was a magnetic field from which he could not and did not appear to want to escape.

Martha, on the other hand, in spite of all appearances, was also deeply involved with her mother, whom she had not spoken to for over twenty years. Her cutoff from her mother was just as intense as George's attachment to his. Cutoff and having nothing to do with the previous generation betrays an intense attachment that is denied but equally powerful. The projection process on her side acted through a huge amount of punishing negativity coming from her mother to Martha. Martha saw her mother's actions toward her as hostile, cold, rejecting, and very much unlike how she was with Martha's sister.

Martha's hatred of her mother betrayed her attachment to her mother. Her father, now long deceased, had never intervened or established his own relationship with Martha. He had remained distant in the family. Not surprisingly, she married a man who also could be distant, rejecting, and hostile toward her. She deeply wanted his support and approval, but rarely got it except for when he brought some of his business clients home for a meal she prepared.

In my counseling, whenever the parents present their child as the problem in the family, I gradually convince them of the importance of my working with them (the parents) rather than with the child. As the parents continue in counseling they slowly begin to see, primarily through my questioning about family process, how anxiety works in their family, and how this can focus on the child. They begin to connect the child's behavior and their own. For people who have long lived the way they have, it is difficult to see any alternatives to the patterns they have established; it seems normal to them. Slowly the sense develops of how much of their thinking is bound up in the child. They begin to see how this is not appropriate for the child, and how they are avoiding their own concerns by this focus. As the couple begins to defocus on the child, it is normal for issues around the emotional distance in the marriage to be exposed. Underlying marital conflict often emerges.

George and Martha used the mechanisms of emotional distance and marital conflict, but projected very little of their anxiety to their twenty-two-year-old son. I had a session with him to get his input on how he saw his family life and to assess how he was doing. He was open about the pros and cons of their family life and appeared free to get on with his own life while his parents battled away. As long as conflicted parents can continue to be appropriately attentive to their children's needs and behave responsibly as parents, marital conflict does not cause major problems for children. Marital conflict affects them most when they are triangled into it and asked, in one way or another, to side with one parent against the other, or when they are involved in the projection process.

PART 2

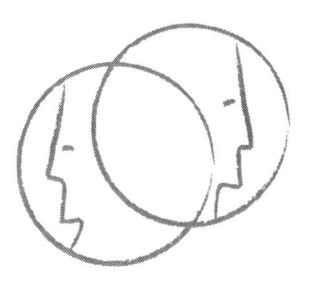

FAMILY SYSTEMS THEORY IN COUNSELING

8

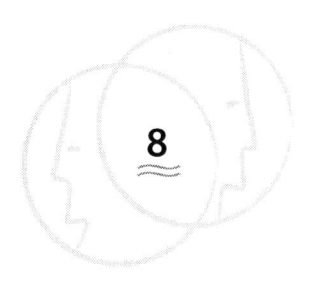

The Counseling Relationship in the Bowen Theory

There are no simple ways to talk about how we humans are intricately involved in the relationships around us and how this affects the act we call helping. We have a certain amount of free will and an ability to shape our lives, but we are also involved in influential emotional/social amalgams. These are powerful and we spend much of our emotional energy reacting to them. We all modify our lives in some way either to avoid or to accommodate the people we are involved with and care about, and they do the same with us. These various emotional systems inevitably affect the way we understand helping and how we go about trying to offer help.

When counselees come into our office to talk about their problems, they bring all of this with them. As we listen to them talk about their difficulties and what they want from us, our own relationship issues get stimulated. Then, as we sit together and interact out of our two emotional systems, we form another emotional system that also functions according to the concepts in the Bowen theory. The primary factors that keep us on track in our efforts to help are: (1) our understanding of theory; and (2) our ability to live the principles of that theory within our relationships.

The Counseling Relationship as Cure?

Almost universally, the various strands of psychotherapy tend to see the counselor's relationship with the counselee as the essential ingredient in helping the counselee. Most major schools of counseling, in spite of their many differences from each other, paraphrasing Bowen, assert in some form the common ideas that:

1. The individual's emotional difficulties develop in relationship to powerful and significant others, usually early in life; and
2. The relationship with a counselor is the treatment of choice for dealing with these emotional difficulties.

This common assumption about the cure being in the relationship with the counselor contains a split between theory and practice. What most counseling is saying (in some form) is, "Your difficulties began over there, in that emotionally powerful group of people (your family), but we are going to work on them here, in this relationship between you and me." What is often unstated but clearly implied is that "You need a healing relationship with a relationally competent, caring person like me to get better."

It is from this way of thinking that the broad professional field of counseling arrives at its almost universal concern with "the therapeutic relationship." A great deal of counselor training is focused on the helping relationship itself and much less on a general theory of human functioning. The helping relationship has built into it some forces that create a potential for abuse. Because of this potential and because of the anxiety we have as trainers, most training programs focus on the helping relationship and ignore the larger theoretical issues.

Bowen Theory, Counseling, and "Individual Problems"

As Bowen's research developed, he saw this theory/practice split in his work. The implications of his thinking led him to a position described somewhat like this (although he never said it just this way): "Why should we impose a one-sided relationship (that between therapist and client) as the way to be of help to clients, when the client's emotional difficulties began in relationships with others?"

The clear implication is that counseling can be a roundabout way of working with people and their problems. Why not keep the counseling focused on the client's original relationships, and the emotional energy invested in those relationships, rather than on their transference to the counselor? Or focus on where the problems are presently being played out, and work with the emotional process going on there, in people's real lives, and not in a one-sided relationship with a counselor?

The individual model of human functioning sees the problem as resident in the individual person. It is his or her problem even though it may have been created in another context, like within the family. The counselor accepts the counselee and understands what life is like for the person (empathy), and the counselee begins to feel better. However, the other relationships in the person's life do not improve all that much. While not usually stated this clearly, the lack of improvement in those relationships is attributed to "those other people's problems." The implication then is "They should be in their own counseling. They should be more like my counselor is with me. Then we could all get along."

From the Bowen theory perspective, whether the presenting problem is focused in a person or a relationship, everybody in the emotional system shares that problem. One person, or relationship, becomes symptomatic, but "the problem" is not restricted to that person or relationship. The individuals are only one piece of the puzzle; they are just a part of the difficulty.

This is not blaming the family. Generally, family members are doing as well as they can. Family members want to be responsible and helpful to each other and it only requires a family systems focus to move the process from hurtful to helpful. Bowen theory helps people become more responsible family members by becoming more responsible for self in relation to the others, and stepping out of the fused emotional togetherness process that keeps things stuck. They can learn to do togetherness in a more differentiated way.

Emotional Latitude and Differentiation

People in families vary in the amount of emotional latitude and flexibility they have around changing. This is about their level of differentiation of self. This means some are in a better position to change self within the emotional process than others are. As a result, in the Bowen approach, there is a tendency to focus on the healthier (less symptomatic) family members as a source of change rather than to focus on the more impaired or most symptomatic family member. Those healthier people often have more ability, or the emotional latitude, to create some change in self and behave differently within the emotional system. When one person changes, others are challenged to change.

Here is one somewhat dramatic example. It represents one of the few times I could not get a husband to come in with his wife. He absolutely refused to have anything to do with counseling. The wife, in her early fifties, came in because she felt depressed and thought she might have a breakdown. It quickly became clear that she overfunctioned in relation to both her husband and her family, including her family of origin, within which she was a caretaker for a number of people. Her four children were nearly all launched in their adult lives, but she still felt a great responsibility for them and was there to help and come up with solutions for whatever problems they had. She was not doing the things that she really enjoyed and wanted to do for herself. She felt stuck in being helpful to, caring for, and supporting others. In her church, where she was also quite active and valued, she was regarded as a good and helpful Christian.

Much of her anxiety focused on her husband, who did not like his job. He felt a lot of pressure in his business; he was always worried about it and what his boss thought of him, even though he was successful. She had become his major emotional supporter, helping him with the work he brought home from the office.

As we looked at her overfunctioning pattern, she slowly found ways to get herself unhooked from doing for others what they could do for themselves. She learned not to respond to the anxiety they or she felt as this emotional unhooking took place. The rest of her family members could handle this better than her husband could. Whenever she would let go of her overfunctioning with him, he would get disturbed about work and begin to talk about what a failure he was. As she gradually did less for him, he became more depressed. Occasionally he would have major outbursts of anger at her over little things that had nothing to do with her. He talked about shooting himself and putting an end to it all. This created huge anxiety for the wife; she would fall back into helping him. He then would calm down, but then she despaired of ever having the life she wanted.

The threats of suicide hooked her. We talked about all of this and she sorted her way through the emotional issues regarding who was responsible for what. While maintaining a warm relationship with him, she got herself extricated from his work life and began doing some of the things she personally enjoyed. The big step was her getting into a master's degree program. He felt abandoned by her, became very depressed, and talked more about suicide. He had a gun in the house under his lock and key, but he absolutely refused to talk with anybody (like me) about his depression.

She went to a medical library at school and checked out a book with pictures of people who had "blown their heads off" with a gun. She showed it to her husband saying, "I just want you to see the mess I am going to have to deal with when you kill yourself." This dramatic act did it. He could see that she was unhooked from his threats. His rages and his depression calmed down and he began to function better for himself, while she got on with her life plans. Eventually, over a year's time, he began to focus on things that were more pleasurable to him as well, and he obsessed less about his work. And the two of them got along much better.

I considered myself to be doing marriage and family counseling even though I was seeing only her. The issue was anxiety in the family, including the larger family, and the wife was highly sensitive to it. She wanted to alleviate it in others so that then she could feel less anxious. By changing her part in the emotional process in the family, others were forced to change and adapt to her new level of functioning. I met with her four children and they adapted more quickly to the changes in their mother. Eventually the husband came in for one session because, he said, "I want to meet this guy." It was a friendly meeting. He agreed that his life had changed for the better and he was happy that his wife was happier. Overall, my work with this family took just over two years.

The Counselor's Family History

All counselors come out of families and, as we participated in that intense emotional process there, we continue to operate out of many of those patterns as adults. Education, degrees, and sophisticated concepts do not change these emotional realities. We may lay an intellectual veneer over the underlying family-based experiences enabling us to fool ourselves into thinking that we are more grown up with our new knowledge. Subjectively, we want to believe that we have grown out of those old patterns; but objectively—if a hidden camera could observe our current functioning in relationships—it would be easy to show this statement as false, personally as well as professionally. We are not all grown up.

Given enough anxiety, we are all able to fall back into our early emotional patterns in family. In a phone call home to our parents, how long does it take before we begin to feel or act like an adolescent again? One student is the best quick example I have. He had a PhD in psychology and was doing postdoctoral work in my family therapy training program. Very early in the training, before he really got the complexity of the concept, he said, "I am going home this weekend to differentiate myself from my family." I did not bother telling him he was not getting it. When I saw him the next week I asked, "How did it go?" "Terrible," he said. "As soon as I got off the plane, I lit a cigarette. Then I met my mother, and the very first thing she said to me was, 'I see you're still smoking.' I immediately said, 'I'm a grown man. I can do what I want.' And the whole weekend went like that. Nothing had changed."

The Counseling Relationship in a Larger Perspective

If a counselor can manage to keep a moderately intense relationship with the counselees, then the counselees and their emotional system will normally calm down, at least for a while. This is true of most any counselor regardless of theoretical framework. This relationship has the effect of draining anxiety or tension out of the system. Counselees are relieved by the existence of this important relationship and feel better. This is, in fact, the function of a standard triangle. In addition, if the counselor takes on the anxiety him or herself, and even becomes responsible for fixing things, the counselee will feel even better. The counselee can relax, and those involved with him or her may say, "He/she is getting better."

If the counselor becomes more emotionally important to the counselee, however, and they become more intensely involved, the counselee may well distance from emotional contact with the other family members, who will then become more disturbed about the relationship with the counselor. A significant new relationship with any type of helper, be it friend, minister, teacher, as well as counselor, can have a calming effect in the larger system. Even a secret affair can do this. However, continuing with this example, if the affair becomes emotionally overinvested or more intense, then the person may become alienated from the family system and tension in the system will increase. Usually, at that point, the suspicious spouse becomes a detective, alert to all signs that have been previously ignored, and discovers the affair.

There are professional affairs in which the same kind of effect can result—whether they involve a doctor, a counselor, or a pastor. Some counselors have professional affairs with their counselees, although not sexualized, and they themselves feel some of the benefits of these emotional involvements. It is not unusual for the one spouse in counseling to indicate to his or her spouse not in counseling that the counselor is a wonderful person and too bad the spouse cannot be like the counselor.

Here is another case when the husband absolutely refused to participate in marital counseling. I became aware of the importance both parties were assigning to me, and of some of what the wife was saying to her husband about how wonderful she thought I was. This caused the husband to see his wife and me in cahoots against him. I told the wife that I wanted her to tell him that I said she "didn't understand him at all." In addition, I wanted to know what he said in response.

She was offended because she thought she understood him perfectly and I was disagreeing with her; but she did what I asked. This served to create some distance from me in the triangle, to lower the level of intensity and make me less important. When she told him, the husband said, "He's damn right about that!" Not long after that, he was willing to come in for counseling with her. I was no longer the enemy to him, or the hero to her. I was just important enough.

The Assumed and Assigned Importance of a Significant Other

In the training work I do with my students, we start with one simple sentence from Bowen: "The successful introduction of a significant other person into an anxious or disturbed relationship system has the capacity to modify relationships within the system" (Bowen 1978: 342). This is a statement about helping and change that can apply to almost any type of counseling or helping process. It is consistent with his theory, and shows how other approaches to helping, or other therapeutic modalities, could also be helpful, even though they use different theories. Bowen focused on several variables in this statement, and it would be worth the reader's time to see how he expanded on it in his book.

The significance of this other person can be either *assumed* on the counselor's part (how the helper thinks of their importance to others), or it can be *assigned* (how the counselee thinks about the helper). As Dr. Bowen pointed out, leaders of cults, healers of various types, and charismatic leaders of spiritual movements can take on importance for one family member. Other family members may have negative reactions to this. Their reactions may be for emotional reasons, like loss of love and caring from the person who becomes involved with these people ("She doesn't care about us anymore"), or for material reasons ("He changed his will and is giving everything to that swami").

Someone who represents God can bring this intensity out in family members. This phenomenon can make pastors and pastoral counselors suspect for some family members, and more trusted by others. Such a helper could say in effect, if not in actual words, "Believe in me," or "Trust in me," or "Have confidence in me." This leader or helper assumes great importance and/or the importance is assigned by the believer. There may be some kind of a conversion experience and an instant change of sorts can result in the way the person lives. His or her daily life and behaviors may change, but the family is often quite put off.

Another element is how much thinking/feeling time the counselee devotes to the relationship and how emotionally preoccupying it is. Counselors can also have overly positive or negative feelings with regard to their counselees that preoccupy them outside of the counseling session itself. This is an indication that things will not go well. This kind of reactivity, of either sort (experienced either as looking forward to seeing the counselees again, or dreading to see them), needs to be discussed with a supervisor.

A more common example of this phenomenon is a new "in-love" romantic relationship in which each partner will likely have an overvalued image of the other. We can see the changes in a person who is in love and how they reorient their lives around the other person. Friends and family of the person in love may say things like, "I don't know what she sees in him." In this case, a very high degree of assigning and perhaps of assuming of importance is involved and we marital counselors often deal with the fallout of this process when it collapses.

Charismatic people, whatever their role, whatever they are selling or doing, often assume as well as attract the assignment of importance. They do this through exuding a great deal of warmth toward the other person, making them feel special. Those who are in need of this warmth will be susceptible. In my work with clergy involved in sexual abuse cases in their church, they have usually been more charismatic and warm, empathic types in their style of leadership. When they encounter people who are in need of love, attention, and acceptance, then the abuse may happen.

Bowen's Different Approach

The Bowen theory approach to the pastoral care and counseling relationship with counselees is quite different. The relationship is intentionally less intense. When I started counseling from this perspective, there was a kind of loss for me. I had enjoyed the warmth and emotional intensity of involvement with counselees. After making the change in theoretical orientation, I work at a somewhat greater emotional distance from my counselees, hopefully inspiring less assigned importance to me from them. I would not now want to return to my previous way of relating to counselees.

The effort, as much as possible, is to keep the intensity of emotionality where it belongs, within the counselee's family system; to be more reality focused there in terms of the functional aspects of those emotional relationships, and not to encourage the transference to the counselor or to intensify that relationship. I work at ways of downplaying the role of assigned importance to me and do not assume undue importance.

It is very difficult for many clergy to do this, not only because of what their parishioners bring in terms of their projections and triangular expectations, but because of the models of pastoral care and counseling they have been taught, or that they automatically fall into. That kind of intense caring relationship is one of the "benefits" many pastors look for in their work. It might even be what led some into becoming a pastor. They thought, "I'm good with people; I enjoy caring for them," or some version of that.

In the family systems theory approach, the caring is in the skills we have and that our clients can develop for differentiating a self within their family system. It is not in the relationship with us. I think of this as a very caring approach and that there is nothing better I can do for the people who come to me for help. The help I can offer is not through a warm, one-sided relationship with me, but through them getting along better with the people they live with. The former encourages a dependency on me; the latter encourages more autonomy in relationship with others.

The Expression of Feelings in Counseling

In my pre-Bowen days, I had become quite good at getting counselees to identify and express their feelings. This automatically intensified the emotionality of the relationship with me. I should have been good at it—I had spent six years working at this in my own life and relationships. Lois and I had been doing the kind of marital work that Harville Hendrix eventually described in his books; the latest version of that kind of work is Sue Johnson's Emotionally Focused Therapy (EFT). Both involve intense affective work.

However, Lois and I did not experience any lasting changes in our relationship in spite of the greater emotional intensity. We, as well as my counselees, would say, "I didn't realize I had so much pain (or anger, or fear, or sadness, or whatever) inside me." As with Lois and me, I was not seeing my clients' actual relationships change all that much, even though they were going "deeper" into their feelings and expressing them more.

As I see it now, the intense feeling focus maintained the following in me and in my counselees:

1. Essentially a victim stance within key triangles; that is, a kind of other-focused way of seeing life where other people create my

experience by their behavior and expressed feelings. This stance is most easily invoked in counseling by that famous fusion-based question: "How does that make you feel?"

2. This stance allowed us to avoid taking full responsibility for our own lives since we believed others made us how we were. If they were not nice to me, I felt bad, and I would feel better when they learned to be more respectful and to take better care of or relate better to me. Lots of energy went into trying to get this to happen.

3. It also maintained an inability to see that feelings go with our positions in an emotional system. *If we can change our own functional position in an emotional system then our feelings change. The objective position in a system determines the subjective experience.* For example, anyone who has ever been promoted or demoted in a work system has experienced this, and it is a similar phenomenon in the family emotional system.

Knowing about the objective elements of emotional-system relationship functioning, and especially about triangles, can keep things much more fact based and reality oriented. This avoids or reduces many of the subjective, feeling-based transference issues. Of course, transference is always there. The issue is whether we counselors do things to enhance and heighten it or not. People come to pastors and pastoral counselors with much of their transference already in place—expecting certain things of us because of our pastoral identity. They project these expectations on to us.

Counseling as Coaching

The counselor/counselee relationship looks so different in Bowen theory work that many of us, rather than speaking of counseling, call our work *coaching*, or even *supervision* when referring to counselees' work in their own families. I like the term *coach* because it takes the focus off of the counselor/counselee relationship. It makes clear that "the game" is "out there," elsewhere in the counselee's life. It is not primarily about the relationship between me and the counselee "in here." My office is on the sidelines and I am talking with the counselee about what they are involved in out there on the playing field, and it is more about how the counselee is able to move, relate, and be with others out there.

The challenge is to modulate the close/distant relationship with counselees, to discover how to be important enough or close enough so that we are seen as having interest in and relevance to their issues, without becoming too important. It is possible to meet this challenge if we have a good functional understanding of emotional systems theory and have worked on our selves within our family systems. The point is to relate actively to the system and stay outside of it at the same time. We do not offer or promise our clients any other benefits except what they are able to accomplish through their own responsible efforts to learn about self and change self within those other important relationships.

Neutrality and Pastoral Caring

The helper has to find a place of emotional neutrality or detachment with each person in the emotional system. This is a very tricky issue, especially for us as clergy. It is tricky first of all, simply because people tend to hear the word *neutrality* as meaning uncaring or uninvolved or not having a position of our own. But the concept is really about the emotional side-taking that happens in triangular relationships.

Here is the basic counseling strategy for couples in the Bowen theory. *The tension within a two-person system can be resolved when in the presence of a third person (the counselor) who does not take sides, stays in equal contact with both parties, is curious about how they behave with each other, tracks with them their emotional process, and leaves responsibility for their thinking and behavior with them.* This curiosity may include not just their objective behavior, but also the more subjective thinking, feeling, and intentions that go into the behavior. We do not ignore feelings, but we do not focus on them exclusively.

We as helpers have to live in a genuinely neutral place for this to happen at all. We cannot be "trying to get some change in the system." If we secretly side with one partner, or have more sympathy for one partner, change will not happen no matter what our behavior is. Our own secret emotional side taking is more powerful than our outward behavior. The counselor's neutrality is the only way solid change is going to happen.

Being neutral does not mean we do not have our own thoughts about responsible behavior in relationships. It does not mean that we let go of our own beliefs and values. It does affirm that other people have to figure things out for themselves. That is part of what growing up (or growing into our full humanity) is about. It means becoming responsible for our own beliefs, values, and behavioral principles in relationships. This is critical in defining a self.

Most of the people I work with, because they are referred through secular sources, do not know that I am a clergyman and I do not make a point of saying it up front. At some point, usually later in the counseling, they may look at degrees on my wall and say, "You are a minister?" to which I say, "Yes. Do you have any questions or concerns about that?" That usually is as far as it goes.

What is so interesting to me is how many of my counselees get involved or reinvolved with a church at some point later in counseling, without us ever discussing it. Usually this happens as they work on issues of self-definition in their family, as they begin to think about what principles they want to base their life on. When they tell me about their renewed church involvement, my typical response is usually, "Really? What led you to do that?" Their response is usually some version of, "We have talked so much about what I believe and how I want to behave that it has gotten me to think about the basis of some of my values. I thought church would help me with this." At these times, I think I have fulfilled my John the Baptist role.

Emotional neutrality goes against the core of what many of us have dedicated our lives to, and against many forms of counseling, but with neutrality, we can be much better observers and understand the emotional functioning of the system more clearly. If the counselor can remain outside the system while relating actively to it, freely moving about within it, relating to anyone in it at any chosen moment, then solid change is possible.

9

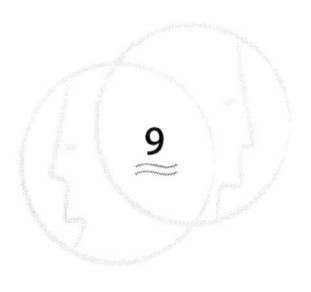

Getting Started and Assessing the Couple

The two primary, interrelated personal goals for doing counseling based on family systems theory are: (1) to define self; and (2) to stay neutral within triangles. Defining self is one way of demonstrating neutrality with the couple in conflict. It requires the ability to manage self, with a relatively lower level of anxiety, within powerful emotional fields. There is a definite art to doing this, unique to each counselor, but this art is based on a scientific understanding of the functional facts of relationships.

The First Contact

From the first contact, which is usually by phone, potential counselees will invite us into a triangle. This is normal. Anxious people are always looking for vulnerable outside people to help them with their anxiety. It is our job to keep defining self and not take up a function within the triangles.

I never allow my first contact with counselees over the phone to become a counseling session. They will, quite automatically, tell us about the problem from their point of view. They may have already diagnosed what the problem is, who is at fault, and suggest what we should do to help. Without labeling the caller's efforts or being judgmental, we just do not discuss the caller's ideas. From the beginning of the call, we have to begin to see the web of relationships around the caller, and inquire briefly about these.

I do not go into detail with the caller about what the problem is. Generally, a couple of sentences from the caller about the nature of the difficulty, with perhaps a few clarifying questions from me, should be enough information to decide whether or not I am the appropriate person for them to see. Other phone discussion focuses on who will come in for the first appointment.

One common opening gambit is for a caller to request an individual appointment for a marital situation. For example, a wife might say, "I have a marital problem and I would like to come in and talk about it with you." I might say something like, "Tell me why you are thinking about coming in on your own." I never argue with callers about this issue, but I have a number of ways of saying, "It would be best if you came in with your partner. Your concerns would have a much better chance of being addressed if I could see both of you. When just one partner gets involved in marital counseling, it often does not turn out well." In most cases this is all that needs to be said. If the wife persists in wanting an individual appointment, I ask her, "Does your husband know you are calling me? Have you asked your husband to go to counseling with you?" If she says no, then I suggest that she talk with him and let him know how serious she is about wanting to do it. I may coach her in how to talk with him. She could say to him, "I need to do this because I want to be happier in our relationship. I am not happy now. I want to be more loving to you. And I would like to have your cooperation in this."

If the wife says she has asked him to go to counseling with her and he said no, then I ask her, "Tell me how you asked him. What exactly did you say?" Very often her request would come off as a threat, or as some kind of "You"-focused statement that he needs to be fixed in order to be a better husband. This guarantees lack of success. Then we rehearse another approach like that above.

Ninety percent of the time the other partner agrees to come in for at least a first session and typically they remain in the counseling thereafter. What they fear might happen in counseling (being "ganged up on" and blamed) does not happen, and they are surprised to find themselves more comfortable than they expect. On rare occasions I agree (sticking with this example) to see the wife alone with the primary goal in my head of getting the husband in as well. I just do not want to get into the marital issues without him present.

In the session with her, if she indicates she has said the right things to him, I ask her, "What would it be like for you if he came in with you?" This question helps me to discover whether she is undercutting the invitation in some way, out of her own anxious concerns. It might be some version of, "I don't think I could say what is on my mind if he were here." Now we are clearly in the territory of marital openness. I say in response that there is no better way to work on this than by doing it.

If I think she has done her best at inviting him in, and really does want him involved, but he just will not agree, then I say, "Would you mind if I called him right now?" When she agrees, I call him with her sitting there, even if he is at work, and say something like, "Mr. ———, this is Ron Richardson, I am a counselor at ———. Your wife has come in to see me with some of her concerns about your marriage. I believe she has mentioned them to you. She is sitting here with me now, listening as we speak. My problem is that I feel like I am only getting half of the story. I would really like to hear your side of the story. There are always two sides to these sorts of issues and I am sure your side is just as important as hers is. Would you be willing to come in and talk with me?" Usually he agrees to come in.

A couple of husbands have still refused to come in. I make one final effort. "Well, here is part of my concern, Mr. ———. The research is pretty clear that when only one partner becomes involved in counseling for a marital issue it often does not turn out well and ends in divorce. I would like to avoid that possibility as would, I'm sure, both of you. It would help me if I could at least meet you once and hear your side of the story. Would you agree to one appointment with me?" I rarely have the other partner say no to this request. After they come in, they normally decide to continue. Of course, this has to do a great deal with how that first conjoint appointment is managed.

Avoiding Secrets

When callers request an individual appointment, I do not tell them (because I am not going to argue the point) that I do not want to be a part of a secret; that contributes further to a closed system and puts me right smack in a problem triangle. This would especially be a problem if I were this couple's pastor. If I was engaged in some pastoral act (as simple as a coffee conversation) with her husband, and I knew what the wife was saying about him secretly, this would affect what I might say or do in relation to him. Secrets make us sensitive to touchy or difficult issues and, as a way to deal with them, we may avoid any related topics when talking with people who are not in on the secret. We may also just avoid those people.

Secrets are common in these more anxious families. At a minimum, they are not open with each other. They bring this closed style of functioning to us, looking for us to be their confidant, the "one person in the world" they can talk with freely. It does not matter whether we are seeing a whole family, a couple, or just one person, we are still involved in the family system. We become part of the secrecy system if counseling itself is a secret in the family. I rarely talk with one member of a couple about their marriage without the other partner knowing about it. The only exception would involve dangerous physical abuse in the relationship.

Keeping a secret can cause more problems than the content of the secret. When people know a secret they tend to become more guarded and less open with related others. They have to be careful not to reveal the secret and this becomes a primary focus in managing the relationship. Typically, they do this by distancing.

If the family knows about us as counselors, then we will be discussed by them and what is said about us, even by our counselee, may not be told to us. We will be in their triangles whether we like it or not. It is amazing what counselees tell others about what they think we think and have said. We will be used in the family triangles as a part of its emotional process, in one way or another. The phrase, "My counselor says..." may be used on a regular basis, and what is repeated may not bear any resemblance to what we actually said.

Dual Relationships

Because so many readers are church-based pastors, this is a good place to talk about dual relationships. Nearly all professional counseling organizations have an ethical rule against having any other kind of relationships with counselees, and for good reasons. The dual relationship that gets the most attention is having a sexual relationship with a counselee. This is actually sexual abuse due to the hierarchical power issues involved. There are other kinds of dual relationships. I will not catalog them all, but this issue is particularly challenging for pastors who counsel parishioners.

In essence, the problem in dual relationships is that the counselor could have another agenda going on with the counselee. For example, perhaps the counselee is on the pastor's church board. A difficult issue may be before the board on which the two people either may or may not agree; it does not matter which. At some point in the counseling, the pastor may think, and maybe even say out loud, "So that's the reason you oppose me/support me on this issue before the board." It does not matter whether the pastor says this or not. There could be many examples of this.

The rule against dual relationships is designed to keep counselors from getting into these situations to begin with. However, counseling relationships can be abusive in any case, with or without a dual relationship. Not all dual relationships have to be abusive. The issue is a combination of the character and the responsible stance of the counselor, along with a knowledge of boundaries (triangles) and how to manage self around them. It requires an ethical clarity that knows when certain lines could or should not be crossed. If I, as a pastor, decided to do counseling with one of my board members, then this issue has to be openly highlighted and discussed between us, up front, at the beginning of the counseling relationship. We would both have to be alert to any sign that a line had been crossed and be able to discuss it immediately. However, given the hierarchical nature of the relationship, this is more our responsibility than theirs.

Doing Assessments

Assessment is an ongoing process. I have a specific way of doing the initial assessment that I will describe here. Assessment differs from diagnosis in that I am not labeling anybody with a psychological label. This is one reason I do not participate in an insurance scheme that asks for a diagnosis. For example, it is quite common to refer to people who drink heavily as "alcoholic," but they are so much more than that.

There are many facets to their lives and the alcohol abuse would be just one aspect; it does not really summarize who they are and how they function in relationships.

Assessment is about getting a picture of the couple's emotional system, their nuclear and multigenerational family, the key triangles that are at work, how each partner functions within those systems, the nodal events in their history, and dating the emergence of symptoms. This also includes which of the four mechanisms they use to manage family anxiety and fusion. I attempt to make some determination about their functional levels of differentiation. The goal of the assessment is to develop a plan for how I will proceed with the couple.

I start with a three-session assessment process for couples. I have a first session with the couple together, and then I see each one separately. A fourth session, with both together again, is called "the completion session." This refers to completing the assessment and, normally, it is the beginning of counseling. At that point, in the fourth session, we jointly decide whether and how (who I would see and when) to continue to meet.

I run a relatively structured assessment in order to accomplish certain goals. I loosely time these sessions based on what I wanted to do in each segment. There are often exceptions to what I can accomplish within a session for a variety of reasons, usually having to do with the particular circumstances of the couple. What I do not accomplish in these three sessions I return to later.

First Session with the Couple

Once we are seated in my office, I think it is important for people to hear themselves speak about something that is normal and non-anxiety generating. I might ask, "Did you have any difficulty finding us?" or something of the sort. Then I fill out an intake form in which I ask them their names, their address, and phone number. I go over how they like to be addressed, and mention how they may address me. It is important to get this basic information at the start. If, for example, in the midst of the session someone rushes out of your office in a suicidal panic, you want to know where you can reach the person.

Then I put down the form and ask, with my eyes moving back and forth between the two of them (I do not want to single out one of them as the spokesperson), "So what brings the two of you in to see me?" This is the "statement of the problem" phase. I spend around fifteen minutes on this, not going very far into the depth or content of the issues and certainly not working with them to solve the problem. I want to get a sense of the primary concerns they have, something of the history of the concerns, and show them in my responses that I have some understanding of what they are talking about. I take minimal notes during this phase while maintaining eye contact with them as well as taking note of their body language.

Quite often, the couple will be inclined to get into their latest fight, or go more in depth about their complaints. I am very active in attempting to abbreviate this while also not wanting them to have the sense of my cutting them off. I explain that we will have plenty of time to go into their concerns in greater depth later, but that right now I want to get a general sense of their concerns. Before moving on to the next phase of this session, I ask if they have any other concerns or problems, not yet mentioned, and then clarify those.

Ideally, at this point, usually no longer than twenty minutes into the session, I change course by saying something like, "Let me tell you how I like to proceed in this sort of situation. After getting a brief statement about what your concerns are, as we have just done, I like to spend the rest of this session on getting a history of your relationship, so that I know something about how things have developed between the two of you over time. Then, I would like to have an individual session with each of you, get some of your own family history, learn about the time before you met each other, and get to know each of you separately. The point of all of this is for me, in as short a time as possible, to get on board with the kind of life course you have each traveled over the years, separately and together, and how you got to this particular point in your lives. How does this way of beginning sound to you?" They normally say it sounds good and thorough.

Those with the most intense forms of conflict usually want to get into the counseling and solutions right away. It could be easy for a counselor to get caught up in their anxious concerns and go with their request for immediate help. Unless someone is going to move out and start a separation right away, or someone is going to be hurt in an abusive situation, I ask them to go with my plan even though it seems like a slow start. While not saying this, my assessment process is a kind of intervention. It helps to put them more in touch with the bigger picture and to see themselves in a larger context.

Then I say, "Okay, but before going on with the history of your marriage, let's talk about the fee we charge for a fifty-minute session. We work on a sliding scale that is determined by family income and the number of people supported by that income." Then I hold the fee chart out between the two of them and ask, "Where do you fit on this chart?" They identify a fee figure. I say that this is a suggested fee and then ask them, "How does that work for the two of you?" Then we agree on a figure and I write it down on the intake form for the secretary to see at the end of the session when they pay.

Why do I personally do the fee setting? Why not just leave it to the front office, as many counselors do? I want it to be clear that they are entering into a contract with me personally, a certain amount of my time for a certain amount of their money. That is the deal. They are contracting with me, although the fee goes to my agency.

After setting the fee with the couple, I say something like, "Okay, tell me how the two of you first met and how this relationship got started." This question is not addressed to either one. At this point, I also start taking extensive notes. After one speaks for five minutes or so, then I ask the other, "Is that how you remember it? What stands out for you around how you met?"

I get specific dates for events along the way; how things developed between them, and what all of the following topics were like for them: their engagement, when and in what circumstances they got married, family reactions, divorces and remarriage, places they have lived, births of children, deaths of family members, job histories while together, and so forth. Of course, I want to hear about the development of the marital conflicts and how or whether that might coincide with any other important events or dates. I attempt to get right up to the present before the session ends.

In doing this I never make interventions or say things like, "Well, do you see how that decision to get married coincided with your father's death?" In general, and throughout counseling, I rarely make such interpretative statements. Of course, I take note of such connections in my own head, but making interpretations generally inspires reactivity like compliance, rebellion, argumentative power struggles, and so forth. At most, we can be curious, wonder or muse aloud, and perhaps invite them to wonder with us.

In this part of the session, I want to make sure that both partners have a chance to tell their side of the marital history. I want them to both have the sense that their side is heard and respected. I want to comment on the positive elements I hear in their story and let them know of the strengths I perceive in them and in their relationship, as well as getting what the challenges are. I work to make sure that neither partner walks out feeling worse than when they come in.

Very often, doing the marital history has a positive impact emotionally for the couple. I do not do the history for this reason; my goal is to learn about them. However, it does often put them back in touch with the good things they have forgotten, what originally brought them together, and what they like about each other. Even couples like George and Martha, who were at great odds with each other, had some positive feelings after doing the marital history. In addition, they do not feel like total failures in front of me. At the end of the session, I set appointments for each of them separately, and an appointment for meeting with them together again.

Finally, before we end the session, if their conflicts are intense, I ask them not to discuss their issues during the week. They should save their arguments for when we meet in the office. Most couples comply with this request and appreciate that they do not feel obligated to carry on the battles. It gives them some relief and generally, it creates a better atmosphere between them.

Second and Third Sessions (with Each Individual)

I begin the second (individual) session by asking, "I wonder if, after thinking about it, there is anything else you want to add that wasn't discussed in our first session together?" This is a chance for something like physical abuse to be raised if it had not been acknowledged, or was denied, in the first, conjoint session. It might be some issue that one of them was uneasy talking about in front of their partner. Or the person may say, "I know we are asking for marital counseling but I have really decided to get a divorce. I can't take it any longer." Or it provides an obvious time for one of them to say, "I debated telling you, but I am having an affair." One man told me, "I think you should know that I have been having affairs with various women for all twenty-six years of my marriage, beginning on the day we got married."

Any of these topics would be serious enough to warrant further discussion before getting into the person's individual history. Some counselors avoid having individual sessions so they will not become privy to these kinds of secrets. I would rather know them up front because they are going to keep the counseling from going anywhere and I would probably eventually find out. In each of these cases, some determination needs to be made about how we will proceed with the counseling.

As counselors we have an ethical responsibility to maintain the confidentiality of our counselees. I tell them this. But we also have to wonder, at what cost? As I have explained, I am against having secrets, which I distinguish from privacy. I never reveal one person's secret to the other. I would work for growth toward openness. However, do I think it is right for a person to reveal an affair that is now over? I tell them I do not know what they should do about that, and ask why they would or would not tell. That often seems to be the more important question. Whenever a secret emerges, we discuss how to proceed from this point.

In taking a personal history, I begin with where and when they were born and what they knew about the circumstances of their birth. I want to know about their development over the years, within their family. I ask, "Tell me about your mother and father," and see where that goes. I want to know about sibling relationships and where they fit in the birth order, about the relationship with other important family members, and how the person now functions within their family. There are questions about social development, school history, and how well they did. We talk about adolescence and how that went, both within and outside of the family, dating, sexual development and experience, and then further education and/or career history. In all of this, I get a sense of the person's life course and how they have managed it.

Fourth Session (with Both Partners Together)
This session with both partners represents both the completion of the assessment phase and the beginning of counseling. I begin the session, right off the bat, with the intent of getting them started in doing the counseling. I ask them, "So, I am wondering what the two of you

have been thinking about since I last saw you together." Occasionally, in response they say something like, "We were wondering what you were going to tell us today." I say, "That makes sense, and I will have something to say later; but first tell me what other thoughts you have had about your marriage."

This is usually enough to get the ball rolling. One or both launch into the marital issues that concern them. I then begin to work with them as I would in a regular counseling session. Depending on what I have to say, I wait until ten or fifteen minutes before the end of the session to make my general recommendations as a completion of the assessment. I want first to provide them with an actual experience of what the counseling with me would be like. Toward the end of the hour I say something like, "I want to say some things before we stop but first, could you tell me what the last thirty-five or forty minutes have been like for you?" Usually both would say some version of, "It's been good. That is the best we have ever been able to talk about our fights."

Then I say, "Good. Let me share some of my thoughts with you before we stop. There are a number of things I could tell you about marital conflict in general, but let me just say that you are good candidates for marital counseling. My recommendation is that we do more of what we have just been doing. What do you think?" If they agree, then we talk about frequency of sessions and the times.

I say that I know from personal experience that the work is not easy, and how difficult it is to let go of reactivity, but that the best results in counseling come when individual members of a couple can focus on who and how they want to be in life and in their relationships. My final note is one of hope, emphasizing that I have seen many couples improve their lives together and I believe they can as well.

One of the benefits of my way of doing assessments is that the heavily structured approach puts me in charge of the process. I want to continue to be in charge of process throughout the first phase of the counseling work, so this structure creates a momentum for this. One of the negatives of my way of doing assessments is that it also puts me in charge of the content. This is due to my asking specific questions about history. Doing the counseling, I want to back away from being in charge of the content and shift that focus back to them.

At the end of the completion session, I find a way to tell them this. I explain that I have asked many questions about their background and history and this meant I was guiding the focus of our talks. Now, I am not going to be doing that anymore. I say to them that, as we had just done in this session, the ball is now going to be in their court. Where we start each session is now going to be up to them. I tell them that I hope, between sessions, they will attempt to do the best thinking they can about their difficulties and that, when they come in to see me, I will be interested in how they are sorting things through or attempting to understand what is happening.

At the end of the next full counseling session, I show them their family diagram (see appendix 1 for the symbols) that I developed before the session, and give them each a copy. I have it on a clipboard on my lap during that first counseling session (and all succeeding sessions) and refer to it from time to time by looking at it or by clarifying who people are when they come up during the session. As an example, see below the simple diagram I first developed for George and Martha. I add to my copy of the diagram as sessions continue and new information is revealed.

The copy I give them has some of my notations with names and dates, births, deaths, moves, and any nodal events that I know of up to this time. I explain to them that this family diagram is like a map of their emotional territory; it helps me to get on board with the events and experiences of their lives and to put their present circumstances together in some larger perspective. I say I am interested if they ever have any new information they want me to know and to add to the diagram.

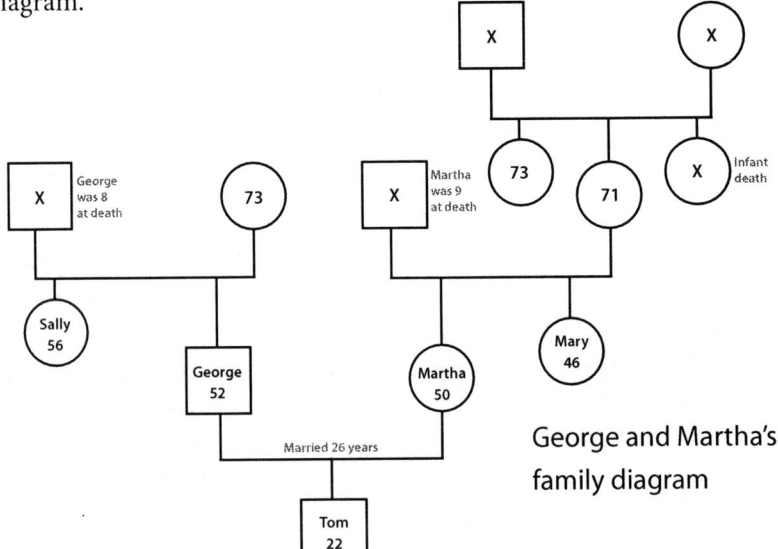

George and Martha's family diagram

Assessment Criteria for Moderate and Severe Marital Conflict

Being clear about the differences between moderately and severely conflicted couples affects both our sense of their prognosis and how we will go about helping them. We know that severely conflicted couples will make progress more slowly and they will have more relapses. The primary differences between the two groups are in their levels of chronic anxiety and differentiation of self.

Typical couples in my counseling practice are highly conflicted and polarized. This has usually been a chronic condition. When they have been conflicted for many years, we have to wonder what brings them in for counseling now. In George and Martha's case, their son had left home about four months earlier. They had transitioned to becoming empty nesters. Then things started heating up more than normal for them. Most couples have other situational stresses develop. For example, a job loss and increased financial pressures could trigger them to come in for counseling. A change in the parental family of a partner, like the death of a parent, could increase anxiety. It is important to ask them, "What brings you in for counseling now since the conflicts have existed for a long time?"

In some cases, a series of stressful events has occurred and things are beyond their ability to cope. Their reactivity increases exponentially. Cluster stress adds to the level of chronic stress that already exists. These couples may improve as they became more aware of this and are able more thoughtfully to address their sources of stress.

An intense level of conflict usually emerges out of the expectations each partner has for how either their partner or their marriage would fulfill some strongly held hope. Through various maneuvers over the years, they each may have attempted to get the partner to comply with these hopes and when these efforts failed, conflict usually was the result. Expectations can come from many different sources (popular culture, our cultural heritage, keeping up with the Joneses, our beliefs and commitments). However, the major source of emotional expectations is experience in the family of origin. The unresolved emotional attachments with family will heighten the expectations over which the couple fights. This is normally what provides the intensity to their fights.

One of the first strongly conflicted couples I worked with in Canada was a first-generation immigrant Chinese man and a first-generation Romanian woman. They met in their English as a Second Language class and fell in love. After marriage they developed a business together and only then did they discover how different their expectations were, both of what a marriage is and of what a marital partner is supposed to do. In addition to all of the cultural differences involved, their difficult family-of-origin experiences (which were part of the reason they had emigrated to Canada) were a major source of intensity in their arguments. Another couple had emigrated from the former Yugoslavia where young girls were sent off to "marriage preparation camps." There they were beaten and terrorized into learning to submit to their future husbands. When this couple arrived in Canada, the wife quickly took to our more liberal legal and cultural traditions for women and refused to be the submissive wife the husband expected.

Sex is usually infrequent for conflicted couples, although one memorable couple came in saying they were planning to divorce, but they wondered what was wrong because they still had "great" sex twice a day, every day, and maybe three times a day on weekends. They did divorce, thus proving that good sex, while usually a help to a marriage, is not the answer to good relationships. Usually the sexual relationship improves on its own as the conflicts subside and, ordinarily, I do not focus much on this. Occasionally, I provide counseling aimed at specific sexual issues if I think it will improve the marital atmosphere.

Both moderate and heavily conflicted couples have usually established pursuer/distancer patterns. In the more heavily conflicted, often the usually pursuing partner begins to feel hopeless and decides to leave the marriage. He or she stops pursuing and starts distancing. At that point, the normally distancing partner begins a strong pursuit and may even be the one to say, "Let's go get counseling," when before he or she would have nothing to do with this idea.

Anxiety is not usually an openly obvious issue, but it is always pervasive and deep. People will be very guarded and protective of any vulnerability, which they will be hesitant to discuss. As the intensity of the conflict increases, they will be significantly more other focused and most often see their partner as the primary problem. They might say that they know they are both to blame, but they do not really believe it. Unlike more moderately conflicted couples, they show little curiosity about what is going on between them; they usually think they have figured out what/who the problem is and what/who has to change.

Moderately conflicted couples might be open to systemic experiments like reversing their usual pursue/distance patterns or their over- and underfunctioning patterns. Exercises can be prescribed for them and they usually do a decent job of performing them and learning from them. They show some curiosity, ask real questions, and are able to hear some teaching about what happens with couples in conflict. There is usually no point to prescribing exercises for highly conflicted couples. They will only be occasions for fights, as they will argue over the rules of the exercise and who was supposed to do what.

With highly conflicted couples, one or both of the individuals will have a strong sense of having sacrificed self in the marriage, and they will be highly sensitive to any suggestions on the part of the counselor to "compromise." They claim their whole marriage has been a compromise and they are not doing it anymore. More moderately conflicted couples can find ways of compromising that do not also feel like losing self.

Usually there are very intense triangles associated with the strongly conflicted couples, with affairs being one of the common types. There can, however, be other kinds of relationships that are equally if not more intense. George had, in some powerful ways, never left home. His involvement with his mother established him and her as the close twosome with Martha in the outside position. There are many other kinds of triangles, which I will discuss in chapter 11.

Philip Guerin and his colleagues, in their volume on marital conflict, speak of the "expectation to alienation progression" in highly conflicted couples (Guerin et al. 1987). This describes how bitterness can build in one or both spouses so that a kind of invulnerable stance evolves in which they will not allow themselves to feel hurt anymore.

One couple was typical. The wife described eleven years of trying to get her spouse to be the husband she wanted. He refused to make any changes. Then she gave up and felt very bitter toward him. This went on for many years with both maintaining a quietly hostile distant stance. Then he learned that she had dinner with another man and this shook him up. He became the pursuer and did everything he could to win her back. He became what she once would have regarded as the perfect husband. He pleaded with her to go for counseling. When they came in, she said to me, "It is so ironic. He is doing everything I once wanted him to do, but now I don't care. I just want to be away from him. I feel nothing for him anymore." So much bitterness had developed that she said she was not motivated to work on the marriage and there was no chance she would ever love him again. They divorced.

This bitterness progression is one of the most useful things I learned from Guerin and his colleagues. They use the image of a "bitterness bank." As one or both partners experience frustration of their wants, feel hurt, and then blame their partner for this feeling, they become more and more bitter. They then make "deposits in their bitterness bank." As these deposits build the partner becomes more alienated from his or her spouse. They see themselves as the victim of their partner. Eventually they move onto the "island of invulnerability" where they no longer feel anything. They say, "You can't hurt me anymore." This is a defensive maneuver in order to stop feeling pain.

Often these partners come from a family where this bitterness style was used in the parental marriage. It is part of a multigenerational process for handling hurt. In order to make any progress in marital counseling, this style or way of trying to take care of self has to be unearthed and addressed. Partners have to get out of the victim position and begin to take responsibility for their part in the relational difficulties. Sometimes it helps to look at the functioning in the parental family as a way to get some objectivity on self's own functioning in the marriage. Later I will show how this was done in the work with Martha.

Assessing for Physical Abuse and Fighting

During the assessment phase of counseling, it is essential for the counselor to get an accurate sense of whether any physical abuse is taking place and the nature of that abuse. If this area is ignored and violence is taking place, the counseling will go nowhere. Apart from the possibility of injury, it will be nearly impossible to achieve the level of safety required to develop greater openness in the relationship.

When couples describe their fights to me I often ask, "How hot does it get?" This open-ended question leaves it up to them to mention any physical quality to the fights. If they do not say so, then I get more specific. "Do you get physical in your fights?" If they say yes, then I ask, "What is the nature of your physical fights? Has anyone been hurt in these fights? Has anyone had to go to the hospital? Have the police been involved?"

Clergy may too easily assume that their church members do not have physical fights as a part of their emotional arguments. My training in psychotherapy in the early 1970s never mentioned physical abuse. During my residency in Arizona, I was working with a conflicted couple who were church members. After many weeks, we were getting nowhere. Finally the wife said to me, "Ron, you don't understand how we fight." I asked, "What do you mean?" Then she described a recent fight where she got so angry that she threw a hot iron at him. Luckily, it missed. He blew up and chased her. She escaped out of the house and waited for him to cool down before she came back. They both agreed that their fights were often out of control physically. In this case she was a big, strong woman and she could, as she said, "give as well as I get." Obviously, this lethal situation needed attention. Because I had no training in this area, I referred them to another counselor in the agency.

I attempt to distinguish between the kinds of fights my counselees have. For some, because of their physical proximity during arguments, one partner ends up pushing or slapping the other, or throwing minor body punches that never land with any real force. No one ever gets hurt. In reporting this, the couple, typically, are ashamed of their behavior and, in some cases, have already managed to stop it by themselves. Because of their openness and their believable resolve to stop fighting in this way, I decide I can work with them in marital counseling. Any fighting that is more dangerous than this is not usually appropriate for marital counseling until this fighting behavior is under control. Personal work is often required, perhaps for both partners. Sincere apologies and expressions of remorse and guilt are never enough of an indicator that the abuse will end.

Physical fights are quite often a result of the normal fight/flight stress reactions in which less well-differentiated people have not learned to be more in charge of their reactions. They involve a high level of blame and a fused sense that one person, in one way or another, is in charge of the well-being of the other, and that the one has a right to demand the continued presence or removal of the other. Another version of this is where the one being left threatens violence against self via suicide.

Alcohol abuse is another indicator that physical abuse of a partner could be present. Alcohol removes the inhibitions people might normally have related to hitting. We must not assume that church members do not abuse alcohol. It is more common than we believe, and it will contribute to family conflicts and abuse. Where this is a typical pattern, then substance abuse counseling is primary before doing marital counseling.

While gender and power debates, like the issue of male dominance, have relevance to these issues, I tend to see many physical fights as indication of runaway emotional processes in which both partners can participate. Both partners help to create the emotional environment in which physical abuse might happen, but the victim is never responsible for being attacked. Some men use physical intimidation to control women and to keep them from acting independently. When this is the intent of the physicality, marital counseling is not an option.

Physicality is often called "power-oriented controlling behavior," but this can show a lack of understanding of the sense of the dependency, weakness, and fear that lies behind it. For example, a male abuser may say it is the duty of the wife to stay with him, obey him, and support him. He will do whatever he can to keep her there. Clearly, this fear of abandonment comes out of his family of origin experience.

Abusive men (or women) may have grown up in families where physical fights were normal for dealing with disputes. Some of the abusive men (and a few women) I have worked with grew up with all male siblings. As brothers they fought a lot with each other and it became a "normal" way of dealing with conflict.

In doing more in-depth assessments on this issue, several areas need to be explored:

- What sort of drinking behavior takes place?
- Did either partner grow up in an abusive household?
- Did they have fights with their siblings?
- Is there a pattern of coercive control and physical violence in the relationship?

- Has such a pattern existed in previous relationships (for example, abused women may have had previous male partners who abused them)?
- How violent is the language that they use in fights?
- What threats are made and images used?
- Are there issues of extreme jealousy and accusations of infidelity?
- Is there a pattern of always monitoring the presence of the partner?
- Is there a pattern of physicality outside of the marriage (for example, a man who gets in fights elsewhere)?
- Is there any history of violent crime?

Questions for counselors to consider are:

- Can the couple stop their fight if it approaches the limit of physicality?
- Is there any sense that, for one of the partners, engaging in counseling is coercive?
- What is the level of respect of the partners for each other and recognition of physical boundaries?
- Does one partner show any signs of fear of the other and is he or she able to say whatever is on his or her mind?
- Can one partner tolerate hearing the other partner talk about how the one is angry?
- Are both aware of how they can escalate the fight to physicality?
- What evidence do they show of being able to manage their anger and interrupt its expression?
- To what extent can each be responsible for his or her behavior?

10

Goals for the Counseling Process

The primary method for accomplishing the goals I describe in this chapter is by asking questions. Our work is like being a *researcher* of relationships rather than being a *fixer* of relationships. It involves being curious about how the couple actually function with each other. The questions are a way to engage people's thinking and to widen their understanding of what is going on. In asking questions, we are using our curiosity to enlist theirs. We are asking them to teach us about themselves and, in the process, responding to our questions, they have to think about how they function. We are not functioning as educators, although learning will happen; nor are we functioning as fixers or healers, although things will get better for each of them and between them.

As counselors, we do not need people to change in order for us to feel personally adequate. I see this need in many trainees; it leads them to push their counselees, to interpret things to them, and to encourage them to make certain changes. If the counselees would only do what was suggested, then the counselor could feel like a good and competent counselor. This represents fusion in the counselor.

Reducing Anxiety

An immediate first goal in counseling, and one that continues throughout the work, is lowering the level of anxiety. As anxiety goes down, so will the couple's reactivity. People will be better able to sit and listen to each other. They will be able to think more clearly. They will become more open about self and able to develop a self-focus. This will help them prepare the ground for change.

There are no techniques involved in doing this. A lower level of anxiety in the counselees usually results from a lower level of anxiety in the counselor who is able to keep reasonable emotional contact with them while they act out their reactivity. A counselor who is able to sit with a couple who are in heated conflict, maintain a sense of self, and not get caught up in the fusion of triangles, will demonstrate a less anxious presence with the couple. The couple will appreciate this and begin to use it for themselves.

I do not tell them to "be calm." That is an other-focused approach that is more about the counselor's anxiety than about them. It is saying in effect, "I can't be calm and work with you until you are calm." It is not their job to help us to be calmer. Saying something like "Calm down" can, in itself, create a certain amount of reactivity in them and it certainly reveals our own. Just like anxiety can be infectious and spread through a system, so can calmness—and it starts with the counselor.

One way people can become calmer is when a counselor listens to their story, shows an understanding of it, and validates the feelings involved. This is a universal way of functioning for almost all counselors. When this happens counselees feel like they have connected with someone who understands them. Standard counseling skills like reflective listening show that we can understand how painful or upsetting the situation is for them.

We have all probably had counselees in tears just because they felt a relief like, "At last, someone understands what life is like for me." This is not so productive toward change but it can help some with their level of anxiety. Just one simple example was a couple who had four nearly grown sons. At some point early in the process I said to the mother, "So what has it been like for you being the only woman in a family with five men?" She immediately began to cry. She appreciated that I got what she felt she was up against. I did not go further with this. It was enough that I had connected. I came back to it later in the counseling when her thoughtfulness was more engaged.

There are at least two problems with doing too much of this sort of empathic listening and reflection. If we wanted to enhance the transference to us, and the emotional dependency on us, we would do more of this; but, as discussed earlier, this is not a useful thing to do. We do not want to become too important to counselees. If we focus, as is the case in a lot of counselor training, on being empathic, we will start solidifying that kind of "very important" relationship. They will start focusing their emotional energy on us, looking forward to talking with us more than focusing on their difficult relationships.

The second problem is that we can quickly get into a triangle with the counselee. They can begin to think we are on their side. Their partner could begin to think this as well. After making the comment to the wife in the above example, I had to balance it with a comment to the husband about the challenges of being the father of four boys. The art of this work has to do with being able to modulate how close we get with each partner and still stay neutral in the triangles. We do not want to be too close or too distant.

Generally, being able to relate calmly to the counselee's stories requires us to have developed our own lowered levels of anxiety by doing our own family work. When we have learned to be calmer in our families of origin, in the midst of the powerful emotional issues that can get stirred up there, we will be better able to do it with our counselees. If we find their emotionality too intense, or they remind us too much of our own family situation, we will start to distance and not effectively relate to the counselees.

Because of a counselee's similarity to our own story, we may barge into it and start trying to fix it, just as we may do in our families, or would like to do. Presented with similar kinds of "bad guys," we may want to take them on and confront them, or get them to do what we think they should. Traditional bad guys in couple counseling are often labeled as distant or autocratic husbands/fathers or as controlling or bitchy wives/mothers. They are often seen, in our own emotional dramas, as the oppressors and as the cause of family problems. When we take on this view and use these labels, we have jumped right into the middle of the family triangles, both theirs and ours.

Another area of inquiry for the beginning counselor is to discover whether there are particular kinds of people or situations that tend to stir up our own anxiety. Early on, I found I could act in anxious ways around counselees who I would have then described as "whiny, dependent women." My anxiety showed as an internal experience of near disgust. This limited my ability to relate and be of use to them.

I distanced and could not figure out how to relate to them in the midst of their emotional experience.

The label "whiny and dependent" said as much about me as about them. I rejected those parts in myself that could be like that and then projected it back onto those women, treating them in the same way. I needed to learn to become more comfortable with my own dependency. Also, I had a mother who, in spite of her relational difficulties, never behaved in this whiny way. When she divorced her first three husbands she never asked for alimony. She never asked my father to pay child support. She assumed she would make it on her own and did not want to be dependent on a man. I admired this and thought she was "gutsy." She was my norm for how a woman should be. So dependency was a family theme for me as well as a personal one.

Altering the Emotional Climate

The major way of altering the emotional climate is by functioning with the couple in a way that interrupts their automatic reactive behaviors. For example, as I pursue the pursuers and do not pursue the distancers (see chapter 12), a different emotional experience begins to happen for both of them. The distancers begin to feel safe enough to see something of value in the counseling for themselves. They will not see this if their energy is going into distancing from my pursuit. The pursuers eventually begin to appreciate learning about self, usually a previously unexplored territory.

In order to run sessions in this way, to engage with both partners, and alter the emotional climate, we have to be willing to take charge of the process in the room. We cannot be laissez-faire about this. If we let one partner carry on a big rant about the other, and then turn to the other and say something like, "What do you feel about that?" it should be clear what will come next. If one partner starts out with a negative focus on the other, I ask questions until I can get that focus elsewhere, ideally on the self of the one speaking or on a relationship with someone other than the partner in the room. Only then do I turn to the other.

I am interested in exploring the automatic quality of their experience. There is a tendency, especially in our "let it all hang out" society, to go with our spontaneous feelings. We say, in our arguments, "I'm just telling you how I feel." There are plenty of times, in other contexts, when going with our spontaneous feelings is a happy, productive, and positive thing to do, leading to good or enjoyable outcomes. When this repeatedly gets us in trouble, however, and we get into repetitive negative cycles that lead us to spiral down into unhappy holes in our relationships, then it is time to interrupt this pattern.

Change involves being able to activate our more objective, observing, and thinking self in order to decide when and how we will interrupt our automatic behavior. When people begin to think about their behavior, rather than just react, the emotional climate begins to change in their relationship. Learning, for example, that our pain comes from our expectations and not just from the behavior of other people, helps us feel less like a victim. We can decide whether we want to keep the expectations or modify them in some way.

Humor can reveal a different twist or angle on the relationship. In its most profound sense, humor is about casting tragedy in a different light. This is what the logo for the theater tries to communicate with the two faces, one laughing and one crying. Both are about the same events, seen from different perspectives. Woody Allen once made a movie in which he told the same story twice, once as a tragedy and then as a comedy. People who have observed my counseling sessions have remarked on the amount of humor there is; not in telling jokes, but in just seeing different angles on things. Respectful humor is a useful tool.

Being in Charge of Process

I do not expect nor want the partners to talk to each other in counseling. Instead, I want each one to have a conversation with me about their personal experience, within their relationship, while the other one listens to what is said. I know what would happen if I said something like, "Why don't you two talk about that with each other." It would not be long before they would be in an argument. I want to talk with each of them about the emotionality that lies behind their arguments. It is important also for their partner to be able to sit and listen, and not have to react.

The number one self-defined issue that conflicted couples bring to counseling is "We don't communicate," and they imply that this is what they need to learn to do in counseling. Teaching heavily conflicted couples communication and negotiation skills pushes them together, deeper into a fusion process, and that will lead to them becoming more reactive to each other. They may be able to do it with us present in our office, but they are not likely to be able to do it on their own. Unless they are only moderately conflicted couples, with more differentiation, such homework will set them up for feeling like failures.

It is the individuality force that needs to be supported in counseling. People who distance from closeness typically have trouble being a self in the togetherness. The togetherness force will take care of itself. We do not need to push for more togetherness as do many approaches to counseling. Couples will find their own way to be together better and to communicate when they feel less anxious, less fused, and more like a solid self.

Interviewing each partner in the presence of the other introduces him or her to a new way of relating. By being emotionally separate individuals, having their own thoughts and feelings, they can become closer. Often, at the end of counseling, people report that, "As I listened to him/her talk with you, I began to feel closer to him/her." In cooperation with the process of differentiation, individuality provides a way to be together that will offer true intimacy (the closeness of two recognizably different people), rather than the fused togetherness (closeness as sameness) that will generate anxiety and reactivity.

One of my early goals is to enlarge the complexity of what lies behind their arguments with each other, not to let it stay at a simple level of who is right or wrong. I want to look at the multidetermined, systemic qualities that feed into their interpersonal issues. This could involve many other stressful, extra-family aspects of their lives. This often involves family-of-origin and multigenerational material. Using what Bowen called the "wide-angle lens," we see that their conflictual fights are just the conclusion or the tail end of some much larger process that is not being recognized or talked about.

Whoever starts the counseling session by speaking first is my focus for a period of time. Early in counseling, I normally spend no more than ten to fifteen minutes with one person, moving back and forth, interviewing one and then the other. Later, when they have started using counseling to do some solid thinking about self, I might stay with one partner for up to thirty minutes, while the other simply listens. In this way, they gradually learn that the way to get out of their difficulties lies through thinking more clearly about self, what self brings to their encounters, what is personally important, and what self will or will not do in various circumstances.

When I switch and talk with the other partner, usually physically turning my body to them, I ask, "What have you been thinking about while I talked with your husband/wife?" I have one rule for when I do this. I do not do it when the person I am talking with has just talked about the partner in a negative way. This automatically sets up the partner to react as if in an argument.

Even though, normally, the person I am talking with has started with a focus on the problems of the partner, I try to take this in a direction that has more to do with self or with others in that person's life, where there was a similar dynamic. So it is relevant to that person's experience with his or her partner, but focused elsewhere. The intent in doing this is to create some space between them, to help each see that the subjective experience being talked about is not limited to the partner and is more about self, thus making it easier for the partner to listen and be less reactive.

When I turn to the other partner, in early sessions, quite often that partner is still back with something the speaker said about him or her. They often say, "I was thinking about what she said about me and how wrong she is." This listening partner now wants to engage in a fight, or to justify self and to turn it back on the other. For example, with George, if I was intending to stick with him, I might have let him say something out of his reactivity. Then I would soon say something like, "Well, you know, as Martha talked about her experience of anger, and who else she got angry with, I was wondering about what this was like for you. How do you experience your anger?" In this question, I am trying to stay relevant to the experience of anger for George, and broaden it out to others, as you will see me do in the verbatims later.

In doing my interviews in this way, talking first with one and then the other, I am showing interest in them individually. I am not treating them as "a couple." Some people implicitly or explicitly resist this idea. They want to be thought of as "together." Their identity is tied up in being part of a twosome. The idea of individuality is "wrong" for them. It may have selfish connotations. My own view is that the fused togetherness approach is more selfish, in that one is attempting to get the other to "be more like me." This idea of togetherness is what will lead to conflict, or to depression for one of them.

Tracking the Relational Process

I regard specific conflicts as the content of what the couple argues about. It is very material, for example, for the couple to decide whether to have children or not. It is a decision with big consequences in either direction, and I certainly do not know whether they should or should not. I am much less interested in the outcome of this decision, however, and much more interested in what each brings to the conflict emotionally.

A counselor-training aphorism says, "The process is the content." This means that how people behave with one another is more important than what they say. Their behavior is the real content of their relationship. There are two levels of process that I track in counseling: the interactive one between them, and the inner process within each of them. The two go hand in hand. In tracking the behavioral, interactive process, I am interested in questions that start with who, when, where, what, how, and much less interested in why questions. The answers to why questions are more content focused and they are unending. They often become one justification after another.

Often content and process can conflict, and what we need to pay attention to in counseling is the process, not the words. When a wife says, for example, "I love my husband," but then she finds many occasions and ways to push him away, one has to wonder what is going on. Once, I was having Sunday lunch with a minister and his family. In the course of discussion, he asked his oldest daughter what she had learned in Sunday school that morning. She said they had learned about "loving our neighbor." Her younger sister began to tease her and said, "Eh, what was that you said?" The older sister repeated herself, and the younger one kept on asking, "What did you say? Speak up, I can't hear you." Finally, in frustration, the older sister took her Bible that was sitting on the dining table, turned to her younger sister next to her, and began pounding her over the head with her Bible saying loudly, "I said we learned to love our neighbor!" Clearly content and process were in conflict.

In addition to the interactive process, there is also an inner process. It is about how people process information internally, what they focus on, how they perceive others, and how they make decisions about how to behave toward the other. Often there is a significant lack of awareness of this internal process in conflicted couples. Because of fusion, they are unable to separate thinking and emotionality. Their reactions to each other are automatic. They say, "Who wouldn't feel or react like me?" They often do not realize that there are choice points.

Tracking the inner process in each of them also opens up the fusion between them and within self; it leads to more clearly defining a self, and then getting different behavior in relation to the other. By "tracking," I am referring to following how things work, how people get from the perception of what the other has done or said to the decision to behave a certain way in response. I want to introduce the idea that there are choice points in the process. We can wonder with counselees what might happen in the interactive process if some other option were followed, and then what it would take internally to do that.

In the early stage of doing counseling, I want to focus on and open up both the interactive and the inner process. The following verbatim, from the first counseling session with George and Martha, shows some of what I am talking about in this chapter.

First Counseling Session with George and Martha: Exploring Reactivity

In this relationship, George has been the distancer and Martha the pursuer. He came to counseling reluctantly. I did not pursue him. I wanted him to start moving toward me (rather than me toward him) and to see some value in counseling for himself. Part of what I did in this situation was to pursue the pursuer; I kept my focus on her, asking her to look at self rather than letting her talk about him. I do the same when the pursuer is a male. What follows is the first post-assessment counseling session.

Note: In the verbatims I give in this book, most of the counselee quotes are shortened. I want to focus on what I say or do, so I give more of my own words. The actual balance of who talks most is not the way it appears here.

Martha: He is such an idiot. [She starts right in as they sit down.]
George: I didn't understand that it was that important to you. I was . . .
Ron: [I interrupt him and turn to her.] Martha, what is going on?
Martha: He promised he would be home early to help me with getting things ready for our son's birthday party. I had lots of things I was counting on him to do.
George: I really did plan to get home but I had stuff to do at the office.
Martha: That's him, always making excuses. [Looking at me in a way that says "we" get what he is like.]
Ron: So is there more you want to say about this, Martha?
Martha: [She goes into the story a bit more, saying he did not even call to say he would not be there. In early sessions I let angry people blow off more frustration than I do in later sessions. This is not so evident here. People need the sense of having been heard.]
Ron: Okay, so this might be something that is typical of what happens between you two? [She nods "yes" emphatically and is still steaming, partly as a result of telling the story.] So when George does something that you are unhappy with, what goes on with you?
Martha: He is just such a selfish jerk; he never thinks about anybody else. He won't even put himself out for his own son, let alone for me.
Ron: [Interrupting] Yeah, okay. I got that part. But when you experience him being what you call "a selfish jerk," what happens with you?
Martha: Well, he is so uncaring about anybody . . .
Ron: [Interrupting again; I really don't want her to go on about him.] Let me stop you, Martha, for a moment. I want you to hear what I am asking about. What happens with you when you think George is uncaring?
Martha: What do you mean?
Ron: Simply, what goes on with you?
Martha: When he is so selfish and uncaring I get angry.
Ron: Okay, how do you get angry?
Martha: I get angry!
Ron: Gotcha, but different people get angry different ways. Some go quiet and become sullen. Some smile and carry on, and you'd never know they were angry. Some hit and beat up the other per-

son. Some blow up and verbally lay into the other person. How about you?

Martha: I blow up. I yell at him.

Ron: Then what happens?

Martha: He kind of snivels around making excuses. I get more upset then. Sometimes he fights back and will argue with me and then we usually have a real blowout. We don't hit. We never hit. I attack him and he attacks me. We don't ever get anywhere. Maybe it feels better to him to argue like that, I don't know. Because then, at night, he wants to get all lovey-dovey and I tell him to go sleep in the guest room. Actually, we hardly ever have sex anymore. I'm not interested. It only happens on the rare occasions when we have drunk too much at a party and I kind of let my guard down. But mostly we hardly even talk. I don't want to. I don't want anything to do with him.

Ron: How long do things stay like that?

Martha: Usually days. It used to be that I would keep the fight going, but lately, during the last few years, I just go quiet and stew.

Ron: Okay. So when George does something that you don't like or, as in this situation, fails to do something you want him to do—like help you with the party—a little dance happens afterwards. If we had a silent movie of it, we would see you move toward him with an angry expression. He would sometimes act as if he had his tail between his legs [she nods], and other times his face would go angry and he would move toward you, just like you move toward him with anger [she nods again], then the encounter ends when someone, what, walks out of the room? [She nods again.] And then things stay like this, a lot of physical distance without any intimacy. He tries to move toward you, perhaps sexually . . .

Martha: Sometimes he just wants to talk but I'm not interested.

Ron: Okay. But eventually the two of you come a little closer and sort of get back on even keel again?

Martha: Yes, I guess that's about it.

Ron: [I turn to him.] George, you want to say anything about this whole process?

George: No, that sounds pretty accurate. [He goes silent and I don't pursue with follow-up questions. I want to show him I can pursue her and I do not want to elicit his excuses.]

Ron: Martha, over the years, when these things happen, have you ever tried anything else besides getting angry and blowing up?

Martha: I don't think I know what you mean. What would you do? Who wouldn't blow up if they were married to an idiot like him? [She is back to a focus on him.]

Ron: I don't know what should happen. But in this silent movie of the dance between the two of you, have you ever tried any other kind of dance step? Gone a different direction in the way you move?

Martha: I don't know if I get what you mean, but no, probably not. I remember blowing up on the first day after we got married. I remember the look on his face. Actually, it was almost comical; his look, I mean. And I can remember what I blew up about. I should have called it quits right there, but for some reason I hung in. I thought he would get the point and things would get better.

Ron: Yes, I remember both of you talking about some of the good things you had. And, as I remember, the sex was pretty good, too. You both enjoyed it. And there were other good times. [Turning toward George] George, is there anything you want to add here?

George: No, I don't think so. I never have figured out what she gets so angry about. It never seems like that big a deal to me. I just . . .

Ron: [I interrupt him. I can tell he is going to launch into excuses and I don't want to get him started down that road.] Thanks, George. [Turning back to Martha] Martha, what if George really was an idiot? I mean, really. What if he didn't have the capability to understand why things are important to you and he really didn't understand what you expected of him? [Turning to George] No offense, George. [Then back to her, waiting for her response]

Martha: [More thoughtful, with a slight smile] Well, I'm pretty sure I wouldn't get angry at him. I wouldn't expect things of an idiot. There would be no point.

Ron: Okay. So your expectations are part of the dance. Right? You move toward him with the expectation that he will meet your wants. He doesn't and then you blow up.

Martha: Well sure, isn't that what marriage is all about? Why wouldn't I expect things of him?

Ron: You got me again on that one. I don't know what should be. But I find the idea kind of intriguing. Surely you have heard the saying about digging yourself into a hole; I don't know how it goes exactly, but it says something about maybe it's time to stop digging. I am wondering what it would be like for you if you stopped expecting anything from George. I don't mean he is really an idiot. But then, well, I don't know what would happen. It would be a different step in the dance, I guess. But if you acted that way, and had no expectations of him, I wonder what would happen. I guess, from what you say, if you truly had no expectations, in reality, then at a minimum you would have no anger. Is that right? What is your thought? . . .

In this scenario, I want to show that there is no magic or anything special or tricky in this way of working. I do not regard the behavioral experiment I offer as "brilliant" work. With intensely conflicted couples, we will go back over the same reactive patterns repeatedly. The more fused the couple, as with George and Martha, the slower this work will be.

In this section of the interview I was simply trying to develop some self-focus in Martha, and not get deeply caught in the triangle by going after George. I wanted to inspire some thinking, hopefully in both of them, about the interactional sequence between them. I wanted Martha to begin to connect her anger with her expectations as much as with George's behavior. This will put her more in charge of her experience and eventually she can develop options for how to be when George fails to come through in the way she would like. I want George to see me pursuing her and not him, since he thought he would be fingered as the bad guy. I do turn to George a couple of times in the session and try to get something other than excuses about his behavior.

My message about George ("What if he really was an idiot?") toward the end of this segment was intentionally ambiguous, but I hoped that he might find it provocative without feeling too offended. Martha found the idea of not having expectations kind of amusing and volunteered, as we talked about it, that she would try the experiment for a week. She discovered that it created a different subjective experience for her. It did not lead her immediately in the direction of thinking that her anger was her responsibility. However, the experiment loosened up the fusion just a little bit. Somewhat surprising to her, she found George to be more forthcoming and helpful during the week. Of course, I knew this new dynamic was not going to last, but it gave them an insight into a different way to be together.

Interruptions and Being in Charge of the In-Office Process

When one partner interrupts while the other is telling their story—as they will nearly always do in heavily conflicted couples—and tries to begin telling their own version of events, then we have another opportunity to define ourselves in the triangle. I do not want the counseling session to become an extension of one of their "he said/she said" arguments. If they walk out at the end of a session in which this is all they have done, they will certainly question the benefit of counseling. They do not need to pay me so they could argue in front of me.

I generally interrupt the interrupter, not to lay down some rule of "No interruptions in here," but with some sort of comment like, "Okay, George, I hear how this could be difficult for you and you have your own version of these events. I want to hear about that and I will get back to you in a little bit. First I want to ask a few more questions of Martha." I am not asking George's permission to do this, so I do not say, "Is that okay?"

If the interruptions continue, for whatever reasons, my next move is to use my hands as a kind of traffic officer. I lean forward in my chair, hold up the symbolic stop sign with my hand, with similar words as above. Next, I put my hand in between them and gesture to open up some space between them, creating some imaginary separation in the air, and say, "George, I really am going to get to your side of this." Then I turn back to Martha and say, "Martha, you were saying . . ." Having said this to George, I have to make sure I switch to him fairly soon, but I am not going to do it at his demand.

Nearly always, the person in George's position eventually learns to shut it down, be quiet and not interrupt; but this takes time, depending on the level of anxiety. With the most conflicted couples, it is not easy for them to stop interrupting each other. They cannot stop the reactivity going on inside of them. I usually say again what I had just said, and redo the hand actions, and add, "If the two of you just redo your fights in here, we are really not going to get anywhere."

Increasing Self-Focus

The primary goal of all marital counseling work is to increase the level of differentiation of the participants. As this happens, the couple's marital relationship will improve, as will their family life in general. Differentiation of self is the way out of the anxiety and fusion that leads to reactivity and the symptoms that make life less satisfying.

An essential step in doing this is for each partner to develop a self-focus. When each one can be more objectively aware of the interactive process between them, and how self participates in that process, we are laying the groundwork for change. For example, with significant levels of expressed anger, I ask questions like, "What do you have to do that will guarantee that you get yourself good and angry?" They have never thought of it as something they are in charge of and as a decision they make. Their angry reactivity is a simple, automatic response. I want to expand those automatic moments into discrete little segments. Then, when they have their fights at home, they will start observing themselves more, in the midst of the fight, and learn how this contributes to their way of being with one another. In a later session I might ask, "Have you learned anything more about how you make yourself angry?"

The self-focus eventually becomes a means for each person to set some goals for self, both in how each wants to be with the other and in life generally. What principles or beliefs about being in a relationship would they like to be better able to portray with the other during stressful or difficult times? This is about changing their focus from reactive to proactive. As objectivity develops, and they can reflect more accurately on self in relationship, then they can begin to measure their own success and how they get themselves derailed from their goals.

When the agenda for each partner begins to change from "How do I show my partner how wrong she (or he) is?" or "How do I get him (or her) to become the person I want him (or her) to be?" to "How do I become the person I want to be in this relationship?" there is a real change in the emotional climate of the relationship. As typical fights get started, at some point one of them will be able to step back and think a bit more about how he or she wants to be at that moment. If they can change this, even to a small degree for a short period of time, then the change has begun. When they come in for the next session and say, maybe in a dejected way, "Well, I was able to do what we talked about for about ten seconds, and then I lost it." I say, "That is progress. I am interested in how you could make that happen for ten whole seconds. What did you have to do to make it go for so long?" or, "You say that you lost it, but tell me what you had to do so that you changed your focus from how you wanted to be, to getting back at your partner?" This focus changes it from being a passive experience to an active one.

I will have more to say about developing self-focus when I describe the early phase of the counseling process in chapter 12.

Engaging Both Partners and "Resistance"

To be of help to people, they have to want to come back each week. This requires engaging with each partner, and that is not always easy with heavily conflicted couples. One way to subvert engagement with both partners is by becoming a part of the triangle. This will bring back one partner, but the other will be reluctant and often be seen as "resistant."

If we think of one partner as resistant, this is really about us. A systemic view of resistance understands it always happens in response to someone wanting the resistant person to change in some way. The resisting person is responding to the pushy person. I do not engage people in order to change them. Changing them is not my job. Change is always up to the individual person. My job is to be there, be involved, be curious, and occasionally share something that I might know about relationships or, at a minimum, function with them out of that knowledge.

Most people who become counselors tend to be emotional pursuers in their own relationships. The primary training maxim I use with them is, "Don't just do something, stand there." This is in contrast to their usual way of being with others. It is quite normal for pursuing-type counselors to join in with the pursuer in the couple and to go after the distancing partner. They can pursue that partner right out of the counseling. Early in the counseling with George and Martha, she was eager to talk and he was hesitant. I did not push him to respond to my invitations to say something. Very often, the relationship pursuers watch me with the distancers and they are amazed at how open the distancer becomes with me. They ask how I got him (or her) to talk so much, even about feelings.

An amazing number of counselors simply do not like or are critical of the people with whom they are working. Their negative views will sink the counseling effort. A whole variety of subjective feelings and attitudes can get in the way of a good working relationship. If we use labels for counselees like defensive, hostile, argumentative, or threatening, this is really as much about us the counselor as the counselee.

Some counselors have, for example, a clear gender bias, or other kinds of biases (like class, racial, ethnic, religious, political, cultural, or sexual orientation) that will affect their work. Quite often, they think they do not have such a bias, but repeated failures to engage the particular type of people involved will make this clear. Some people tend to see females as inevitably more problematic than males, or just the reverse. Some, based on their own family experience, will automatically take sides around these kinds of stereotypical issues. They will be unable to engage these people.

Shifting the Relationship Process

As partners become slightly more objective and self-reflective, their relationship process will begin to change. Their togetherness time between sessions may change. At first they may not be able to alter their argumentative patterns, but they find themselves thinking about what they each did, and what they might want to try to do differently. Or, they find that after having the argument, they can then talk sooner and more calmly about what happened.

I always know we have turned a corner in the counseling when one partner is more open and vulnerable about self's sensitivities with the other. The expression of vulnerability tends to be heard and, very often, the response of the other exposes some kind of vulnerability of their own. As long as this is not a blaming statement (What you do to me), they will begin to make headway.

The open expression of vulnerability implies a growing sense of safety. It is not safety when it is other focused (as in "You make me feel safer"), but it is based on a stronger sense of self. Ideally, it means there is more trust in self and that self cannot be so emotionally damaged by the reactions of the other. This is part of a move toward greater differentiation.

As you will have noticed from the verbatim of George and Martha, in talking about the interactive process between the couple I like to use the image of a dance, and of the steps each one takes in doing the dance. I might refer to the music or, as in square dancing, who calls the steps or, as in English country dancing (à la Jane Austen), each dance having its own music. I might talk about how professional dancers coordinate their moves with each other, and yet each has to be skillful and competent in performing their own part. I often speak about the couple rewriting their choreography and developing new steps. With a very combative couple, I might talk about their being fighters in the ring, and I wonder what the bell is that calls them out from their corners to start throwing punches. I try to move the images from being more pugilistic to being more like the dance. Boxers do a dance also, so I move the images in that direction.

The point is to create the sense that this two-step, while appearing to be automatic, can be altered as each one begins to master self's part in the dance. They can become better dancers rather than stepping all over each other. It is a great way to talk about fusion and differentiation, or togetherness and individuality. Good dancers have to be very much in charge of self, but they can also coordinate and cooperate with others.

It is possible to give homework to more moderately or less conflicted couples, and they will usually do it. For example, after spending some time unpacking the elements of their pursue/distance dance, I ask them to try a week of reversing their positions. I ask the husband to become the emotional pursuer, wanting lots of nonsexual togetherness time, and for the wife to be the emotional distancer. They almost always learn something about self with this exercise.

I also ask these moderately conflicted couples to play with their over- and underfunctioning patterns and to reverse them for a week. I am interested in what these experiments do to their subjective experience of self in the relationship. I may suggest to a more moderately conflicted couple, after a few weeks of working with them, to take a short holiday from the struggles of the relationship. I suggest they get back into their early dating patterns, maybe give the kids to a trusted babysitter and go away for an overnight. I tell them not to talk about anything they usually fight about and to do the fun things together that they used to do.

I would not do this with a more heavily conflicted couple, although I do suggest they give the "relationship talks" a rest. Pushing them into greater togetherness will only heat things up for them, and going away together could prove a disaster. They will not have enough unfused individuality to draw on. They will become more anxious and find a way to have a fight as soon as possible.

I do not directly focus on "the relationship" with these couples. They have been fighting over the relationship for years. Each will try to define what it is. One says, "It's fine." The other says, "No, it's terrible!" "Well, it wouldn't be so terrible if you would just . . ." Fighting about "it" is a frequent topic for conflicted couples. It is one of the topics that they will try to triangle with us around, since we are the relationship experts. Instead, I suggest we put the relationship as a topic on the back burner and look to see what can be learned about self, about what each one brings to the relationship, and this is where I consistently put my focus.

Thinking about Family

In the first phase of counseling, I want to expand the couple's understanding of their problem and begin to connect each person's emotionality to their own families of origin. This goes more slowly with heavily conflicted couples. I explore with them their emotional progression from frustration of expectations with each other to hurt and then anger. The amount of emotional intensity we bring to this process is almost always related to our unresolved emotional attachments in our family of origin. In working with one partner back through this progression of feelings, I clarify the emotional expectations that begin the progression. For example, a wife might say that she wants to feel special and prized by her husband; or a husband could say that he wants to feel valued as someone to be relied on and thus feel important.

As the expectations become clarified, I usually ask, "How did this wish of yours, to feel special, get to be so important to you?" Quite often the first response will be, "I don't know." Then I ask, "Would you say that, before you met George, this expectation was present in your other dating relationships (or marriages)?" The answer is usually yes.

Then I ask, "So how did this hope of yours work in those relationships?" I then explore these other relationships and the role of their expectations there.

The point of looking at these other relationships is to discover whether and, if so, how pervasive the expectations have been in the person's life, and to better connect them, subjectively, with the feeling experience involved. I do not ask about feelings per se, but they come out as people describe these other relationships. Better connecting with the emotional intensity of these other relationships helps people to own and explore the expectations they have. The better connected they are with the subjective feeling experience they have had in other relationships, the better they will be able to relate it to family when I do, eventually, ask about that. More often, as a result of going slow with this process, they connect the issue with their families themselves.

Often, in response to my questions, more moderately conflicted people jump right into their family of origin as the source of their emotional expectation. If in the process of exploring the expectation in other relationships the person's family is never mentioned, I casually ask something like, "So you say you have always had this hope for your love relationships, and we have looked at a couple of examples. When you say "always," it makes me think that this is something you had within you before you ever started getting serious about dating or getting married. Would that be true?" At this point people often mention their family. If not, then I might ask, "So this makes me think about the family you grew up in. Would you say that the kinds of feelings you describe and the underlying hopes you have relate to your family in any way?"

If the person has not yet made the connection, then often a kind of light will go off in their heads, and they will say, "Why, yes, I think they do." Then we explore how this expectation developed within their family experience. They can connect the subjective feelings in the different relationships back to their feelings in family and how they began to formulate their hopes and wishes for their life as adults. People who are more phobic about family may deny any connection of these issues to family. That is fine. We have to wait until they are more comfortable and not pursue them on the importance of family until then. I had to do this with Martha. She refused to talk about her family in early sessions.

As we talk about family, each person begins to take more ownership of their own emotional frustrations and focus it less on their partner as the source of this frustration. As arguments continue to happen we can keep connecting their intensity back to this originating experience. More and more, people will take responsibility for their issues and do less blaming of their partner. The issue is theirs to deal with. Doing this sort of work does not change the fact that they still feel badly that their hope is not being met, but they now hold it in a much wider context, as a kind of personal life theme. Eventually, I want it to be clear that these themes relate to family.

As this happens, in working with more moderately conflicted couples, they will be in transition to doing middle-phase counseling and beginning to do family work. I arrive at this point with some of these usually better-differentiated couples as early as session four or five. A few will feel attracted to thinking about self in family, and perhaps begin to address it in family before we discuss it in counseling. Family is, for these people, a less toxic issue and they probably have good enough relationships with family to be able to address their concerns. Most people move much more slowly around these themes.

More heavily conflicted couples are usually hesitant to look at family. That is part of why I have described a process of approaching it slowly. If we rush too quickly into family-of-origin themes with them, they will reject them and shut down explorations that go in that direction. They remain convinced that the problem is solely with their partner. They will say, "No, there is no connection with my family." If we push it they will say, "Look, I told you I don't want to talk about them. They have no meaning for me anymore. They are not relevant to what is going on here." A lot of groundwork has to be laid before these folks are willing to talk about family. It has to become clear to them, through their own exploration of the feelings and emotional issues, that family is relevant.

Here is an important note: *I want to make clear that talking about family in this way is not the same as doing family-of-origin work.* Many types of insight-oriented counseling approaches can talk about family and it can be useful, but, in my experience, it does not change much of the subjective experience for the counselee. It can simply be an interpretive intellectualizing of the experience, or a way to blame family. They will still feel trapped in an unhappy world because now it is clear that, while it may not be all their partner's fault, it must clearly be their family's fault. This is not change, and this is not family-of-origin work.

Family-of-origin work involves actively reengaging the family and relating to them differently. I will talk about doing this work when I talk about middle-phase counseling. All that this sort of exploration does, as a part of first-phase work, is to place the themes or emotional issues back in the family context. Most heavily conflicted couples will not be ready to reengage their family members in a useful way to do this work. With them, the relevance of family experience to current marriage experience has to be seen repeatedly so that, at some point, the implications are inescapable.

For all of us in general, but for heavily conflicted partners in particular, doing family-of-origin work takes a tremendous amount of courage. For many people it feels like going into a war zone. I make clear that there is no such thing as courage without the context of fear. Then, they are often quite amazed, as we prepare for doing it, that their fears do not actually materialize; but they do not have any way of knowing this ahead of time. As they do the work, their feelings about it usually begin to change and then they develop enthusiasm for doing it. We just have to be very respectful of people's need to do it at a pace that is comfortable for them.

11

Addressing the Triangles in Counseling

The whole point, for most people, of going to a counselor is to bring a third party into their emotional issues, spreading the anxiety. Part of the importance they assign to us as counselors is that we will understand their experience and see with them, automatically, what the situation is. As people tell their personal stories a kind of magical spell is cast. Much of traditional counselor training, with a focus on things like empathy and establishing a good relationship with counselees, has served to set up counselors for participating with clients within these triangular forces.

Paraphrasing Dr. Bowen, let me restate the basic principle for change when working with couples in conflict: *The tension in the original two-person system can be resolved when contained within a three-person system, one of whom remains emotionally detached or neutral.* This is the magic of the work. It offers a productive outcome with the least input of time. When this process is followed, one or more members of a system will eventually work at differentiating a self within the system, be able to function more responsibly, and be better able to relate to others.

This chapter is central to my thinking about the neutral stance of the counselor. The primary challenge in engaging both partners and becoming a resource to each of them has to do with how the counselor manages self within the helping triangle. The more anxiety and stress there is for a couple the more triangles they may have and the more intensity there is in the triangles. As counselors, we are only the latest triangle the couple will try to involve. Our responsibility is to manage ourselves in this triangle. We do this through our actions; less so through specific words. Remaining neutral, defining self, and living out our level of differentiation are the key elements. We demonstrate a way to be connected without taking sides. We maintain our own autonomy. We do not take on their anxiety. We keep pushing it back at them. The magic is that as we do this the couple will become better able to deal with their issues.

We do this not only in the conjoint marital sessions. It is especially important to be vigilant in individual counseling sessions. I sometimes think counselors in training should be allowed to see individual counselees only when they have shown an ability to stay neutral with couples or families. Doing individual counseling, we always have to be aware of the triangles to which we are susceptible.

One-to-one relationships are the antidote to triangulation. People will tend to escape the one-to-one with a counselor by focusing on someone else and talking about them. Thus, both counselor and counselee could be anxious about sitting alone together and will feel more comfortable talking about another person, whether they are present or not. We challenge this behaviorally by keeping our focus on the partner we are talking with, and his or her experience, as he or she tries to shift the focus over to the other. Eventually he or she will learn to feel safer in staying focused on self.

Defining and Managing Self in the Counseling Triangle

Where I, as a counselor, choose to put my interest and the kind of things I am curious about are the primary ways I define myself to counselees. In the way counselees tell their story, which is nearly always a kind of invitation to take their side in the story (something along the lines of "See how awful she/he is?" or "See what I have to put up with?" or "Don't you agree?"), they are asking me to see the problem the way they see it. Martha's implicit message in the triangle was "You see how uncaring he is, and what he does to me. Will you straighten him out?"

In choosing where to focus, I rarely ask questions that invite the speaker to say more about their partner or even about the fight. For example, a question like "What did you think he was up to?" invites the speaker to speculate about the partner's motivations. This will not go well. One of our favorite other-focused activities in an argument is to draw conclusions about other people's motivations and tell them what they are "really" doing.

As the counselees tell their story about the other person, I ask process questions about themselves. These questions ask the person to think about his or her part in the interactive or the personal, internal process. Again, I do not lay down rules in counseling for how they should behave, or what they should focus on; I just act on my own beliefs about where to put my focus. I do not need their cooperation to do this.

Another, more direct way to define self in a session is to tell them some general thought I have, related to what they have been discussing/arguing about in the session. These comments are never interpretations about them but just observations about how we all, myself included, tend to function. "You know, what you are describing seems to be a pretty universal thing about us human beings. When someone does something we don't like, we get all stirred up and we react. Often that becomes a fight with that person. Does it work that way for you?" Then I ask, "What do you know about how you get yourself stirred up?"

The better-differentiated couples will take this kind of question as an opportunity to reflect on self. They respond with a thought that says, essentially, "I can't quite figure out why I get so worked up. What he/she does is not worth a death sentence, but I just can't stand it." My follow-up questions focus on the inner process in that person and what kind of a path they follow to get into a fighting stance.

In early sessions with more heavily conflicted couples, I do not make such general statements very often. It depends on how thoughtful they are capable of being versus how reactive they are. When people are in the midst of their reactivity it is not a good time to try to shift the focus to some thought of yours, and certainly not to do any teaching. Teaching will be seen as a distraction, or it will be used as another way to put the blame on the other person.

George and Martha had a sense of humor and could get the point of my comments more easily through humor. Not all counselees are like this, so we have to be careful with humor or it will come off as sarcasm. Once, early on, when George was focused on Martha's nagging, I told a joke. I said, "Have you heard about the couple where the wife thought her husband had a drinking problem? He said to her, 'I wouldn't drink so much if you didn't nag me so much.' Then she said, 'I wouldn't nag you so much if you didn't drink so much.'" They both laughed. Then I clarified for him what I was asking about with regard to him. What was his own experience when she nagged? I was not asking him to say more about her nagging. The lightness helped him to refocus.

Working with the Couple's Triangles

In working with a couple on their triangles, I first want to uncover the major triangles in their lives and get a sense of how the triangular process works: who does what, when, how, and then what happens, and then what, and so forth. Then I clarify with the couple descriptively what a specific triangle is about and how it functions. With the moderately conflicted couples, I explicitly label it as a triangle and we can talk about the concept.

With more conflicted couples there is always the danger that they will misuse the teaching. They will not hear it or will only hear it selectively, as a way to continue the fight with their partner and to diagnose or label them like, "There you go being a distancer again," or "Stop being such a pursuer," or "You're trying to triangle me." This continues the other-focused quality of the relationship. Once people have begun to reflect on their own part in the emotional process, then they can make use of teaching information to develop their thinking about their own part.

I attempt to elucidate what is difficult about engaging each other directly, rather than take the anxiety elsewhere. I also ask about the other person in the triangle. "So what does your good friend Jane say to you when you complain to her about George?" Jane can either intensify the anxiety, adding more fuel to the flames, or minimize the anxiety. In either case, I am interested in how useful it is to hear Jane's response. "Does what Jane have to say help you in your relationship with George?"

When it is clear that a particular triangle is not being helpful to the marital issues, I talk with the partner involved. A good example of this is a woman whose friends were encouraging her to get out of the marriage and talking down men. I asked her what this was like for her and what the impact of this process was on her; then I asked if this sort of advice was helpful to her in her own goals for her life. I asked if there was someone she did enjoy talking to who did not take a position about her marriage and who could simply listen to her without taking sides. She did have such a friend and started seeing her more. This friend helped her to think things through for herself without asking her to defend whatever position she decided on.

As she began to recognize the triangular process, she went back to the other friends who advised against continuing the marriage, and started asking them about their own personal experience. Where did their stance come from? Her questions to them got them into a more thoughtful place and their discussions about marriage improved. One of those friends, the one who most vociferously advocated divorce, became hostile around her questions, and that person ended the friendship.

Generally, people are quite unaware of what drives the triangling process, so my questions help them think it through. Questions like: Who do you talk with about these things? What do they say, and what do you do with their advice? When do you feel most like you want to be with your buddies? How does being with them help you? What do you get from talking with your mother about your marriage? Were there ever times when you felt like you didn't want to be with her (the affair) and would rather be with your wife? At what points do you find yourself wanting to be more with one than the other?

In George and Martha's case, the parental triangles with their mothers were central, with George being hugely overinvolved (at a daily contact level) with his mother and Martha being hugely under-involved with her mother. George and his mother could be a close twosome where Martha was often in the outside position. Then, when George was unhappy with his mother, he and Martha could be the close twosome against his mother. They did not talk about Martha's mother, but she was a silent and unseen presence hovering over their lives, as was George's mother. Their triangles did not involve their son, but in many marriages, the children will become involved in the marital conflict.

Some Examples of Marital Triangles

Philip Guerin and his colleagues suggest eight common triangles that can be involved in marital conflict (Guerin et al. 1987). They are:

1. the extramarital affair
2. friends or the social-network triangles
3. professional triangles (as with a doctor, pastor, or a therapist)
4. the in-law triangle
5. children-oriented triangles
6. stepfamily triangles
7. the primary parental triangle of each partner
8. sibling triangles

The first three are extra-family triangles, and nearly always represent leakage of the family triangles into the larger arena outside of family. I am not going to discuss all of these but I will touch on some.

Professional triangles have much in common with affair triangles (which I discuss in more detail below), especially given that the latter do not have to be sexual. Counselors can have professional affairs with their counselees. The seductive moves, initiated by either person, can have a different manifestation (other than sexual) and intent, which can be simply to create an alliance; but the effect on the marriage or other family relationships can be the same. The counseling relationship can become more important than other normal relationships and there can be, in a real sense, through this closeness, an "alienation of affection" in relation to others. The counselee thinks, and may say, "If only my husband/wife/family members understood me the way you do." We cannot stop a counselee from thinking this, but through our behavior, we can minimize this kind of thinking and keep their focus outwardly on the relationship with others, rather than on the relationship with us.

All cultures know about the *in-law triangle* and the issues that can happen around this. In some cases they cause only a certain degree of alienation, and in others they can become literally deadly. They happen when the partners have not differentiated a self well enough from their parents. They have not clearly defined with their own parents that their partner is now first in their lives and is where their primary allegiance lies. If, for example, a mother and daughter-in-law are regularly at odds, usually this is due to the husband failing to make clear to his mother that he is now devoted to his wife.

In a real sense George was not fully married. He had not left his mother and "cleaved unto" his wife. Emotionally, we all have some difficulty growing up and leaving mother, but this was more extreme in George. He had significant difficulty defining himself to his mother as separate from her, in his thinking, feelings, and actions. George had an older sister who had long since distanced from their mother and rarely had contact with either her or him. She was not any better differentiated than George and they both acted out the flip sides of the same coin. She had some of Martha's style about her and their mother could focus negatively on her with George. All of their mother's intensity, in the projection process, had gone to George as "the little man of the family" and his sister had resented the attention he got. She did not consider herself lucky in this matter.

Although it was often a source of friction between them, Martha was somewhat accepting of the situation between George and his mother since it took some of the emotional heat off of her. Whenever George got more upset with his mother than with her, she was off the hook and no real intimacy was being asked of her other than to commiserate with him about her. Of course, other times Martha came up short when compared to his mother and how "caring and involved" his mother was, and also how his mother got more time than she did.

George's mother was especially focused on his career, and she wondered out loud how much Martha helped him with this. When his mother visited their house over the years, she tended to give Martha "tips" on how she could be of more help to George. She was not often overtly critical of Martha, as can happen in some cases. In those cases, one partner can ally with a parent (including an in-law parent) to shape up the other spouse around any number of issues. A similar type of triangle is where the daughter is very close to her father, and the husband comes up short in comparison. Sometimes the triangles are three-generational, with the grandparents fighting with the parents around their grandchildren's treatment.

As George began to see that things were cooling down between him and Martha and he was feeling less anxious in that relationship, he was more able to put energy into thinking about the triangle with his mother and how he was going to manage himself there. She often wanted to have regular, even daily, contact with him, treating him in some ways like a partner. She had not put energy into developing her own social connections and a life of her own. Any attempts by George to suggest that she do this were rebuffed. She continued to rely on him to do jobs around her house even though she could easily afford to hire someone to do the work. He was always readily available.

As his work on self progressed, slowly it became clearer to his mother that his primary loyalty was to his wife. George did not attack his mother or tell her to leave him alone; he just behaved differently and also let her know clearly when he was not available. He also initiated contacts before she called him and, eventually, this was when he usually pursued the family-of-origin agenda. I will say more about his work in chapter 14 on middle-phase counseling.

The *good friend/best buddy triangles* can have their own problems, whether they take a position for or against the marriage. The very best friends do not usually (except in cases of severe physical abuse) take positions about the marriage. Their level of differentiation and instinctive sense of boundaries will automatically keep them from participating in triangles. They will stay focused on their friend's own experience and behavior.

Those friends who have their own unresolved emotional attachments and, for example, have an agenda around the opposite sex, may strongly advocate certain ideas. This may or may not feel comforting to the one with the difficulties, but it will not be of help. This situation is much like adolescents who distance from their parents and fall in with a group of kids who like to talk negatively about parents or authorities in general. They form a like-minded pack, but they are simply moving from one form of fusion to another. The process is the same. The person needs to think for self and needs help doing this; they do not need to be told what to think or do.

The *primary parental triangle* for each partner is usually the most relevant to the marriage. The partners each developed their own level of emotional maturity in their family of origin and it was there that they also developed their functional styles and relational sensitivities. In doing assessments, I am always interested in the ongoing relationship with parents, and how well a person can both be connected with them and be a self with them.

Triangles and Change

Bowen did not invent this process of detriangling; he simply put a label on it. Down through the ages there have been people, friends or family members, who have had this skill as they related to others. Here is one example of how it might have happened. Not long after marriage, the new husband and wife start arguing. One day the wife decides to leave her husband and move back in with her parents, who accept her back.

The wife starts talking with her mother, telling mother all of the awful things the husband said or did. The point of these stories would be to ask the mother to agree that the wife was right to leave him. Mother is expected to have a sympathetic response and to support her daughter by agreeing with her. In this triangle (mother, daughter, husband) the mother has several possible moves:

1. She could agree totally with her daughter, as the daughter hoped, and join in with the daughter telling other stories of the husband's awfulness. The mother might even say, "I had my reservations about him all along but I didn't want to discourage you. You were right to leave him." This might extend to telling the daughter about her own husband's misdeeds and then generalizing to "all men."

2. Or, she might say, "I told you he was the wrong man for you, but you never listen to me. Maybe you will start listening to me now." She is agreeing with the daughter while also attacking her poor judgment.

3. Or, she might not agree with her daughter at all; maybe even be on the husband's side, and say, "Look, you are just being the baby you always were. He is good for you. He is right to be critical of you. You need to grow up. He is criticizing you for your own good." Even if he is abusive she may say, "Maybe he can knock some sense into you." Another version of this is, "Whatever he says or does, you have to learn to be submissive and to serve your husband. If he is not happy it is your job to please him and make him happy with you. That is the wife's role in life."

It might be that, after the daughter has been home a while, she begins to remember why she wanted to leave home in the first place. Mother (or father) may become more critical of her and they begin to argue just like they used to do. Eventually her husband does not look so bad to her and she goes back to him. When they are reunited, she has changed her position in the triangle, and she begins to tell him about the awful things her parents/mother said about him. This husband has the same options for responding to these stories as the mother had, and so the triangling will continue through the years.

However, there have always been some wise, better-differentiated people in families who saw other options to the three triangular moves listed above. There are at least two other options:

1. In response to her daughter's awful stories about the husband, mother could be interested in how her daughter managed herself in relation to him. She could ask the daughter lots of questions, not about the husband, thus eliciting more negative comments about him; but with each story, she could ask about what the daughter did or said in response. What made her say or do that? What sort of thinking has she done about the situation? Had she thought of any other ways she could have responded? What do her friends say about all of this? What does the daughter think about what they said? How does she go about evaluating her own behavior? The point would be to invite the daughter into thinking about herself, her situation, and how she could handle it.

2. Or, she could tell the daughter about herself and her own marital history and how she decided to manage herself in her arguments with her husband, especially when he was critical of her. She could talk about what she learned in particular about what she would do when he was angry at her, what sense she made of it, how she sorted it through for herself, and then what she decided to do. Then she could talk about what the impact of that was, and whether she needed to refine what she did or said. The point of this would be to show the daughter something of her own experience and thinking process around her marital conflict.

She would show how she defined herself in her marriage. She would allow the daughter to draw her own conclusions, but the mother would not get pulled into talking about the husband in any form, whether it was to try to understand his intent, or to make excuses for him, or to be critical of him. She would only talk about her own experience in marriage, and not much about her own husband.

Both of these responses keep the discussion and the emotional process between the two of them, mother and daughter, talking about self with each other, rather than talking about someone who is not present and who would have his own version of what transpired in the marriage. Both responses could be combined. They are examples of a one-to-one relationship. In doing so, the mother would become a resource to her daughter by providing the daughter an opportunity to think about her situation, how she could better define herself, and what she was going to do about it. This enhances the daughter's own autonomy and responsibility for self.

This sort of natural wisdom has existed in some better-differentiated people down through the ages. The mother defined herself and stayed neutral in the triangle by not taking anyone's side. She did not distance from her daughter and say, "Don't bring this to me. This is your mess. You deal with it." She stayed connected to her daughter and was interested in her experience. She did not criticize anyone, or tell her daughter what she should do about her husband or the marriage. That was the daughter's responsibility. This self-defining stance is similar to how we can be a resource to our counselees as we invite them to think things through for themselves and work at their own self-definition.

The Affair Triangle

One obvious triangle in marital conflict is the affair. Very often, when couples come in for counseling, the affair has just been discovered and they are in crisis. Up to the point of discovery, the affair triangle may have helped to stabilize the marriage and it was a place for the one partner to take his or her anxiety and to feel more comfortable. It drained off anxiety from the marital relationship and may have helped calm it down.

One couple in their seventies came in to see me. Nearly every evening after dinner the husband told his wife he was going to the local pub, but he actually was going down the street to spend the evening with another woman. He said that now they rarely had sex; they just listened to music and talked about things they were both interested in. He had been doing this for twenty years and the marriage had been quite placid with the wife suspecting nothing; she enjoyed having her evenings to herself. When she discovered what he had really been doing she blew up.

When affairs are discovered they normally become the emotional focus for the couple. The one not having the affair blames the one who is. Sorting through the issues of who is responsible for what is important. The person having the affair is always responsible for his or her behavior, but both partners create the conditions in which the affair took place and continues. In the case just mentioned, the wife went along with her husband's absence every evening. She was comfortable with his emotional distance and she could engage then in her own activities. This is the pre-affair situation we want to address after dealing with the emotional fallout resulting from the affair.

If the affair has not ended when they come in to see me, I take the position that we not do marital counseling. I say that counseling for the marriage depends on having no other emotional involvements that drain off energy from what is happening in the marriage, and we would be wasting our time to try it. Whenever anxiety goes up, the person could just take it to the third person and feel better. The positive aspect of anxiety, to help generate movement and change, would not exist.

After doing my normal assessment, I then schedule individual sessions with each partner (with occasional conjoint sessions) to address whatever issues exist around the affair. The goal of these sessions is to get to a place where marital counseling can begin, with the affair ended and most of its emotional fallout addressed. The point of this phase of the work is to get back to the kind of relationship they had just before the affair began.

When I say to the people having the affair that it has to stop if they want marital counseling, and they say, "Okay, I will break it off," but show no pain or upset around this, then I suspect that they are lying and do not intend to give it up. In individual sessions, without being confrontational, I address this suspicion. I make clear that they could try to hide this from me and proceed with the marital counseling, but that it really would be a waste of time and money. Normally the person fesses up to what is going on and we can then work on that.

Often the partners not in the affair knowingly allow it to continue because they are too dependent on their partner, emotionally or financially, to have a bottom line that says, in effect, "You end it or you move out of the house. As far as I am concerned, the marriage is over." Without this bottom-line position, there is tacit permission for the affair to continue. My individual work with this partner tends to focus around whether there is a bottom line (they do not have to have one) and if so, how they deal with it.

If I discover during the assessment phase that there is an affair going on and the partner does not know, I would rather know about its existence than not know, even though it presents a quandary. I say to the person that I cannot recommend marital counseling in this case, until the affair is finished. If not, then I recommend counseling with each of them separately until there is some resolution of the situation.

I never reveal the affair to the other party; that is not my job. I do not even take a position around whether the partner should be told or not. Often, when the person having the affair is tempted to reveal it, I ask what they imagine would result from doing so. The only time I take the position that it probably should be revealed is when one partner has suspected the other of having an affair and runs into continuous denials from the one having it. This can be crazy making for the partner, to have the reality of his or her perceptions or intuition denied. They even may be told they "are crazy" to suspect such a thing.

On occasion, I have sessions with the other woman (or man) and discuss with her what has gone on for her around the relationship. I tell her the same things about triangles and how things change at some point down the line, when the wife (or husband) is no longer in the picture. I might even say that the likelihood of this relationship with the husband ending in him having another affair is quite high statistically. These sorts of comments rarely change the outcome, but people remember what I say and one or both parties often return for counseling some time later (maybe years later) saying, "Well, it went just as you predicted. How do I avoid doing this again?"

I regard affairs as different from one-night stands, but they can result from the same sort of emotional conditions in the marriage—typically, significant emotional distance. The person having the one-night stand could say, "It was just for the sex," and I accept that, but it would be indicative of the couple's inability to address their sexual issues because of the emotional distance. That has to be addressed in order to get to the sexual issues. David Schnarch's book *Constructing the Sexual Crucible* is about the Bowen theory, differentiation, and sexual intimacy (Schnarch 1991). While Schnarch's focus on certain themes is more intense than mine, his thoughts can be useful in these discussions.

Affairs differ by how emotionally important the lover is to the partner having the affair. The emotional distance is still the issue in the marriage and the person having the affair is attempting to deal with it in this new relationship. When I ask this person to give up the affair if they want to have marital counseling, this is difficult when the affair partner is emotionally important. They are giving up more than the sex. If they agree to give it up, then we spend some of the individual counseling sessions grieving the loss of this relationship. They might learn from it in order to bring those emotional issues back into the marital work.

There are cases where a marital separation has already occurred due to the affair. The affair has continued, but neither married partner has initiated divorce. They stay stuck in that fixed triangle, sometimes for years. Verbally, one or both will say that is not what they want but behaviorally neither one can decide what to do. I might spend a few sessions with them on this because one or both could be in genuine turmoil, but my basic position is that things will not change until one of them makes a decisive move.

In these cases, I have one strategy that usually creates movement. It depends on the partner not having the affair being able to pull it off emotionally and not all can do it. Let's say this person is the wife. I say to her, "What would it be like for you to meet and get to know the other woman?" She is horrified at this suggestion. I then ask what she knows about this woman, and ask a bunch of questions related to her husband's attraction to the woman. Very often the wife has fantasies about the other woman that may be quite wrong and that involve her denigrating herself. It is this fear that the other woman was "better" in some way that would inspire her to keep her distance.

I ask questions like, "What do you know about what your husband is telling her about the future of their relationship and of his marriage with you?" A number of questions of this sort begin to get the wife curious. Often, she gets herself into the place where she can go visit the other woman, who is also very hesitant to meet with the wife. Whenever these meetings do occur, and the wife has the intent of just getting to know the other woman, in a semi-friendly way, and not to attack or judge her or blame her "for breaking up my marriage," then movement begins to happen in this stuck central triangle.

This is a powerful detriangling intervention. The husband is often furious but he can no longer keep things as they are. He becomes the outsider. The two women compare notes on what he said to each, and they both then have a better picture of what is happening and what they might do. It definitely helps the wife move from fantasy to reality. The filling in of gaps in the information helps her to make plans for herself.

This does not always bring about a marital reconciliation because, in these sorts of circumstances, the husband really does not want the marriage to continue but for a variety of reasons (often financial) will not be clear with his wife around this. This forces him to declare himself. Both the wife and the other woman are freer to get on with their lives with the increased sharing of information between them. The husband may decide he wants individual counseling to clarify what is going on with him. As always, family issues are involved for all parties. The other woman may come in for counseling with me just because she liked what has happened and it helps her get out of a stuck position that she did not like. She wants to move on in her own life.

Opening Communication

Sitting with a couple is a process of sorting out and externalizing their fantasy, feeling, and thinking systems, expressing those out loud, and getting each to talk openly. They often say to one another, "I never knew you had such thoughts or feelings." Then the other says, "I never dared tell anyone, especially you." The counselor attempts to get each person, through asking questions, to think through their own participation in the emotional process. When eventually someone announces an "I" position, what he or she has decided to do and not do in the relationship, then there is the chance for progress, if he or she can maintain it against the opposition. The opposition is often one of anger or hurt or accusations of selfishness.

This approach to helping can be done on a short-term basis, which may be more symptom focused, or on a long-term basis, which deals with underlying processes and leads to greater differentiation of self. For short-term purposes, this approach will work best with people who are not multiproblemed and who are more capable of calm reflection about their lives. More anxious people, like George and Martha, will need more intensive, longer-term work simply because of the difficulty of getting a grasp on all of the anxiety and reactivity that exists in their emotional system.

In a typical couple doing this work, one partner will move forward, differentiating a bit of self, and then the other will do so. Each will do it in small steps, as they learn the skills involved, usually requiring work in a number of different areas within the emotional field. Those who take on doing their own family-of-origin work and drop a focus on their family of procreation usually do the best; but this happens in only half of my cases. Reluctance to do family-of-origin work usually shows where the limits are in what can be accomplished. However, I have numerous counselees come back years later, saying they now feel ready to do the family work.

12

The Counseling Process: Beginning Phase

Working for Self-Focus

At the start of counseling, each partner is usually more of an expert on the behavior of the other than of their own. One approach to their heavy degree of criticalness of the other is to talk with them about their huge investment in the other, as a form of caring about how they want things to be better. However, I wonder with them how well their strategy is working and what the likely or apparent effect is of their approach. If, for example, I ask George, "Do you have some sense of what you could do right now to get Martha to move away from you and be more distant?" he would know. He replies, saying that it would be some form of criticism. Then I ask, "Is that distance what you want to have happen?" He denies that is what he wants, but then I wonder with him, based on the regular outcome of this approach, if maybe he does want that distance. I ask, "Let's just play with this idea a bit. Let's say that distance was a goal of yours. If that were the case, that you wanted her to back off and be more distant, and you could get this by being critical, what would that be about for you?"

In the more moderately conflicted couples, this sort of question is heard as a direct invitation to talk about self, and they do. In the more heavily conflicted couples, they hear this question as an invitation to talk more about the partner. George starts telling me how Martha is "always" doing something that bugs him, or how she "never" does anything to please him. I then ask, "Tell me what happens with you when she does (or does not) do this." It takes him some time to get what I am asking. He tries to talk more about her, but I would interrupt as below.

Ron: Okay, but I am asking about you. When she is not being the way you want, and you criticize her, what might your need for greater distance be about?
George: I see. Well, I just want some relief from her constantly being at me. She is being critical of me so I come back at her.
Ron: Okay, tell me what that is like for you, when she is at you.
George: Well, I don't know. I hate it. I just feel hammered down and she won't let up.
Ron: So this sense of being hammered down is pretty powerful for you? It's almost a physical thing? [He is shaking his head affirmatively.] When you feel that pressure, that hammering, what do you want to do?
George: It depends. Sometimes I just want to get away from her, but I don't walk out of the room anymore because then she really blows up. So I might just go silent. Other times I come back at her. I guess I hammer at her. I want her to know what it feels like. Then we have a real blowout.

After I spend some time focused on George, I then turn to Martha and ask, "I wonder what you have been thinking for the last ten minutes?" If she starts being critical of his sensitivity, then I interrupt her and ask, "I wonder if you heard anything in what George was saying that rang bells for you, or where you said, 'Yes, that's how it is for me too?'"

These kinds of questions, going internally to inner process and/or then to the interactional process would be how I spend most of my time early in counseling. I want each of them to learn more about their own part in the emotional process, and to take more responsibility for self. As this happens, the perception of the other as the enemy, who is the source of their difficulties, will begin to diminish and the person will begin to see self's own part in the difficulties.

On another occasion, talking with George in a fairly early session, we had this exchange.

Ron: So, George, we are back into this dance of Martha pursuing and you distancing. Is that right? Maybe you don't agree, but would it be fair to say that you were distancing again from Martha at that point, like we have talked about before?

George: Well, yes. I guess so.

Ron: You were feeling hammered at again? [He nods.] I wonder if you have thought anymore about what goes into this distancing on your side of the dance?

George: Well, it's just that she is so controlling. She just wants things her way. You know it's not just me. I hear plenty of guys talk about their wives as controlling. They sometimes use less polite words to describe them. [Here he invokes his "buddies" triangle.]

Ron: I can imagine. I do hear this fairly often that someone finds another person "controlling." Women say it about men as well. But let's stick with you. I wonder just how that works. Do you mean she physically puts your arm in a lock behind your back, the way the police would, for instance, and makes you do what she wants?

George: Well not physically, but it's like that. That's the way it feels.

Ron: And at those times you just start to feel powerless and want to get away. [He nods.] And yet sometimes you have energy for getting away; it's not as if you collapse in a heap on the floor and say, "Uncle." [Pause. He nods again.] But there are other times when you decide to stand your ground. You get angry and you shift the blame back to Martha and go on the attack. Is that right? [He nods.] The dance move is different. And at some point in those arguments she might storm out of the room, right? You don't feel so powerless at those times, like you are being controlled by her. You feel like you have the upper hand.

George: Yeah, that's it. I just say, "Enough," and come swinging back at her.

Ron: Okay, so I wonder what makes for the difference between these two kinds of dance moves you make, but . . . Well, here is another direction. I think there is a similarity in both moves, a similarity that could be true of both of you. We are at the end of the session and we are going to have to stop, but here is my thought. I wonder if it isn't the case that in the distancing, when we feel powerless and "controlled" by the other and blame them with angry attacks, if in fact we aren't just abdicating responsibility for self. We would rather make it someone else's fault and say, "They are controlling." I wonder what it would be like just to say, "I am responsible for me and I decide what I will or won't do." Well, I need to stop here so maybe the two of you can just think about that and let me know what thoughts you have next time.

During these early sessions, the partners would likely ignore this comment and start again with their latest fight. I could easily work my thought into that discussion and ask if they had any further thought about it. The intent always is to bring it back to self and ask, in a variety of ways, for people to think about responsibility for self in terms of their thinking, feeling, and action. In their fusion, how the other partner is, is so much a part of how self is. Self-focus interrupts this. It has two aspects: (1) reflecting on and thinking about a person's inner emotional process connected to the larger emotional system; and (2) that person's actual, behavioral functioning within the interactions of the emotional system.

The Essence of Change

Remember, *our subjective feeling experiences go along with our positions in emotional systems.* Someone who functions less adequately in family is going to feel less well about self, have lower self-esteem, and be more reactive than someone who functions well. This means we can "work" forever on our inner feeling life and not experience change. In fact, this feeling-focused work might further embed a person in their emotional system in the functional position they have always had. Subjectively this person will continue to feel it is other people's fault that they are treated as they are and they can only wait for others to change, or do something to try to change them, like get angry at them, or punish them in some way.

In terms of what creates change, I am interested in getting people to take more responsibility, to reposition themselves and move differently within their emotional systems. What hinders this is our commitment to our subjective feeling experiences, the stories we tell to support them, and to the beliefs they embody about our place in the emotional systems of which we are a part. The more fused we are, the more rigidly we will hold to these commitments and beliefs. We lack the objectivity to see that there are any options to how we are present within a system.

With more moderately conflicted couples I sometimes simply ask people to suspend what they believe, and to act out of a different set of assumptions, to kind of "make believe," or to pretend to be different. It is a kind of pretend repositioning. When they engage in this "as if" behavior and act differently, they find they also feel differently, and they are able to sort these things through for themselves more easily. More heavily conflicted couples do not want to participate in anything "make believe" and usually will not try the exercise. However, when a person finds another way to move within their emotional system and to function differently, they are often amazed to discover that their feelings change. So, *feelings reflect the position in the system, and changing feelings has to do with changing the position.*

A Verbatim Example: Starting to Develop Self-Focus

With more highly conflicted couples, I spend more time than with less-conflicted couples on their inner emotional process. By working on the inner process, I want to loosen the internal fusion and create the experience of having more options around how to function differently in emotional systems. This comes about as a result of exploring the automatic reactions that happen so quickly that people believe it is their only way to be in response to how others are. As we open up options for how to be, then, slowly, they may be able to try out different ways of being with others.

In this segment with George and Martha, still early in the counseling, as I move the discussion away from the argument between the two of them, I want to give an example of trying to develop a focus on the inner process and how that connects with their interactional dance. I start working primarily with Martha but then George opens up as well. I had been ready to outwait him. They come in to the session while in the midst of an argument that they try to continue with me.

Martha [to George]: You're tired? What are you tired from? You don't do all that much. You don't do anywhere near what I do in a day. You just don't want to talk.
George: Yes, I do, but just not now.

Martha: You always say that. I have never known you to want to talk. You always have an excuse.

Ron: Okay, Martha, so you find that George rarely responds to your invitations to talk about things you would like to discuss.

Martha: Never. He never does.

Ron: Okay, so what do you do with that?

Martha: So here we go. Me again? When are you going to talk with him and get him to tell you why he does these things? I really want to hear that.

Ron: [Ignoring her question, I do not want to explain what I am doing; I am not asking for her permission for how I behave in the session, and I do not want to turn to him when she tries to direct things in that way.] I understand that George doesn't always let you in on what is going on with him. He has said that when he thinks you are angry with him one thing he does is shut up and withdraw; he distances from your pursuit. He hasn't found a way to hang in and calmly talk with you at those times. [Implanting an idea for him] But I really would like to hear more about what you do with that experience. Would you help me understand that?

Martha: Okay. [Resigned] So what do I do with it? You ask some hard questions. I really don't know what to say. [She wants to distance from her inner experience. This is typical for the person in the pursuer position.]

Ron: Earlier, you said that the way you experience anger is to blow up and sound off, right? [She nods.] So I hear that this happens when George displeases you in some way. We tried the little expectations experiment and you saw something of how that works. Do you blow up every time he does something you are not happy with?

Martha: Hmmm. [Thinking] Well, I guess maybe I used to but it seems like I am doing it less in recent years. I just say to myself, "What's the point?"

Ron: Okay. That's interesting, isn't it? When you ask yourself, "What's the point?" what has happened when you get to that place? What does it mean to you?

Martha: Well, I suppose it means that I am just giving up. It's not going to go anywhere.

Ron: Would it be fair to say that when you are in that place you feel more hopeless about the relationship?

Martha: Right!

Ron: So, expressing your anger, blowing up at George is a sign of your hope that things could change between the two of you and get better, [She nods thoughtfully. I pause just to let that sink in for both of them] that maybe you could have an impact on him and get a different response? [Slight pause] But when that doesn't happen, you feel hopeless. [She is nodding.] What happens next?

Martha: I don't know. [Thinking] I guess I eventually shut up and walk away. I feel pretty bad. It brings on a lot of upset and sadness. It seems like my whole life has gone that way. [This is a very important statement. Here is some of the family material—"whole life"—but I do not want to go there yet. I know that it will reemerge at some point later. I stick with the relationship with George.]

Ron: What do you then want to do with that experience?

Martha: I just want to get away. I hate that feeling. He makes me feel so bad and I just want to leave the room. I may go out for a drive, or to shop, or take a walk around the neighborhood. [I can hear the experience with her mother here, but I leave that alone.]

Ron: Okay, so at that point then you distance from him. And then?

Martha: And then I start thinking about divorce [As in moving out of the house with her mother].

Ron: Okay, so that is distancing big time. And when you come back home?

Martha: I'm quiet. I don't want to talk. George tries to be friendly with me, and nice, but I don't want anything to do with him. I keep my distance. [I decide to turn to George since she has stayed with her own experience.]

Ron: George, what's been going through your mind as Martha and I have talked?

George: Ah, well, I guess it all sounds pretty accurate as to what happens. She can be pretty moody. I can't figure it out. [He makes a small statement about himself that I grab on to. Initially, we have to listen hard for these embedded "I" statements since they can be rare early on in counseling.]

Ron: Tell me how you try to figure it out?

George: Oh, well, hmmm, I guess actually I try not to think about it too much, really. I don't like to hear her talking about divorce, but maybe that's the answer. I don't know. I don't think things are that bad.

Ron: What's it like for you when Martha gets to that hopeless place? By the way, have you ever thought of her anger as a sign of hope?

George: No, that was interesting. But I still don't know what to do with it. [Pause] I get kind of uneasy when she goes out of the house at those times. On the one hand, there is some relief that she moves away from me in this dance you talk about. [He stops to think.] But then I start to worry that she is really serious about leaving me. [George is opening up more about himself than he ever has. There is a good deal here about self and his vulnerability. This means to me that he is feeling safer in the counseling. I decide to go further with him, but I don't want to push too hard. Martha is interested. She has never heard him talk about this.]

Ron: So if she did leave the marriage that would have a big impact on you?

George: Yeah, sure. Big time. I really don't want to lose her.

Ron: Yes, that makes sense. Let me ask you something quite different. Who else in your life has gotten angry with you and what is that like for you?

George: Hmmm. Well, we occasionally get angry with each other at the office. The guys I work with don't mind sounding off with one another, and I suppose I do it as well. But we get over it quickly and move on. It never seems like it is a big deal. And my son and I have had some pretty good arguments over the years, especially as he became a teenager. But I don't think there are any lingering bad feelings there. I don't know.

Ron: Right. That's it? No one else ever got angry at you? Just your work buddies and your son?

George: Well, my mom sure has been angry with me over the years. A lot. She still is at times.

Ron: And what do you do with that?

George: Hmmm. [Thinking, long pause] I don't know. [He is starting to distance on me. But then he decides to proceed.] I guess it is sort of like with Martha. I can never figure out what is so upsetting to mom. I mean I know I screwed up at times, and I would apologize, but somehow that didn't end it. [He goes quiet.]

Ron: Okay, so you and mom can do the same dance that you and Martha do, is that right?

George: Yeah, I guess it is. I never quite thought of it that way. [This is important for Martha to hear and helps to depersonalize her anger a bit. It's not her fault that he behaves as he does.]

Ron: So even before you met Martha, you were already having this kind of experience with an important woman in your life? [Further emphasizing to Martha that it is not just her] And you would distance from her as well?
George: Right.
Ron: [I decide to not pursue the thing with his mom right now. I will come back to it. It will emerge quite naturally on its own.] Tell me, has your boss ever been angry with you?
George: Oh yes, big time. I've probably come close to losing my job a couple of times because of some things I've screwed up on.
Ron: What do you do about that?
George: I make damn sure I do what he wants. I don't want to get fired.
Ron: Right. You resolve to do better. You take responsibility for yourself. You don't just "try" to do it; you do it. [We had talked earlier, in another session, about "trying" to do better, and how that is different from actually doing it.] You change your steps in the dance with your boss. What about with Martha or your mom?
George [with a slight grin]: Well, they can't fire me, can they? [I have a skeptical look on my face.] Ah yes, well, I guess getting divorced is sort of like being fired. [I turn back to Martha at this point. I want to leave the parallels with him to think about.]

In this interview, each partner began to show slightly more self-focus. George was volunteering information about himself, and it was important for Martha to hear it. They began to show some vulnerability; they are feeling less anxious, less sense of threat, and we will build on that in future sessions.

George displays what individual-model counselors call a "passive aggressive personality." I do not see the behavior as about his personality or something deeply inherent in him, even though he consistently shows it. What is also consistent is that he has people in his life who want to change him, and he has fitted himself into this position as a way to deal with fusion. Over the years of his growing up, George never learned fully how to be a responsible self, directly, out in the open, with important people on whom he was emotionally dependent, like his mother and later his wife. It is a way to stay dependently attached to them without actually exercising much responsibility for being a self in the relationship. He can endure their anger at him. Anger does not mean a change in the system. The others have not figured out a way to do the dance with him differently either.

As they each better understand how they function, then options for how to be within their circumstances can be considered. A simple example is one partner can begin to think of their partner's hostility and attacks as defensive maneuvers rather than aggressive ones. Then, I wonder with that partner what the other partner is defending against. Rather than, for example, being the victim of their anger, how is the partner being experienced as threatening? Then the partner can think about how better to approach the other person.

Starting with some sort of criticism or upset between them, I begin to unpack the underlying emotionality that feeds their own part in the conflict. I am not interested in trying to get them to communicate their feelings as such, or to negotiate a settlement between them on some conflictual issue. They are smart people; they will be able to do that on their own when the fused emotionality is reduced and each can be a stronger, less threatened self in the relationship.

The kinds of questions I ask in order to track the inner emotional process start with clarifying what they pick up through their senses. This begins their reactive response. The primary senses are what we "hear" the other saying, and what we "see" the other doing. This is not just the words we hear but also the tone of voice and the emphasis. We also see facial expressions and postures or stances that can trigger our reactivity. Our automatic reaction to these sensory perceptions, accurate or not, is usually instantaneous.

These reactions are part of an equally instantaneous interpretation of what the other is saying or meaning. These automatic interpretations support our sense of threat and produce the automatic feelings based on them. All of this is reflective of our position in the system. We then act in response to the perceived threat in order to feel safer. I inquire into these automatic reactions, this inner process, to break them down into their constituent parts and slow them down. The following verbatim shows how I proceeded with George.

The full, automatic inner experience of a person, as one part of an emotional system dance, is: sense—interpret—feel—intend—and then act. Each partner goes through the same inner process and responds to the other's behavior. They only see or hear the other's behavior. They are not privy to the inner process that results in this behavior. The questions I ask can be about any part of this sequential process in order to help a person become more aware, more thoughtful, and to begin to consider an option somewhere within it.

Ron: So what gets you going in a fight with Martha? What will trigger you so that you react?

George: What do you mean? She gets angry at me and I react and come back at her.

Ron: Yes, that makes sense. But not all of us would get angry at the same things. Someone else might just say, "Well, that's just how Martha is." Is there something that happens in her anger that is the trigger for you? Beyond the words, do you hear something, or see something that really ticks you off?

George: Okay, yeah, she gets this look, and, uhhhh, there is this tone of voice. When those two things come from her together, I lose it.

Ron: [Then I ask him to describe his sensations in depth, exactly how does she sound and look to him? This can take a little time, with a number of questions, and I want him to get into the experience of these sensations as much as possible.] Okay, Martha gets this particular look, and there is this particular tone in her voice. You sense these things coming from her, what she says, how she looks, and the tonal quality, and then you go somewhere with that. What do these things mean to you that you get so ticked off?

George: What do they mean?

Ron: Yeah. How do you understand them?

George: Well, they mean that she thinks I am a complete idiot. I hate that. She always treats me like that and I just can't stand it.

Ron: Okay, so when you see those looks or hear that tone of voice, you interpret them to mean that Martha thinks you are an idiot. What do you do with that?

George: That's easy. I get angry. I react, I guess usually with something critical of her. And then we are into it. Yeah, that's usually how it goes.

Ron: [Here I might have gone with his intentions in his reaction, but I stick with the feeling experience.] Okay, that makes sense. But I wonder if you also feel anything else, besides the anger? [Slight pause] If you didn't feel angry, or if we could strip it off, like a veneer, what might we see underneath it?

George: [Pause, thinking] Well, it feels really bad. It's like I'm just this dumb little shit who doesn't know anything and who is kind of worthless at living his life.

Ron: Tell me more about that experience.

George: Oh, I don't know. I don't think much about that but it feels really bad.

Ron: So could we say that this feeling is hurt? [He nods.] Okay, you have this hurt, but what you show Martha is anger. I assume you don't say, "Ouch. That really hurts." [Here I am implanting an option around intention and behavior.] "You cover over this hurt, which you don't really experience consciously, which is very powerful for you. But it goes by so quickly you don't notice. Instead you get angry. And when you get angry, what do you think your anger will do for you? [Now intention] It may sound funny to put it this way, I know you may not experience it quite this way, it is so automatic, but what might be your intent in getting angry at Martha when you see things and hear things that to you mean she thinks you are an idiot, and then you hurt?

George: Well, you know what? I really just want to hit her. I never would and I never have, but I think it would just feel so satisfying, you know like that old Jackie Gleason TV scene where he winds up and says, "You know, Louise, one of these days. Pow! Right in the kisser." That's what I want to do. But instead I just blow up at her.

Ron: Okay, I hear you. And congratulations on not following through on wanting to hit her. I don't think that Ralph Cramden ever followed through on hitting Louise either. You show some good control of your reactivity at this point. Hitting Martha would only make things worse. I imagine she might want to hit you at times, but you both show some good control around this. [Looking at her] Right? [She nods assent.] Okay, George, what you say makes perfect sense to me. We all have these vulnerabilities, these sensitivities, or hurts, these tender places that we protect. It is kind of a threat when people touch on them. As I see it, we get anxious at those times when we think something is a threat and could hurt us. And when we get anxious we automatically react to the perceived threat. We can run away, and we have talked already about distancing, and [looking at Martha] pursuing. Or we can stay and fight against what we perceive as threatening. And one of our favorite ways of doing this is to get angry, to fight back and attack the threatening person. But it is all so automatic and quick we don't even think about it. Does this make sense, George? Does it fit for you?

George: Yeah, it does. That's a pretty good way to describe it.

Ron: [At this point I could go back to the intent of his anger, and talk with him about other ways he could address trying to take care of his hurt, and explore these with him, but I decide to look more at the background of the hurt.] You know, a little while ago, when I asked if you felt hurt, and you said yes, you looked quite subdued. I suspect you were feeling some of that hurt at that moment. Can you tell me more about that feeling? [Asking about feelings is always a tricky thing. My training was to get people to go deeply into these feelings but eventually I decided that was not ultimately helpful. However, there does need to be some connection with the feeling in order to do what I want to do here. I want, at the same time, to keep the thinking, observing self for George present, and not have him overwhelmed by the feeling. So I am asking him to describe it without being deeply into it. He is, at this point doing good self-focused work and Martha is paying attention.]

George: Well, I don't know. I'm not aware of feeling it all that much but it's true that it's there. It just feels awful, like I'm kind of worthless. I don't know what else to say.

Ron: Okay. Is there anyone else besides Martha that you can have this feeling with?

George: No, I don't think so. I don't feel that way with my son or the guys at work when they get angry at me. I can just sort of slough it off. [It is clear to me that he is ignoring his mother, but I don't want to be the one to say it. I move toward family in a tangential way.]

Ron: How about with your sister?

George: No, I don't think so. [Pause] But yeah, well, this is sort of interesting. I think I got compared to her a lot and I did feel like I didn't measure up. I remember feeling that way with Dad before he died. She was always smarter than me; I never felt like I could catch up to her. In that sense I could have this feeling with her, but she didn't give it to me.

Ron: Okay, so a lot of younger siblings can feel this way. She was what [looking at his family diagram on my lap], four years older than you? That makes sense. But somehow, in other ways in your family, you could get this feeling?

George: Well, yeah. I remember it some with Dad, but then he died so early in my life. Sis was closer to him. She knew him better than I did, and it seemed he liked her better. [Pause] But I guess I could also get it with Mom. [Another pause] Yeah, as a matter of fact, I still get it with her. Yeah, that's right. I always feel like I haven't grown up when I am around Mom. I mean . . . , yeah, this is funny. I spend a lot of time with her, as you know, and there are ways she relies on me like I'm the man in her life, but I don't really feel that way. Yeah, I feel like I'm "the little man." That's what she used to call me after Dad died! I was "the little man of the house." And you know, I still feel this way with her. It's like Mom made me her project. She actually said she was going to teach me how to be a man, since I didn't have Dad to do that. But I never felt like I became one. I mean, a grown man. You know I feel younger than most of the guys in my office, even though I am older than most of them. But especially I feel it with her. Yeah, that's it. That's that worthless feeling. Wow. Yeah. [He looks at Martha, and then looks down, and I just let them sit there, silent, while all this sinks in.]

Ron: Okay, George, that all sounds pretty important to me. We can spend some more time thinking about all of this. I don't really see it as your mom's fault, whatever her intention has been. But the question you raise is, how you are going to feel like a grown-up man with your mother and others? How do you get out of this "dumb little shit" position? There are things we can do if you are up for it. So we will return to this later, but right now, Martha, I'm wondering what you are thinking about. [Here I will be careful not to let her focus on him but want to take it in a similar direction for her.]

This verbatim is an example of how I develop more self-focus. It is not firmly in place yet, by any means. Both George and Martha still experience others as doing to them, and themselves as having less control over their subjective experience, but we are moving in a more self-focused direction. At this point I am not clarifying that the feelings go with a position in the system, but this will come. We have moved his subjective experience into another interactional realm, with his mother. This takes some of the heat off of his and Martha's interactions. This was a familiar experience for him before he met Martha. The vulnerability that George showed here was critical for moving ahead in the counseling and it was a good sign that Martha had a positive response to it, rather than a critical one. She was getting how powerful this was for him.

George is a great example of someone who has been, both as a child and as an adult, the focus of the family projection process. I am sure it was never his mother's intent to infantilize him. She does not have an evil intent and does not need to be blamed. This is just the result of the way she dealt with her anxiety in family. He has grown up with this process still in place and has experienced limitations in his own life as a result.

The projection process was never so focused that he became a juvenile delinquent or something of that sort, but there is a kind of irresponsible and a not quite up-and-up quality to George. This was a part of his occasional one-night stands. They sounded to me like something a rebellious kid would do when I heard him describe them. In his workplace, as a high-level sales representative, there was a quality of being able to put something over on clients and to "make a killing" in terms of commissions. It did not sound quite ethical. It was as if he enjoyed getting away with things, like a kid breaking the rules. As it turned out, I knew something about his boss and that his boss actually prized this sort of behavior, which made it more difficult for George to look at. But that sort of focus in counseling came very much later in the process, during the middle phase, as we focused more on principles he wanted to live by.

13

The Transition to Middle-Phase Counseling

Markers of the Middle Phase

Couples are moving toward middle-phase counseling when the following markers are beginning to be evident. Each of these markers develops as a piece of a larger whole that we could call the precursors of differentiation of self. In the transition period, these markers are just beginning to show.

1. *The partners begin to make a clearer separation of thinking and feeling.* Rather than just reacting out of their feelings, they are able to step back and develop some objectivity about what is going on in their lives. They are beginning to have feelings, rather than their feelings having them.

2. *They are starting to develop a focus on self rather than on others.* Each person is beginning to make a project out of self, rather than the other. They are recognizing their own issues and beginning to take responsibility for them.

3. *They have an increasing ability to see self's own part in the relationship process and to interrupt their own reactivity.* With their increased objectivity and thoughtfulness, they can each see more clearly what they bring to the relationship difficulties. They can begin to reevaluate their own way of relating, and see what they each need to work on.

4. *They enlarge their sense of "what the problem is."* Their understanding of their own personal history is beginning to shift, as are their beliefs about what motivates others. Their more fused, reactive sense of how their problems came about is beginning to become more diffuse and less certain.

5. *Their presenting symptoms are reduced, so that there is (in the case of marital conflict) less actual fighting or conflict.* While their presenting symptoms still happen, they are experiencing more control over them; their fights are usually less intense and shorter in duration.

6. *A new sense of their family of origin is emerging.* Their understanding of who their family is—something that they thought they had figured out—is beginning to change. There is doubt about their old beliefs about family members and what motivates them.

7. *They are beginning to reconsider some of their beliefs and values, and are developing new principles upon which to base their lives and actions.* As they go into the transition period, so many things could feel like they are up in the air; the couple could begin to feel confused. Beliefs and values might be challenged not by anything specific that we, as counselors, say or do, but because a new sense of how things work is beginning to emerge. For example, parents who think the difficult behavior of their adolescent son was because he was "bad" could begin to change as the parents see their own part in the difficulties. This could lead to a period of confusion and uncertainty around "how to parent."

Looking at Martha's Hurt

I turn now to my tenth joint counseling session with George and Martha. They could still regress back into their old ways of fighting. So much of the work was caught up in their ongoing fights that we had to keep going back over old territory. I have just had an individual session with each of them separately where we began to touch on the issues that emerge with Martha here. We are beginning a long transition into middle-phase work and some of the above markers begin to show.

I have been defining the interactive process between the two of them, and what each brings (their inner process) to those encounters. The work may seem slow, plodding, and repetitive, but it is essential to do. They both appear to be feeling safer in the sessions. There is a lighter and less intense atmosphere.

Martha reports being less angry and that George is less evasive. I see them both as more open and forthcoming. He, more and more, seems to be seeing counseling as something that is for him rather than to make him into something that Martha wants him to be. We have just increased the time between sessions from being weekly to every two weeks and they seem to have managed that okay. I always try to do this as people start showing some improvement so they do not attribute it only to counseling. If people are very dependent on the counselor they may react to this move of spacing out appointments by regressing.

In this session, I begin to explore Martha's feelings of sadness and hurt, and how that connects with her relationship with George. This is much more important than focusing on her anger. It is where she is stuck around better defining her self. This is at the start of the session. It is quite delicate work and, for the sake of brevity, I have contracted much of the session. I want to be very respectful of her inner experience and not oversimplify it, but I am encouraging her to take more responsibility for it, rather than seeing it as something other people make her feel, as if she is a victim of others.

Ron: So what have the two of you been thinking about this week?
Martha: Well, we had another fight. Same old story.
Ron: And you blew up again?
Martha: Boy, did I.
Ron: So you were feeling more hopeful again?
Martha: Right! [She has a slight smile, but sounds cynical.]
Ron: She says cynically. [I smile.]
Martha: Right.
Ron: I would like to learn more about your anger. Do you mind if I ask a few more questions?
Martha: That seems to be what you do. Go ahead.
Ron: Okay, yes, I do ask a lot of questions. I guess I'm just curious about how things work for each of you. If you wanted to get yourself

angry with George right now, what would you have to do? [The question poses it as a decision on her part and something she does.]

Martha: I'm angry at him right now. I don't have to do anything. It just happens.

Ron: Okay, I hear that it just seems automatic.

Martha: Right.

Ron: So bear with me here. If somehow we could focus on your experience just before the anger, then . . . Maybe that's not the way to say it, but if you didn't get to the angry stage, what would you be experiencing? Does that make sense?

Martha: Yes, it does. [Pause] We talked about this some in my session with you. I haven't really told George about this. I know what it is. It's hurt. I just feel so bad.

This part of the interview is *much* contracted. I go slowly. I want her to make some contact with the experience, but not go too deeply into it. I want her to keep an observing eye open to watch the experience. If she starts to tear up then I have gone too far with it. I want her to talk about it without being deeply in it.

I am also monitoring to what extent it is a problem for her that George might hear this, since she has not told him about her previous session with me alone. I do not want her to feel too vulnerable in front of him, and I do not want him to be able to use this material later in an argument. This is very important. I do not want to be an agent of her being slammed with her vulnerability. If he has not also gotten to a place of vulnerability yet, he may do this. So, very often, when one partner in a heavily conflicted couple gets there more quickly, I will set up individual sessions with the other just to explore this inner material—maybe two consecutive individual sessions at the most.

This inner sense of vulnerability is the source of much of our anxiety. When it is touched upon we protect it. We will tend to focus outwardly and, either in our imagination or perhaps in reality (as in physical abuse), see others as a threat. We see them, in our fusion, as the source of our lack of feeling safe. Anger is useful for helping to protect us.

Unfortunately, getting angry usually does not make things better for us, although it may serve to keep us from feeling more hurt. The differentiating process puts us more in charge of our emotional life and, eventually, we do not need the angry reaction. The more differentiated we are the more we can feel both comfortable with our vulnerability and safe. This is because we can feel confident in ourselves and not rely on others to "make us" feel safe. The more this happens the less difficult it is to get close to others. We do not have to be guarded.

Vulnerability is a normal part of life. Normally, vulnerability invites vulnerability in relationships. Better-differentiated people will more quickly talk about it in counseling. When our life feels more tenuous, however, we are not so open to experiencing it, and we are less flexible in how we adjust to our life situation and close relationships. Energy goes into keeping the guard up. We do not need to label people as "defensive;" we can just recognize with them the importance of feeling safe.

I have never found a way to get less well-differentiated people to make a solid change in their functional position in a relationship system until they have recognized this inner emotional process around how they deal with anxiety. It is easy to stay stuck in this place. In a great deal of counseling, people would rather talk to the counselor about their pain, rather than look at what they do with it, and how to change self.

Ron: Okay. So to some extent your anger comes after your pain. Is that right?
Martha: Yes.
Ron: I wonder if anger is like a protective shield for you. Does it help to keep you from experiencing the hurt?
Martha: Absolutely. And I feel much stronger when I am angry. I just fall apart when I feel the hurt.
Ron: That makes perfect sense to me, Martha. I think many of us do that. Would you tell me more about the hurt?
Martha: I'm not sure I want to.
Ron: That's fine. We don't have to go there. [Now I am concerned that she is feeling my pursuit of her inner experience in front of George too strongly. I back off, but then she hangs in with it.]
Martha: But I think it is important.
Ron: Fine. You tell me when you want to stop talking about it.

We go into the experience of the hurt in her present life with George. She says it has been there from the start of the marriage and it has just built over the years. It took major jumps when (ten years ago) she found out about his two one-night stands with women at conventions. I ask her to talk about some of the times she especially remembers the hurt. They are still quite vivid for her even though they are years old. I ask her to describe the subjective experience of the hurt. This is part of the process of thinking about feelings. We kind of walk around it and look at it together, almost like a sculptured work of art.

We counselors have to assess to what extent a person is too fragile to go into this material. If their defenses stay up around it I respect that. I absolutely do not push. They know better than me how far to go and I do not need them to go into it so I can feel like a better counselor. It is possible that less well-differentiated counselees could decompensate around material of this sort. She was not a physically or sexually abused child so the chances of decompensation were lessened—her personal boundaries were stronger. I believed that Martha had enough self to manage it but it was up to her how far we went with it. If counselees are too dependent on us, they may let us lead them into this material and then, when the session is over, they will feel lost and scared.

Martha's feelings of deep hurt long preexisted her relationship with George. She just continued the theme with him. He provided the occasion for her having it and she reacted in a way that was typical for her. It was as if she was a young girl who could not escape a damaging family experience. She had no other resources for figuring out what to do.

Working with Martha's Bitterness

High levels of bitterness often exist in heavily conflicted couples and working with it is a slow process. Increasing self-focus around issues of bitterness is especially challenging, but it is critical to do. No significant progress will be made on the marital issue of emotional distance until it is addressed and reduced.

Bitterness can often exist in both partners, but in different forms. Martha was openly bitter and George did not appear to be. As Martha worked on hers and eventually reduced it significantly so that she was ready to move more warmly toward George, only then did his hurt and bitterness clearly emerge. He was not ready to receive her and to be more open toward her emotionally. He did not want to welcome her move back toward him with open arms. The kind of process I describe below, in the work with Martha, had to be repeated to some extent with George. They were both surprised at his level of pain.

Behaviorally, bitterness shows as a hostile distance. People feel totally justified in maintaining their distant stance. Often they will dwell on the bitterness, maybe even nurture it. Bitter people feel like victims of the offenders. They say, in essence, "You hurt me one too many times, and I am not going to forgive you anymore. I am going to punish you and protect myself with my distance."

Ron: So, Martha, we have looked at how your anger at George came out of hurt, and how your hurt resulted from frustration and disappointment over how your hopes and expectations in the marriage to George were not met. Right? [She nods.] Now I am wondering what else you did with your hurt besides get angry.
Martha: I don't know what you mean.
Ron: Okay. We have talked about a lot of the hurts you had with George. Over the years these hurts accumulated and built up. [She nods.] What happened to you as this went on? Maybe a better way to ask this is, what did you do with the build-up of all of this hurt?
Martha: What did I do with it? Hmmm. I don't know. Ummm. [Thinking] I guess I went pretty sour on the marriage.
Ron: In what sense "sour"?
Martha: Well, I got cold. A part of me just shut down, or turned off, or something.
Ron: Say more about that.
Martha: Well, early on when the upsets happened and, as usual, George would apologize at some point, then I was ready to forgive him. But then, after a while I didn't want to forgive him anymore. I just stopped responding to his attempts to make it better.
Ron: Okay, so would it be fair to say that you became more and more bitter?
Martha: Absolutely. That is exactly what I did.
Ron: This is certainly a common enough experience when our hurts accumulate and we can't figure out what else to do with them. Other than with George, is there anyone else in your life with whom you have been bitter?
Martha: Well, sure, my mother.

Ron: You went through the same sort of experience with her? You could never figure out a way to get around her anger and put-downs of you and eventually, slowly, you went sour on that relationship, too? Your bitterness grew there also?

Martha: Yes, that's it.

Ron: Here's a different thought. I wonder, how do you think this sort of hurt and bitter process might have worked for her? Was she similar in this regard? With regard to the bitterness, I mean.

Martha: Oh, yes. She was a very bitter woman. Not only with me, but with Dad also, and my sister to some extent. Hmmm. Sort of like I am with George. Yuck!

Ron: In some ways you might have learned something about that from her?

Martha: Well, maybe. Yes, I guess you could say that, even though I don't like the idea of me learning to be like her.

Ron: Yeah, I get that. But back to this bitterness—what does it do for you? How does it help you? Or what did it do for your mother? [What we have done here is to show how she has something quite powerful in common with her mother. This has an impact on her even though we do not directly talk much about it here.]

Martha: What did it do for us? I know you will not let me get away with saying, "It just happened." So, let's assume I was doing it to me, for a purpose. Is that kind of what you had in mind? [I nod.] Well, I don't hurt so much. I guess it helps with that.

Ron: Okay, so being bitter is kind of a protective thing? It helps you feel safer and not hurt so much? [She nods.] That makes sense to me. Now let me ask, is there a cost or a downside to being bitter?

Martha: Hmmm. A cost? That's hard to see.

Ron: How about for your mother? Could you see a cost to this self-protective thing she did?

Martha: Well, she was pretty lonely, I think. Oh boy, yeah. That's a cost. [She talks more about this.]

Ron: Well, Martha, let me give you some of my thoughts because what you're saying sort of fits with what I think. While it is fully understandable how it happens, I think of bitterness as almost a self-destructive act. [I go slowly here.] Quite understandably, we get there when we think there are just no options for dealing with our hurt. But it ends up cutting us off from others. Like you say, you didn't want to just keep forgiving George, but you couldn't figure out what else to do, so you withdrew into this hurt and bitterness. Am I off the track here?

Martha: No, no. What you say makes sense and describes what I did. But what do I do with it?

Ron: Yes, that's the question. Let's say, the bitterness protects us and helps us feel safer, but at the cost of being cut off from others, maybe even others we want to care for. After a while it begins to color everything. To live without the bitterness can, for one thing, feel too vulnerable. It's like this big unhappy place you have talked about sometimes, where you just feel hopeless and helpless; so it feels better to us to seethe with anger and be bitter. Often we can feel more justified in this place, and stronger. So, is there some better way we can look after ourselves, but with less cost?

Martha: That's what I asked you. [I smile.] But you're not going to give me the answer, are you?

Ron: Well, actually I have the answer right here in my desk drawer, but you're going to have to guess it. [We laugh, bringing some lightness back to this heavy topic.] Yes, you're right. But I don't know what the answer would be for you. It is a quandary. But it is a very important question. The issue is how to take care of yourself with as little cost to you as possible. The thing is that bitterness is something that we focus outward on others; it is sort of something we think we are doing to punish others, and we don't think about what we are doing to ourselves at the same time.

Martha: That's right. I agree. [We discuss it some more, then I turn to ask George about his own experience with bitterness. He claims, at this point, not to have much experience with it, but he has seen it in his mother. Soon afterwards, we end the session.]

The Next Session and Martha's Emptiness

This comes from our session two weeks later. As with the last session, we have reached a point where we can be much more interactive and I can say more about how I think about these things, with my words being taken simply at face value with no greater or lesser importance than they were just my thoughts for discussion.

Ron: So, what have you two been working on? [As we move from first phase towards middle phase, my opening question is usually this one, rather than "What have you been thinking about?"]

Martha: [Martha is eager.] Well, I've been watching this bitter thing we talked about last time. And you know how we talked about the cost of doing it; well, there is also a cost in not doing it. We haven't had any real connection over the last two weeks. At least when I got angry with him, something happened between us. Now there is nothing. We have barely talked and I feel like I am just letting him off the hook. He goes on his merry way, doing what he's always doing, and I don't even have the fun of giving him a few good punches. If I let go of the expectations of him, and I let go of the anger and bitterness, what do I get from him? Nothing.

Ron: Okay, so you were thinking that if you did these things then he would be different? Is that right?

Martha: Well, yeah. [She is being more thoughtful here instead of more reactive.]

Ron: I suppose my thought was that in making these changes in yourself, your own life might go a different direction. I didn't think of it as doing something for or to George, but as something for yourself, so life could be different for you, and you could focus on something other than how George was being. You could focus on how you wanted to be, not just in relation to him but for your own life. If you don't have George and your upset with him to focus on, what might you focus on?

Martha: Well, then, why be married?

Ron: Well, that is another heavy question that I can't answer for you.

Martha: Yeah, you're a real font of wisdom. I'm glad I didn't climb up the mountain to get the answers for life from you.

Ron: Maybe you have in a way. Anyway, you have worked really hard. It is sort of like climbing a mountain. But, just like all of the other gurus, I'm a charlatan.

Martha: I believe you.

Ron: Martha, I really don't mean to be enigmatic here. I think you have hit a very important place. You remember how I commended the two of you that you have not focused your anxiety and difficulties on your son, the way a lot of parents do, but you have focused your emotional difficulties on each other. In your case, Martha, if you

let go of focusing on George, you discover something like—I'm going to take a guess here—it feels like a big emptiness. [She looks at me somewhat startled, and then sad, and almost teary.]
Martha: I think that's the right word. And it feels awful.
Ron: I get that. It makes sense. It is a loss when you let go of that focus on George. [Pause] But it is also an opportunity to give your life a new direction, something more rewarding and fulfilling maybe than trying to whip George into shape. You can always go back to that and I suspect you will from time to time, just to revisit that old place if nothing else, but I don't think it will be the same for you. [We chat a bit more about this quite profound place she has arrived at, and then I move over to George, but I make sure to ask him a question that will direct him away from talking about Martha. I do not want him to comment on her experience.]

All along, Martha has had this fantasy solution for her life that maybe George could love her the way she wanted and help her feel fulfilled rather than empty. As she faces letting go of this solution she has to learn to be more responsible for her happiness and satisfaction in life. Stepping out of the more fused place to a more differentiated place is not easy existentially. The interesting thing is that, in later sessions, George also begins to feel the loss of not having Martha be angry or nag at him. He is feeling more adrift. How is he going to run his life if he cannot count on her to act in ways that focus his reactive energies and then defeat her efforts to change him?

A Turning Point with Martha and "Old Family History"

A turning point in the work with Martha occurred about three sessions later, after some work with George that opened up vulnerable material for him in relation to his mother. We looked at his hurt and bitterness in relation to her. Doing this keeps things balanced out and it helps keep them more respectful of each other as we do this.

Now the more fused emotional issues and the marital issues are more clearly connected with the multigenerational issues. Family-of-origin material has emerged normally, on its own, from time to time in the counseling. Counselees will often mention it spontaneously in talking about their experience. We just have to listen for it.

This work is not about going back over "old family history." Actually, it is not history. The past is still present—*the problem is that it has not become the past*. This is the essence of unresolved emotional attachment. It is nearly always the case with our difficult family material that it keeps directing our present behavior. When we can (in fact—not in fantasy during counseling) go back to those family settings and work at being different with the original people involved, then change will happen. The past will become truly history. Emotional cutoff, as here with Martha, tends to solidify that old emotionality and keeps it present, very real, and a much bigger deal than it would be otherwise.

Ron: Okay, so we have been talking about what that hurt and the self-protective bitterness is like for you, over the years, in the relationship with George and with your mother. You saw your mother do it also. And gradually, over time, like her, you have built a kind of protective wall around yourself with George so that you don't hurt so much. Anger helps you reinforce that wall and it has been useful.

Martha: Oh yes, absolutely. I think this is part of what has made George so important to me. I really wanted it to be different with him. I wanted a normal family life with him. I was counting on him to provide what I didn't get in my family.

Ron: That makes total sense to me, but tell me more about your hurt and bitterness in your family.

Martha begins to recount her family experience in greater depth. The basic nodal event was her father's death when she was nine. She had been developing a closer relationship with him and we identified the parental triangle of her and father against mother, with whom he had regular fights. Even after he died, as she got older, especially as she approached adolescence, she had taken her father's side in her imagination. Her mother saw this and started taking this out on her as well. It was like she and her mother fought the battles that her mother and father used to have.

When he died, Martha felt alone. Her younger sister appeared to be their mother's favorite. She was not close to her sister, although it was not an openly hostile relationship. Martha's mother also had an older sister with whom she did not get along. After her father's death, Martha's mother went back to work and she expected a great deal of help from Martha. In some ways, Martha was more competent than her mother was, but Martha reported that nothing was ever good enough for her mother, her mother criticized "everything" she did, and she felt like a failure in her mother's eyes. There was constant hostility between them, even as Martha continued to fulfill her household duties.

She did not see her mother as someone she could rely on for help with any of the ordinary life issues growing children face. Her teen years were even more horrendous between them. She resolved that as soon as she had graduated from high school she was going to get a job and move out, which she did. When she revealed these plans to her mother, her mother blew up and really laid into her. Her mother's ongoing anger was so intense that Martha resolved to have nothing more to do with her. She had no sense of how dependent her mother was on her. When she and George got married, she invited her mother to the wedding but did not consult with her about it. Martha's mother sat in the traditional place in the church, but Martha asked an older friend of hers to give her away.

After the wedding, Martha had nothing more to do with her mother. Neither one called the other. There was absolutely no contact and this lasted for over twenty years, up to the time that I began seeing George and Martha. It was a true cutoff. Martha and her mother lived in communities that were only thirty miles apart. They heard about each other only through Martha's sister.

I spent most of this session talking with Martha while George listened. At the end I asked him what thoughts he had. He was quite respectful, saying he knew some of the things she talked about but some of it was new. He said he could identify with parts of what she said even though his relationship with his mother was quite different. He said he had a new sense of how painful it was for her.

I will not recount the verbatims of this work. It was slow and not easy. Martha was hesitant to take responsibility for her own emotional experience with her mother, and this is normal. She was not responsible for what her mother did to her, but she was responsible for what she did with that, and that response was a part of her family-system functioning.

There is a critical factor about the change process at work here. We want to hang on to our subjective stories about the past, and the people of the past, as we tell them. A strong commitment to our story keeps us stuck in the same objective place in our emotional systems. We are hesitant to broaden the stories, to look at other factors, to see how we might understand them in different ways, and to change our place in the system. For example, the idea that her mother was emotionally as well as physically dependent on her was quite new to Martha.

If we were to change our way of seeing the past, and especially the way we see others who are a part of that past, it would mean we would have to change ourselves. Anticipating the possibility of change in self provokes anxiety. That is part of why deciding to do family-of-origin work comes slowly. We do not want to let go of our view of others, as awful and painful as it may be, because we do not know the implications of doing that. Something might be asked of us that looks even scarier. Repositioning self within an emotional system requires courage. It is like entering into unknown territory. It requires us to behave differently and we do not know how that will go.

Some Specific Aspects of the Transition Phase

Some people may want to stop counseling during this time because of the anxiety they feel around these changes. It may be possible for them to look at this desire and discuss it. Feeling like they have lost sight of their original, other-focused goals about what they wanted to have happen in counseling, they may decide this work is not helping. The counselor cannot argue this issue with them but simply accept it and say, "I am available if you ever decide to come back."

Some couples may claim that they have made enough progress and that they do not need to do any further work. They may find that they are happier and fighting less and this feels good enough to them. They take the calmness they have been experiencing as a sign that things are good enough and they do not see the need for any further work. Again, we ought not to take the position of arguing couples into continuing the work even if we think it is only symptomatic improvement.

Couples who terminate at this point often relapse, especially if their level of stress increases, and the issue for us is to have the kind of relationship with them so that they will feel comfortable coming back. We can commend them for their gains, say they have done some good work, and point out that, in general, some couples experience the reemergence of difficulties as stress levels go back up—and that is normal—and it is perfectly fine to come back and talk about this.

Another way things sometimes go in the transition phase is that one partner wants to continue in counseling and one wants to stop. I would agree to this with the proviso that I could, on occasion, invite the other partner to come back in, or that the partner was free to reengage at his or her initiative. The usual sort of progress in counseling, whether only one or both partners continue, is that one tends to make more progress than the other. When one partner has begun to differentiate a self, the other may well react and then, after the reaction is over, be ready to do more work on self.

One classic example of this is the woman who has been a traditional, overfunctioning homemaker who decides she wants a career. She goes back to school or becomes focused on a job and is not as available to other family members as she once was. Much will depend on the woman being able to maintain a direction for self while also, nonreactively, remaining emotionally connected to the reactive family members. I mentioned in an earlier chapter a wife who set a new direction for herself and her very dependent husband becoming suicidal. She did an excellent job of staying on course while continuing to relate warmly to him, but without taking responsibility for his mood. He eventually got through it and they both became more satisfied with their lives.

Most couples will see enough of a new way of being at this point in counseling that, in spite of the anxiety around the unknown, they will press ahead. From time to time we can point to the emerging markers in their functioning as signs of encouragement and comment on them, giving them the credit.

All kinds of powerful emotional experiences can be stirred up during the transition period. These can easily become a distraction in the counseling if they become the focus. On a couple of occasions I have taught some simple relaxation strategies to some especially tense people. They were amazed to discover that as they relaxed they became very sad and began to sob. Their tension, as unhealthy as it had been for them in several ways, had kept them from experiencing their deep sadness in life. This opened up to a new family focus as we broadened the sadness and tension into that setting.

These feelings are what many counselors think (as I once did) is the "meat" of counseling, the real "pay dirt." I believe, as real as the feelings are, that they are simply signs of anxiety around one's position in an emotional system. We do not need to go deeply into them in order to "resolve" them. They go with the territory. I respectfully recognize them and we talk about them, but they are not my focus. The feelings will pass with the change in position of the counselees. If people can begin to experiment with that position within their emotional systems, they will make headway. A focus on the feelings alone will not do it.

Courage does not exist without fear. We have to be able to tolerate the anxiety related to growth if we want to change. We have to be willing to experiment, to be more daring in our thinking about options, and be more playful in their execution. This takes a growing sense of inner safety. This is the main thing I want to accomplish in the first phase. As pastors, we can think of many biblical verses about fear to draw upon, but I would never make doing the work a moral requirement, or a religious cause, or an obligation to myself. We counselors are trusting in God's grace when we say that when and how people grow is up to them; they are the ones taking the risky action.

A Spiritual Crisis

One very powerful experience some people have as they transition toward the middle phase is the sense that their deepest hopes and wishes for fulfillment, their expectations of what marriage or their partner or life in general would provide, are not going to be met. This can be disconcerting. In one case I asked the husband, "What would it mean to you to let go of the certainty that your wife is the problem in this marriage and that your job is to change her?" He took the question seriously and needed a week to think about it. He came back the next week saying that then he just would not know what to do or how to be. He had a clear mission in life when his focus was on her and her problems. He said letting go of this mission felt like giving up on what was important in his own life. I asked how he could have a satisfying

13 — The Transition to Middle-Phase Counseling

life whether he had a wife in it or not, or whether she had problems or not. He said, "I see the point. That is a good question." We began discussions about his having a personal goal focus.

As the stormy or upsetting parts of a couple's life begin to calm down and they are thinking a bit more clearly, they may begin to see that their long-held hopes are not realistic, or at least not possible. Martha discovered this. Both pursuers and distancers keep their focus so much on the other; the other is the reason their emotional goals for satisfaction in life are not being met. As they bring their focus back to themselves and the lack of fulfillment of these emotional wants, they might become depressed.

The counselor must watch for this and be ready to talk about it. Our own level of anxiety with this experience has to be low. We have to be willing to sit with it and not try to do away with it, argue people out of it, or give them Bible verses to challenge them from experiencing it. To sit with them means we have to be comfortable with our own sense of unfulfilled emotional hopes and wishes. Some counselors have called it the experience of emptiness, as seen with Martha above. Some see it as the basic, primary sense of dread or anxiety that many of us seek to avoid by filling it with relationships or material things, with big projects or goals, or with having and raising children, or being religious, or any number of preoccupations that fill up our time and distract us. These are the things that we think can make us happy.

This is a spiritual crisis of the most basic form. There is an enervating quality to it; we lose spirit for pursuing the thing we always thought would somehow save us and make us feel better. We have been worshiping the idols and false gods that cannot provide true security for our anxiety. There may be a sense of being all alone. A few, along with the psalmist, have referred to the experience as like "the valley of the shadow of death." As counselors, we ought not to try to offer some other distraction, some other focus that keeps people from encountering this lack of fulfillment. We can only be with the people in their valley.

Being there, in this place, is a time of reevaluation, of thinking things through in a more profound way. I think that it is a way of beginning to build a more solid self that is not built on "false promises" or empty goals in life that cannot satisfy, and this includes having the "perfect mate" or the "perfect marriage." It is the beginning step in accepting what is, the way things really are—especially ourselves, our families, and our partners in life.

I say none of this to counselees. I do not want to define the experience for them, or help them avoid it with a lot of theory, or with philosophical or religious talk. Having and getting to know the experience is enough. Being able to be in it, to face it, is a way we challenge the reality of our chronic anxiety and discover it is not so terrifying. Nobody dies from it.

This can be a time of solid learning as we clarify the way we have run our lives, as we face the confusion and uncertainty of "What now?" It is important not to run too quickly toward the project of what to do now. This is a part of knowing what kicks up our anxiety and gets us to pursue unfulfilling goals—like changing the people around us—or even (like Walter Mitty) just fantasizing that they or our life might be different, or that we might have some other partner rather than the one we have.

To some extent, this experience may come with vulnerability or with being open about our inadequacy. In my own thinking—just for myself, unspoken to counselees—I think of it as like "the weakness of God." It is that place of forsakenness we symbolize in the cross. With Paul, theologically we could call it a kind of "dying to self"—at least the old pseudo-self and its hopes for avoiding anxiety and gaining fulfillment. In our own theology, this profound experience can go so many directions. My only encouragement is that, in our own anxiety, we not rush counselees toward our answers and beliefs. They have to build their own—they have to create a solid and better-differentiated self, based on their own life principles, beliefs, and goals.

The question is, "What can you base your life on? What will truly enliven your spirit? What are your goals in life?" and from there, "What principles do you want to live your life by in order to achieve these goals? Does you faith suggest anything to you about all of this?" Each person needs to think this through for self. There is no set way to work this through with counselees; each one develops their own path and thinks their own thoughts, and we just walk along beside them, listen, and maybe ask the occasional question. We really do not have answers for them.

The Move Toward Family and Unresolved Emotional Attachment

At this point in the work, the focus is shifting to unresolved emotional attachment. This yearning, this deep desire for someone to fulfill us, to do for us, stems out of our experience in family. The very best place to take this experience is back to family. This is one of the points of family-of-origin work—to take this experience of unresolved emotional attachment back into family and research it there, in that context. It is most likely a multigenerational theme.

Developing a more objective sense of reality, refocusing our expectations, and reducing fusion is the antidote to unresolved emotional attachment. Getting to know our family for real—how it really functions, what our part is in it, and how we want to change our part—is the way to building a more solid and principled life. Again, it is often the less well-differentiated people who are most phobic about taking these issues back into family. They will take longer before they are emotionally ready to do it.

Through much of first-phase counseling work and this transition phase we have been laying the groundwork for doing family work by asking questions—without being pushy—that quite naturally evoke the family context as the source of difficult emotional issues in people's lives. These questions and the discussion that results from them *are not the same as doing family-of-origin work*. They are just making it clear where the issues started. Talking about family is not the same as being in family and working at being a different self in family. There is no substitute for this.

One young woman lost her mother at an early age and grew up with just her father. She considered him "very controlling" and once she hit adolescence they had many terrible fights. When she was just seventeen they both came in to see me and I worked with each one together and separately. The breakthrough came with the daughter. She had held a deep belief that her mother had died to escape her father, and she had felt this deep resentment of him along with wanting him to comfort her and provide a sense of safety.

She made a major step forward when she, at her own initiative, decided to try to get to know her father as a person, not just as father.

This is exceptional maturity for an adolescent. She showed more emotional flexibility than he did. She began to ask him questions about his family, from whom he had cut off. She went to meet members of his family. She learned more about the context of his growing up, the losses he had suffered in that family, and then, dramatically, she realized that, with her mother's death, he had lost a wife to whom he was deeply attached. She had never thought about his loss; she had only focused on her own. When she said something to this effect to him, he began to sob heavily. She had never seen his vulnerability.

Throughout this process her own emptiness was becoming less powerful for her. This moment of tenderness between them did not end their arguments with one another, but those arguments had much less power. They became more about the standard issues that parents and children fight about during adolescence and they did not have any meaning beyond that. They also began to have more warm times together and she continued to get to know him and his family. He did not continue in counseling, but he mellowed as time went on and as his daughter developed a more solid self. Her work affected him positively. He also began to reconnect with his family as his daughter led the way. Normally, dependent teens and young adults have difficulty doing this work, especially if they are still financially dependent on their family.

When people do not know their parents as real people they tend to have unrealistic expectations of them and who they should be, especially who the parents should be *for them*. They focus on what they think they are not getting from their parents, and fail to notice or adequately appreciate what they have gotten.

Also, they fail to notice their own impact on their parents over the years, and how important their opinions are to their parents. Once, as a young man, I said something to my mother (not in anger, but that revealed a misunderstanding of who she was) that had a powerful impact on her and she began to cry. This had never happened before. I had no intention of hurting her, but I was amazed at the fact that she cried over something I said. I knew I could feel badly around something she said to me; I did not realize it worked the other way. The way we function in family, through the whole process of growing up and into adulthood, deeply affects our parents. If you are a parent you know this. It is not just a matter of our parents affecting us. This is one of the things that begins to dawn on people as they do family-of-origin work and get to know about their parents' own emotional context in their growing up.

As couples work through the transition and move into middle-phase work, they will begin to see their issues with one another in a larger context. They will see that they have been trying to solve something with their partner that really belongs elsewhere and eventually, if they continue with the counseling, they will begin to address it in its original context, a context that continues on into the present. This realization dramatically changes the couple's experience with each other.

14

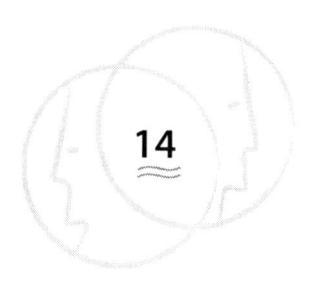

The Counseling Process: Middle Phase

Middle-phase counseling is primarily about doing family-of-origin work. In this chapter I talk about the process leading up to the start of counselees doing the work, and in the next chapter I will talk about some of the practicalities of coaching family-of-origin work.

Unresolved Emotional Attachment

If there were no family process to interrupt it, normal development between parents and children would involve a process of parents taking less and less responsibility for both the physical and emotional lives of their children as they grow older and, as a result, the children taking increasingly more responsibility for themselves. Parents who have trouble letting go and supporting their children's growing independence, or who are overinvolved in their children's lives, taking responsibility for them when it is not appropriate (like rescuing or protecting them from the consequences of their actions), will hinder their children's normal development.

In addition to this, all of us, as we grow, become a part of our family's emotional drama. We interact with family members and, in conjunction with them, we develop a script and play out our roles. This drama becomes a part of who we are. We build a self that depends on how others in our family function in the emotional system. We are actively involved in this, not just passive recipients of scripting by others. This is how our sense of self develops and, depending on the family, it may be more or less fused, and we are tied in with the self of others.

The part of self that is bound up in the give-and-take of family fusion hinders the development of a more solid, better-differentiated self. That part of self keeps us attached to the family emotional process, whether we move halfway around the world and have nothing to do with them for forty years, or live next door and have daily contact. The self of both George and Martha, for example, was deeply involved in their families of origin.

All of us grow up, leave our family homes, and arrive at adulthood with a certain amount of this unresolved emotional attachment to our families. This is equivalent to our level of fusion. In the family drama, those of us who were more dependent on family (or whose growing independence was not supported by family and was hindered in some way through the projection process, or who were overprotected, or who never felt fully accepted by family, or were heavily criticized by family, or never got the nurture we wanted, or the support and direction we wanted, or the attention and recognition we wanted, or, conversely, got even more of this than we needed), then left the family home with a certain amount of unresolved emotional attachment. This can launch us on a lifelong search for getting these things or attempt to keep getting them.

For those who have a greater level of unresolved attachment with family, life will be more difficult. There will be a continuous search for a partner, or a good friend, or a substitute family (like a church community) who will give us what we are looking for. It could involve a search through many marriages, or jobs, or joining different churches to find the right one. Here is a simple example. My mother was not a psychologically minded person but I once asked her how she accounted for her four marriages. She said, without blinking an eye, "I was always looking for the love I never got from my father."

George was strongly attached to his mother in a dependent way. He felt like he needed her approval and rarely got it, but he kept trying. The same was true of Martha. However, Martha was disdainful of George's wish for approval and said she had long ago given up any desire to get approval from her mother. She thought she had "detached" from her mother by having no contact. She said she wanted nothing from her. As will be seen in a verbatim below, she slowly caught on to the idea of unresolved emotional attachment and how powerful it still was for her—and how much it was affecting her present family life.

This emotional attachment lasts beyond the grave. Family members can be long dead but still we may have this sense of deficit and try to find someone to fulfill it. I had some vivid illustrations for that when doing family work with my mother and she would talk about her family experience. For example, in addition to feeling she did not have her father's love, her feelings were still strong for her biological mother who died only three months after my mother was born. She never knew this woman, but she carried her picture with her through all of our many moves. She represented the ideal mother she wished she'd had instead of the "mean" stepmother she grew up with. When mom died, she had her biological mother's picture, as always, on the night table beside her bed.

Here is one other personal family story. My mother was very much of the "Don't ask, don't tell" school about many things in life. She did not ask me questions and I was not encouraged to ask her questions. When I began doing my family work, I asked my mother what my questions were like for her. She thought I was being "nosy" but she slowly grew accustomed to my many questions after she realized she could talk openly without fear of attack or criticism. She even agreed to do a videotape, with me asking her questions, that I would show to my students in clinical training. This was a major step. Halfway through that session, she began to cry. I asked her what the tears were about. She said, "I so wish I could have done this with my father."

Sometimes, the people who chose to terminate with symptom improvements, and who do not do the family work, come back one or more years later and say, "You know, Ron, I have been thinking about all of those family questions you asked me, and I think I am ready now to address them." Pushing people to do this work reveals the fusion needs of the counselor. I know how hard it was for me to decide to do my own family work and I respect that hesitance in others.

Getting Ready for Family-of-Origin Work

Not everyone who gets to the middle phase has developed the level of courage or motivation needed to do the family work. They keep coming for counseling out of appreciation for the kind of thinking they can do around the current dilemmas of their lives, but moving back toward family looks too challenging. For example, this is the case with women who were sexually abused in their families. I have seen such women do their family-of-origin work, even with their abusive fathers, and the outcome is truly powerful for them. But for understandable reasons they have to approach it very carefully and slowly. Most do not do it, and that is fine. For people like Martha, who saw her family as emotionally damaging, they also will be slow and hesitant, at least initially.

Some of us know we need to do this work, but it still seems like a big step and we hesitate. We may become what I call muddlers. I have been a muddler. I chose it over doing the scarier thing. I knew what I could do, but I did not know what would happen next, where this act of reentering family in a new way would lead. As a counselor, I discovered that the only thing I can do is to identify what is happening and leave it at that. We are not in charge of the motivation of other people.

After about a year and a half of working with George and Martha, they entered the middle phase. They could talk openly about their sensitivities or vulnerabilities in front of each other and I had little concern that they would use the information in a fight. They had developed more respect for each other and were more respectful around each other's pain. Their definition of what the problem was in their marriage had changed. They could see much more clearly what their part in the problems were, and were much less focused on whatever might be the problems of their partner. They were becoming more responsible for self, and this is the emotional basis of adulthood.

They also became interested in family systems theory. They asked the occasional question out of genuine curiosity and I gave brief responses. They followed up with more questions, and then I either said more, in the way of teaching, or I gave them some reading to do. Both of them found the theory interesting.

Coaching George on His Family Work

In beginning the family-of-origin work, we invite people to go back into their families with a new focus or intent. They look at themselves more clearly in that context, look at the triangles and functional positions, their reactive patterns, and start thinking about how they can be different. As I briefly described it to them, George said he was ready to do his family work. It was good for Martha to see him taking the lead in this, being thoughtful, and having energy for it. She restrained herself from any comments on how he could do it differently or do it better. She simply let it be his project. Martha was quieter in the sessions when he talked about family and listened closely as he and I talked about what he could do with his mother and other family members. More importantly, when she was present when he and his mother were together, she refrained from commenting to him on whether or not he was able to do what he said he would. This was major growth in Martha.

I coached George on the primary triangle with his mother, where she would come at him either with criticisms or with attempts to tell him how to run his life. While his mother rarely said this, her implication was that Martha was not helping him adequately. Mother saw herself and George as the close twosome and she had Martha in the outside position. He learned about his pattern of reactivity by either emotionally distancing from or more openly getting upset with mother. This was familiar to him already in the work with Martha.

I suggested that whenever he heard his mother doing this he needed to inhibit his reactivity, and then work at getting the outside position by putting his mother together with Martha. I suggested he say something like (whether Martha was mentioned or not), "You know, Mom, sometimes I think you and Martha are in a competition to see who can do the best job of straightening me out. You both have an equal concern for me." In subsequent critical comments, he could say things like, "That was a good one, Mom. I think you are pulling ahead in the competition with that one. Martha's going to have work harder if she wants to beat you." We tried a number of responses like this.

One benefit in this coaching was that Martha was sitting right there as I said this. It addressed her part in that triangle as well. The first time I said the sentence above she gave a "Harrumph" sound, but said nothing. However, it had an impact for her.

Both women disliked being put in the same boat with each other, and George liked the experience of being in the outside position. In this repositioning, he began to have different feelings in response to his mother's critical comments. Importantly, George was able to say these things to his mother with a slight physical move toward her, or a bit of a smile, or even put his arm around her, with a kind of appreciative warmth in his voice. It did not come off as sarcasm or criticism of her. Mother began to offer fewer comments of this sort and George felt much less stung by them when she did.

Apart from the triangle, there were two primary foci in George's family work: first, getting to know his mother better—along with her family and his father's family; and second, telling her more about himself—defining himself even when he thought she would disapprove. This included both being less available to her when she called and expected him to respond, and also initiating contact on his schedule and with his goals in mind.

A major shift happened when he took his mother on a trip to the small town where she grew up. The house she lived in was still standing; they knocked on the door and introduced themselves to the current owners, who graciously invited them in for a look around. They chatted about the house and her memories. Two of her old friends still lived in this town, and they went and met them. Mother shared stories with them while George listened. He also asked them questions about their memories of his mother and her family. They went to the graveyard where some of her relatives were buried and he asked about these people and got whatever stories she remembered of her relationship with them.

Mother found this trip to be a powerful experience, as did George. She became more vulnerable and open with George about herself as a person. They got out of their usual interactions with each other. While he was somewhat uncomfortable with it, George felt "things loosening up" between them. He was able to put his mother into a different emotional context in his head and began to see her differently. It was not all about him. In all the previous years with her, he had experienced his mother mostly within his subjective relationship with her. His view of his mother was shaped by his reactions to her. He did not really see her as the full person she was and that she was shaped within an environment that preceded him. She was not "that way" because of or in reaction to him. Mother had a life before he existed. He was amazed that he had never noticed this before.

The trip began a new kind of conversation between the two of them, with him asking many questions about her life with her family.

He asked about all the relatives and he began to develop a family diagram, which he showed to her. They talked about all these people and her relationships with them.

During successive months, in talking about her relationship with her parents, George discovered some intriguing parallels between his mother and Martha. Mother lost her father when she was in twelfth grade. George had never asked about this before. She described her mother as more distant and spoke of how "alone" she felt. He asked how she coped with that loss. She teared up and simply said, "With great difficulty." She said she probably married younger than she should have, and "poured" herself into that life with her husband, but he also seemed to keep his distance from her.

Then he died. She again felt alone and, without George asking, she volunteered, "The only thing I had in life was you. Your sister didn't seem to need me so much." She allowed that even before his father died, she had established a much closer relationship with George and he was important to her from his birth. He had become "the joy of my life." Later on, in another conversation about these losses for mother, she volunteered, "I suppose that's why I have hung on to you so tightly. I know I shouldn't have." Part of what floored him about this admission was that it did not seem so important for him to get.

George had lost much of his reactivity to his mother and was beginning to see her as a person separate from himself. On the one hand, he found this liberating, but on the other, he found it uncomfortable. He had never really thought of himself as separate from his mother. She was so much a part of who he was. He began to see that a lot of the energy for their "tight" relationship came from him, not just from her. He had resisted changing his view of her.

He also made a rare trip back east just to visit with his older sister and to get to know her better. He was able to ask her many questions about her sense of the family history and about her connections with other family members. He wanted to get out of the "little brother who screwed up" position with her, and be more of a grown-up. This is a position youngest children often get into, and they are amazed at the new respect they get from their older siblings when they do this work.

We talked about how sibling relationships are normally the longest relationships in life—more than with a partner or parents—and how siblings can be a resource to one another as they go through life. He was attracted to this idea. After his visit to his sister, he invited her to come for a visit to stay with him and Martha. This included George's sister having some rare time alone with their mother. I also saw the sister with George for two sessions to talk about family. It was helpful for him to hear me interview her about her experience of family as they grew up. Being four years older, and knowing their father better, gave her a different perspective on family life.

She also talked about how she saw George in the family drama and this was useful for him to hear. The sister had a similar position in family to what Martha had, tending to take their dad's side in arguments (George did not even remember arguments), but at a much less intense level than Martha. She talked about how their mother had focused on George as "hers" and the impact of this on her as his sister. While her cutoff from her mother was not as intense as Martha's, their contacts did tend to be the ritualized, holiday-type thing that involved no real openness with each other. This began to change in this visit. She said, in our second session, "Maybe I have a mother after all."

In George's work with both his mother and sister, it was hugely enlightening to him to pursue them around their life stories, rather than to be the on-guard distancer, and it was somewhat amusing to Martha to see him struggle with this role. However, he did take to it. He was amazed to see his mother be uneasy as he asked questions about her family and growing up, and he began to feel more like a grown-up man with her in doing so. He was changing his position. He was actively moving out of being her "little man" and becoming more his own man. With this position came feelings that were new to him.

Becoming a family researcher, simply learning the facts about family and getting stories we have never heard, is, in itself, a major repositioning in our families. It involves stepping out of the usual way we have functioned in family triangles, and the usual subjective experiences we have with other family members. It becomes a clear demonstration to people, as it was for George, that feelings go with particular positions and as we change positions, so do the feelings.

George made himself less consistently available to his mother and told her, in a nonconfrontational way, that he had others things to do. He did not break off contact (I would never have encouraged that), but when he was with her he often made a point of taking the initiative and asking about her and her family. She, too, became interested in this.

Hearing about George's contact with other family members led to her having contact with relatives from whom she had become distant, and she slowly redeveloped these relationships on her own. This helped loosen the "tightness" with him even more.

He also became more intentionally goal focused with her rather than the passive, emotionally distant son he had been. Over time, George and Martha began to do longer holidays as well as weekends away, and he was unavailable to her for calls and contact. When he came back he reported to her the good times he and Martha had, and ignored any direct or implied criticisms his mother made. She said he was changing and becoming somewhat selfish and uncaring. He simply said in response that he was glad that she had not given up on him and kept trying to straighten him out.

Martha Goes Further into Her Emotional Cutoff

Martha was learning and thinking things through as she watched George do his work but, as will be clear in the next verbatim, she was nowhere close to doing her own work. The following verbatim comes from almost two years into my work with them. We shifted from having appointments every two weeks to three-week intervals. Much of the work focused on George and the relationship with his mother and the larger family.

As George became more intentional with his mother, this had a spillover into his relationship with Martha, as well as at his office. Martha expressed some mixed feelings about the changes, but she appreciated that he was more up-front with her and did not do things such as agree to do something and then not do it, making flimsy excuses.

Also, Martha was able to be different with George if he refused to agree with her in what she wanted. She was more reasonable; she would listen and discuss what happened. George was better able to say No directly rather than behaviorally if he did not want to do something. As he made progress with his mother, he seemed to make progress with Martha. In addition, Martha could set bottom lines as to what she would and would not do with or for him if he was not able to negotiate openly an alternative with her. She was doing a better job of taking care of herself and doing her part in the dance with him differently.

In the following verbatim, after about fifteen minutes of checking in with George on his family work, I turned to Martha and introduced the idea of reconnecting with her mother. However, I did it in the subjunctive mood that she did not hear initially.

Ron: Martha, what have you been thinking about while George talked?

Martha: Oh, just how much I admire what he is doing. It's a whole part of him that I had never seen before we came in here to talk with you.

Ron: Well, that's a nice compliment, George. Martha, here's what I have been wondering with regard to you. What would it be like for you to have a meeting with your mother?

Martha: Whoa! No way! I thought you might be working up to something like this. I am never going to see her again!

Ron: No, no. I wasn't clear here. I didn't ask you to meet with her. I was just asking what it would be like for you to meet with her.

Martha: What would it be like? It would be hell.

Ron: Tell me more.

Martha: After everything I've told you already? I couldn't do it. I hate her.

Ron: Let me ask again. What would it be like?

Martha: I hate to even think about it. I would probably want to say some pretty mean things to her. I wouldn't want to forgive her; I would want to punish her. I couldn't do what George is doing.

Ron: So that anger at her and the bitterness is still a pretty powerful experience for you.

Martha: You bet it is.

Ron: It's not like it is ancient history or anything, is it? It is still present in your life even today, right?

Martha: Yes, I guess so. It doesn't feel so present when I don't think about her, but you're right. I guess she is always there with me. God, even after twenty years of not talking to her I can't get rid of her.

Ron: Well, in my experience, that's the way it is for most people who decide to cut off from an important person like a parent. The cutoff doesn't really change the feelings. The feelings just go underground. If anything, the feelings seem to get more powerful and they influence our other relationships.

Martha: You are probably right, but I'm not going to see her.

Ron: Okay, I hear you loud and clear. But please, just play with me a little on the question I asked. Let me put it this way. If she walked into this room right now . . .

Martha: [Panicked, grabbing the arms of her chair] You wouldn't!

Ron: No, no. Never. But if you were with her right now and you somehow could restrain your anger, so you didn't say anything angry, then what would it be like?

Martha: Oh, you know. I think I would fall apart in tears. I would ask her why she was so mean to me. Why didn't she care about me?

Ron: Okay. So again, it is the hurt that is behind the anger, just as with George.

Martha: Yes. They are very similar. At least I have come to see that. I didn't used to think that, but it's true.

She continued to talk about the similarities in her experience between the two and that, in spite of her criticism of him, she was very sensitive to George's criticism of her whenever he opened up in anger at her. She could also feel like a failure with him. This was quite new to George and important for him to hear. He usually had no sense of his power for her. She spoke about this with enough objectivity and a kind of curiosity that I decided I could do some teaching and see what she did with it. She was moving toward me with interest in this phenomenon.

Ron: I want to tell you about how I think about some of this stuff. All of us, when we grow up and leave home, leave with a certain amount of what is called unresolved emotional attachment. For example, we still have a kind of dependency on our parents, even though we have gotten jobs, brought kids into the world, and appear to be functioning as fully grown adults. This is true whether we ever see them again or not. In George's case it has continued as he has daily contact with his mother, and in your case it continues with absolutely no contact, except for what you get through your sister. Are you with me so far?

Martha: No, I don't get this dependency part. I don't feel dependent on my mother.

Ron: Yes, I understand how it doesn't make sense. Let me try it this way. This is one aspect of what I am talking about. As a part of growing up we all want, for example, approval from our parents. We want to know that they think we are good, capable, and competent people. And when we don't get this, when they continue to be critical of us, we quite normally feel hurt. And, as you know, we can cover the hurt with our anger. If we are angry we feel less vulnerable. Right? This is material we have been over, right?

Martha: Right. But the dependency?

Ron: Okay. The anger and the hurt behind that are a sign of our dependency. I am, for the sake of brevity, simplifying all of this, but we want their approval or love or whatever we call it; that is our dependency. We don't get it, and we feel hurt. As grown-ups, we say we don't want the approval anymore; we say we don't care, but the hurt you just mentioned is a sign of still wanting something from someone that you haven't gotten. We become more sensitive to this issue in our adult lives. We may look for it elsewhere, from our life partner (and you have talked about this), or our kids, or our friends, or work, or church, or somewhere else. This is not stuff we can just turn off. Even not having contact with such a person for twenty years does not turn it off. It is still very powerful for us. Just the very idea of being in the same room with your mother stirs it up. Your attachment to mother and, I want to add, to your father (we haven't talked too much about him but he really is in all of this), did not get resolved. Daily contact doesn't do it [looking at George]. And cutting off doesn't do it. That's the way it is for all of us. It's a very normal thing. The issue is how do we get to a truly adult, emotionally separate, and grown-up place with our parents, or whoever else is important to us?

Martha: Okay, I think I got it. It's true that this has all remained very powerful for me. I never thought of it as a kind of dependency but what you say makes sense. I will have to think some about this. I hate the idea that it could be true. It means that I am still attached to my mother. God! This is awful. I hate it!

Ron: Yes, and even now, this moment, we see the power of it. Right?

Martha: Right. [Pause] Grrrrrrr. [Pause] So am I trapped in this place?

Ron: Not necessarily. There is something we can all do and profit from. It is what George has been doing. As you have seen in the reading I've given you, it is called family-of-origin work. As you have seen with him, it involves going back and having a different kind of contact with those people who are so powerful for us. [Seeing her reaction] Yes, I get it. The very idea makes you shudder. I have been there myself. I have felt a similar kind of dread. In doing this work, we don't reengage with them with the idea of changing them, but with the intent of being different ourselves. It is working at what the reading I gave you calls differentiating a self emotionally in relation to our parents. That is how we grow up. We know we have gotten there when we can be with them, and they do their thing—whatever it is, usually negative—the thing that has always bugged us; they are still the same, and we can be different with them. Am I making sense?

Martha: This is way more than I wanted to think about. But yes, there is a sense to it.

Ron: Well, I am certainly not going to push you to do it. It is difficult work and takes a certain amount of determination and, I think, courage. Everybody has to decide for themselves whether they will do this work and I know plenty of people who have refused to do it. But I wanted to give you a chance to think about it if you haven't already.

Shortly after this, my appointments with them shifted to only once a month. We spent another three months going over this sort of material, with both of them talking about the work. Whenever their anxiety went up for some reason they had their relapses with each other, but they could process them more quickly, and then get back on track. With his trip with his mother as the turning point, George was making good progress in his dual efforts and would report on this in our sessions.

Martha gradually warmed to the idea of contacting her mother. We talked quite a bit about how it might go and how Martha might be, particularly how she might be in charge of her reactivity of anger and hurt. The idea became quite magnetic for her. She got to the place where she did not want to consider *not* doing it, but she could not see how she would do it. We recognized that she would be anxious and considered nonreactive ways she could be more relaxed in her mother's presence. We also talked more specifically about the point of doing this kind of work and that it was focused on self, on how she was with her mother, not how her mother would be with her. She had enough self-focused work with George to understand how this would work. We also discussed the kinds of questions she would like to ask about her mother's family.

Then one day they came in and Martha announced, "Well, I called my mother and we are going to get together." I said, "Oh, yeah? What led you to do a fool thing like that?" We laughed, and then talked about the call and what was said, and the plans they made for getting together. I asked what questions and concerns she had, and then I asked how she thought it might go and how she wanted to be. I did not ask her how she "felt" about this. We spent the whole session on this and I asked George for some on his thoughts about their get-together. I had already given them a copy of my little book, *Family Ties That Bind*, which, at that time, was about the only thing in print for laypeople on Bowen theory and doing family-of-origin work (Richardson 1984).

At the next month's meeting Martha was full of her meeting with her mother and how happy (and proud) she was that she had done it. She said, after some initial hesitance and suspicion, that her mother began to be open with her in response to her questions. These were about her mother's own family life and growing up, not about the relationship with Martha's father or their own history and fights with each other. I strongly encouraged Martha not to ask questions about these relationships like, "Why were you so mean to me?" and Mother even showed interest in Martha's life. She said there was no hint of criticism in her mother and I said, "That's too bad." She said, "What do you mean?" I said, "Well, that's where some of your work will be. She has to do her bit so you can work differently at yours." We laughed and I said that I hoped Mom would be more cooperative and stop being so nice.

She also reconnected with her father's side of the family. She had lost contact with them when her father died and her mother had distanced from them. She began to learn a great deal about him that she had never known. Her picture of both of them, and of their lives together, changed significantly. Another big step for her was to move toward her maternal aunt. Because her mother had cut off from her own sister, Martha had been cut off also. She let her mother know that she was going to visit her aunt, who lived in another nearby community, but she did not ask permission. As it turned out, her mother was fine with this, which surprised Martha. She soon invited them both out for lunch with her and that meeting went very well. Eventually, the two sisters began getting together on their own.

15

Coaching Family-of-Origin Work

As counselees do their own family-of-origin work, the counselor serves primarily as a coach or supervisor. In many respects, family-of-origin work is an informal, naturally occurring activity that more mature, better-differentiated people do normally as part of their own development, without the aid of counseling. The Bowen theory has developed the work into a science, and formalized it into a repeatable process that we all can use. It is a science in that the steps are rational, based on the theory, and lead to a predictable outcome. It is also an art in that each person does the steps in his or her own unique way.

In this chapter, I briefly outline the basic steps and some of the strategies for a counselor to be aware of in doing this work with counselees. I have written extensively about doing this work in other books (*Family Ties That Bind* [1984] and *Becoming a Healthier Pastor* [2005]) and I do not want to repeat here all of what I have said elsewhere.

Each counselee arrives at doing this work in his or her own way. They bring their own level of motivation, and do it at their own speed. As counselors we are in charge of none of this. Once they have entered into this emotional territory, as coaches we can bring a rationale and suggestions for how they might proceed. In both the first phase and transitional phase of counseling, we have been laying the foundation for this work by evoking, through our questions, the relevance of family to their current issues. In the middle phase, people are generally convinced about the relevance, but then wondering are what to do about it.

The work this chapter describes is about us, not just our counselees. We need to remember, for ourselves, the things I say here. We are all in the same boat. We, as counselors, need to have mastered the skills I list below, within our own families, before we can coach others on implementing them.

Reentering the Family as a Researcher

Normally, most of us arrive at chronological adulthood thinking that we have our family figured out. We do not realize that what we think about our family has a great deal to do with how we think about ourselves, and that our experience in family determines much of how we approach our adult relationships like marriage. The intent in doing this work is that we need to begin to get to know our family in a new way, from a more objective perspective. We become researchers of our own family, including our part in its emotional process.

To do this, we need to have an attitudinal shift that should have happened during the earlier phases of counseling. That shift leads to a curiosity about the people we grew up with rather than having a more certain knowledge about them. We focus on what we do not know rather than what we think we do know about them. Properly executed, first-phase and transitional-phase work will begin to move counselees in this direction through the question-asking process.

This step requires a *letting go of our expectations* that family members act in a desired way with us. Part of unresolved emotional attachment is that family members, parents in particular, will "finally" come through with what we are looking for from them. Letting go of our expectations of them means a shift in the subjective idea that they exist for us, that "my" family is about "me." If somebody says to us, "Tell me about your family," we tend to speak of how they are in relation to ourselves, and how they did or did not fulfill our expectations (i.e., "My father was a bastard" or "My mother was a saint"). A surprising number of people do not even think of their parents having a life before they themselves were born.

Becoming researchers of our family means we get to know about them as people, apart from in relation to us. Who are the people they grew up with and focused on with their expectations? We drop all questions about how they experienced, reacted to, and related to us. We want to get to know about their lives in their families, and how they functioned before we existed.

Initially, this involves *gathering facts* and recording dates of births, deaths, marriages, and nodal events in the multigenerational family's life. This fact gathering about family history is a good place to begin because family members will usually be more comfortable telling us this information once they get comfortable with our interest, feel safe with our inquiries, and believe this is not some effort to "get" the family, or them in particular. Generally, family members will join in with this fact gathering. They tend to become curious about what they do not know and will search out these facts for us. As they feel safer, they will collaborate in the research and this is a good thing; it often puts people back in contact with each other when that contact has been lost.

In the process of fact gathering, family members will also offer us free information. This is about things that we did not ask for but that they think we ought to know. This information is often about their view of the family emotional process. When they offer it, then we can be curious about it and ask more questions, up to the point that they stop being open. Our questions, stemming out of our understanding of how family systems function (for example, a knowledge of triangles), will often take them into territory they do not intend. It is fine if they shut up and refuse to say more. We will make note of these areas for future discussions when, hopefully, the level of safety in talking with us is even greater. They will not forget our unanswered questions.

The more this kind of free information is offered, the more willing people usually will be in talking about the family emotional process, and the more our questions can shift over to family functioning and the nature of relationships as perceived by the different players. We have to count on different family members talking about the same events differently. They will naturally tell the story from their point of view, out of their own subjectivity, as if their version is the true story. This way of telling the story represents their own position in the family system and that is what is of interest to us. It is not our goal to "straighten them out" on the "real truth" of these stories. If we challenge the accuracy of their stories (like saying, "That's not true"), their level of safety will go down, they will become reactive, and we will have stopped being researchers.

The point of this information gathering is to get a picture of our multigenerational family and how it functioned over time, starting with the earliest generation people remember or have any information about. We want to get a sense of the various parts or strands of the family down through time. Are there some parts that have done better emotionally, and were perhaps a bit better differentiated, and some that were more fused and more symptomatic? Ultimately, we want to see where we fit in this emotional process, following each line of the generations, and notice how the multigenerational family functioning has affected our own functioning; but that comes later.

One other caveat: we are not engaged in an effort to educate our family members or to teach them about how family systems operate. We are not trying to make them function better or help them. Nor should we take one or more family members into our confidence, enlist them in our differentiating efforts, and tell them what we are doing, even if they ask. That is a triangle. This work is strictly for self. If we do it to or for them they will react in some way, and that will just continue the old family process.

Another obvious attitudinal shift we have to accomplish, in order to reenter our family, is to *manage our reactivity*. We have to learn to see our reactivity as part of the family emotional process that we want to get out of and be different with. The first steps in doing this involve knowing what our reactive patterns are, and then finding ways to hold ourselves back from participating in the process and simply controlling our urges to react. If we become reactive as we listen to the family stories and lose our neutrality in the triangles, people will stop feeling safe with us and they will shut up as a source of information. Their reactivity in talking with us will be a sign that we may have become reactive ourselves.

This is all part of learning to *develop our objectivity* about our family. We have to become like good reporters. At first, I had to think about the Richardson family as if I was not a participant. When it came to my part in it all, I thought about myself in the third person, leaving out words like "I" or "me" or "my." Dr. Bowen would assign people to do a report on their family exclusively using the third person, including for themselves. This was an exercise in learning to look at family in a different way, to loosen the powerful, subjective shackles of the family emotional process that we are a part of.

Developing a Multigenerational Family Diagram

Developing a family diagram for as many generations as information is available is an essential tool. It is also a visual method that many family members will find useful since they will treat it like a family tree. It is useful to give it to other family members we interview and ask them questions like: Is it complete? Do you know specific dates for major events in the peoples' lives like marriages, births, and deaths (family Bibles often record this information)? What were their levels of education, their professions, major physical or emotional illnesses, and how did they do in life generally? Most of this can be recorded on the diagram. Taking successive copies of this diagram to family members as we gather information and revisit it, becomes a useful tool in talking with them.

Not all *family secrets* will be revealed right away and we cannot be impatient about this. There was a secret in my family that took many years to be opened up and it was related to a triangle involving me that I had not even suspected. But it did come. Eventually the safety was there with me so that my mother felt comfortable telling me. I tell about this in Becoming a Healthier Pastor, where I wrote a chapter about my own family work.

One goal in developing this diagram would be to meet, at least once if not more often, every family member that is still alive. I tracked down one very distant, much removed, ninety-year-old cousin living alone in a trailer in the backwoods of Missouri. She was a font of information on family members long dead and whom I had never met. Another distant cousin of my mother's, whom I had never met before, gave me that woman's name and address. These kinds of people will give us a perspective on people like our own grandparents that perhaps even our own parents do not have. It is very useful to take their information back to our parents and report what they have said, the stories they have told, and watch our parents react, often with a sense of wondrous "I never knew that," and see them rethinking their own relationship with their parents.

Differentiation and Triangles

One major result of doing this kind of family history work is that, in itself, it begins to change the relationship with key members of our family. This work lays the groundwork for more of a one-on-one relationship with them, rather than being triangular in nature. The relationships will improve as people become more open with us, especially about themselves. We know how important it is in counseling when members of the couple become more vulnerable with each other, more willing to talk about their underlying sensitivities, and it is the same in family-of-origin work. We do not need counseling for this experience to happen, but there does need to be a sense of safety, and we, as we bring the kind of attitudes I spoke about above, will bring that new level of safety. We create a new kind of connection with people when they reach that point with us.

This greater openness is not, in itself, our own primary goal. Our goal is better differentiating a self within our family. Developing one-on-one relationships with each family member is a part of that. Doing this work from a more objective position is, in itself, part of the differentiating process. We are already acting in a way that is contrary to the expectations of other family members within the usual triangles. Family members will begin to see us differently.

There is an anxiety that goes with this new way of being. It is the anxiety that comes with growth and changing self. Because we are behaving in a new way, we are entering new personal territory. Not only do others experience us differently, we experience ourselves in a new way. It is literally true that my mother and I rarely asked questions of each other. When I began asking lots of questions, I was breaking some kind of rule that felt quite powerful for me. We both had to become more comfortable with this new way of relating.

There is a kind of existential anxiety that goes with being more differentiated. On the one hand we are better connected to others and we will see our family relationships improve, but on the other we become more aware of our aloneness in the world. I do not mean that we are not still interdependent with others, but we experience an increased responsibility for who and how we are in life. We arrive at our own beliefs, convictions, values, and principles for living. We are more able to decide how we want to be.

Interviewing others, gathering facts, becoming more objective and less reactive, means that we have to get ourselves into a neutral place in the family triangles. Take, for instance, the parental triangle. If Mom has always seen us as being closer to Dad and more sympathetic to his side in their disagreements, then she will be more guarded and less open with us about her life and experience. That would be for her like giving information to the enemy. We have to find a way to reposition ourselves in that triangle before information will flow more freely. We have to be able to show that we are not taking sides. As counselors we do this with counselees; we have to communicate to both partners that we are not on one partner's side, but interested in the point of view of both and how each arrived at their position.

A common pattern with parents or other family members is that they want to tell us more about other family members, like their partner, and not so much about themselves. Personally, we do not enter into extended discussions about others, or express an opinion about them (whether we agree or disagree with the person we are talking with), or defend them, or try to interpret the other to the speaker, and so forth. Instead, each time the person we are talking with tells us, for example, an "awful" story about someone else—like our mother tells us about our dad—we ask her some version of, "Well, what did you do with that?" or "What did you say in response?" We find a way bring it back to the speaker.

In doing this, we are keeping it more as a one-on-one relationship, still asking the speaker to tell us about themselves rather than about someone else. It is not wrong or bad that they do this and they are not to be "corrected" about how they "should" respond. It is just about where we keep our own focus. We do not tell them they are trying to triangle us into their difficulties. We also need to remember that emotional distancing is not detriangling; it is just making us more comfortable within the triangle.

In doing this, we are also differentiating a self within the emotional system. Whenever we can step out of our usual functional position in family and get more neutral in the triangles, we are differentiating a bit more. If we have been an overfunctioner and can let go of that, allowing people to become more responsible for themselves, we are developing a self. If we can grow up enough to take responsibility for ourselves, and not let someone overfunction for us, however comfortable and easy it might be, we are becoming more mature. If we can stop our emotional pursuit of others, or stop distancing from them, we are being more real and present.

Another aspect of differentiation, or defining a self within family, can be more dramatic and will generally come later in the family work. In chapter 3 I mentioned the family of eight adult children and mother who were all involved in a project together. When the oldest brother took a position in which he said, "I am no longer participating in this project; I have to get on with my own family life," his position created a crisis in the family. He was criticized and pressured to change back, to be more cooperative and supportive of the effort and not to "abandon" the family. He nonreactively stood his ground and continued in the new direction he had set, while maintaining a warm connection with his family. Eventually the family adjusted to his position and this allowed others to resolve their own ambivalence about the project. In doing this work we will most likely need to take similar steps, but I advise that it come later in the work.

Special Points of Concern for Coaching

There are a number of concerns to be aware of in coaching people as they do their family-of-origin work. Here are a few of them, given in point form for the sake of brevity. They are in no particular order.

1. Differentiating acts, as in the just-cited example, will take many directions depending on the family. Counselees need to be carefully prepared for making such moves and coached in what to expect and how to be in the midst of it. If they relent and give in to family pressure, we cannot be critical of them and imply they are failures. We can say something like, "Well, we talked about how tough this would be, and you know you don't have to do it. You have done some important things in your family and if you can live with things as they are, then maybe that is enough for you." The impetus for change has to be theirs, not ours.

2. Often, when couples arrive at this stage in the work, just one of them may be ready to do it. If the other partner is still willing to

come and listen, as Martha did, that is fine. In fact, she had other things to discuss so she was not left out of the process. Quite often one partner will leave the counseling at this point. It is fine to keep working with the remaining partner, but we will have to work harder to maintain our systems perspective and not get involved in the triangle of being in a close twosome with this "more motivated" partner.

3. In addition, this is a perfect set-up for transference to become heightened, and for the individual counselee to begin to think of this as a special relationship with us. We need to keep the energy and the focus on the counselee and the family, not on the relationship with us. It helps to reduce our importance to counselees by spacing out appointments as they enter this phase. They will need more time between sessions to accomplish the plans made for doing family work.

4. We need to demonstrate what curiosity about family looks like and inspire counselees to become more curious. When they say, "Oh, I know what he is like and he is never going to change," we have to be ready to punch holes in this "knowledge" by asking questions. One goal of this work is to be endlessly fascinated about what we can learn about others whom we think we know. There is always more to be learned about the people we have grown up with. After all, who fully knows us? It is the same for others. Counselees can resist allowing perceptions of others to change. We can explore this anxiety with them.

5. We need to be listening for family reactions to the counselee's efforts (or emergence of symptoms in others), and make sure that their efforts do not include some degree of reactivity, or that the counselee is having unrealistic expectations of others, or is really focused on changing others rather than themselves. It is easy to slip into an other focus rather than maintaining a focus on how self is with others. Families are nearly always reactive to differentiating moves and we need to monitor these and make sure they are manageable for the counselee, and responsible in relation to the family, as in the next point.

6. Some moves in family may be portrayed by counselees as differentiating ones, but really are more reactive. Is the counselee acting for self or having fun "getting others," or trying to get others to come across with what the counselee wants from them? Are counselees having unrealistic expectations of their parents and other family members? *Remember, lowering expectations of others is what makes closeness possible. Raising them nearly always creates distance.* This includes the relationship between counselors and counselees.

7. An expectation that is very difficult to change or lower often represents some powerful emotionality or emotional investment that could be multigenerational. Sometimes there is a whole family history around this expectation and it is interesting to research this as a theme in the family, not just in the counselee.

8. We need to pay attention to the labels counselees use to describe other family members. A sentence that begins, "He/she is so . . ." is usually going to be followed by a label. These may reveal the triangles they are caught in, or the kind of stances they have that will prevent them from connecting well with others. We can draw the counselee's attention to *how labels for others also describe our own position in relation to others*. What do their labels tell about this? In changing our labels for others we can quickly change our own sense of self and our relationship to others. The same goes for the stories they tell about their experience with others. What do the stories tell about the counselees' own positions?

9. As I mentioned in an earlier chapter, particular feelings of profound sadness may emerge when some counselees finally and really accept that family members are not going to be there for them in the way they have always wanted. We simply need to be with them if and as these feelings emerge and help them to think about them. Some have called this a therapeutic depression related to coming to terms with reality. What it is called is less important than realizing that people may enter this place and that some solid learning can emerge from it if we counselors are not too anxious about them getting into this place. Have we dealt with this sort of experience in our own lives and, if so, how?

10. What are the toxic, transgenerational themes in the family? This could include stances around money, death, wills, bad marriages and divorces, problematic children, affairs, or any number of things. When people are feeling more comfortable talking with the counselee, then, and only then, can these things be talked about. Trying to force these discussions will not work.

11. Essential themes to explore are the relationship cutoffs in a family. These need to be inquired into and they will frequently involve triangles in which a counselee will need to reposition self. For example, if a counselee's mother is estranged from her sister and the counselee wants to contact this sister and get to know her, this represents a repositioning in that triangle. It is also called "bridging a cutoff." However, the mother may think of the counselee as disloyal.

12. Remember that there is no one set way of doing this work. Each person's work and family is different, but the family emotional system concepts are the same for all families and it is these that we bring to each unique family. The concepts are our principal guidance system.

Much more can be said about the challenges of doing this work. I encourage lots of reading, and discussion with other counselors who are doing Bowen theory work. It is essential that we, as we coach others, have our own supervisor or coach who is experienced with this work and can talk with us about it.

16

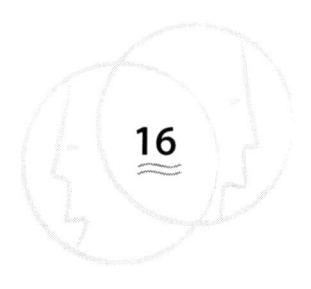

The Counseling Process: The Termination Phase

Premature or Early Termination

Everyone decides on their own when they will stop counseling. I never have an expectation of how long people should continue. These are their lives and I certainly do not know what is best for them. At the end of the first session of counseling, I ask, "Shall we meet again next week?" I ask some version of this at the end of every session right through first-phase work, never presuming that people will continue. Once it is clear they are in it for "the long haul," as we transition to the middle phase, then I drop that question.

People terminate counseling for many reasons. We might question to ourselves why they would end their participation in something that we think would be "good" for them, but that is not for us to judge. In discussing termination, we can explore with them their thinking, make our own contributions to the thinking, and wish them well on their journey. Clearly, we will have our own thoughts about how well they will be able to make it, but I am always willing to be surprised.

In first phase, when people say they want to stop the counseling, it is important to explore their thinking with them. If they announce this at the end of a session, then I ask them to return for one more session so that we can talk about this decision. Their reasons might be based on assumptions or beliefs about counseling that are not accurate, or perhaps they have had some sort of experience with me that was not comfortable or happy for them. They may have heard something in a comment by me that they take as a negative evaluation of them, or that inspired some anxiety, so that they want to distance from me. They may or may not be able to talk about this. If they can talk about these things then sometimes the counseling will continue.

Occasionally there is a mismatch between what people expect counseling to be and what they actually experience. A common expectation among this group of people is that they will be told "what to do" about their situation. When they discover that this is not going to happen and that counseling involves exploring issues, they decide that counseling is not for them. I have had people say, "Well, if you are not going to tell me what to do, what am I doing here?" This usually leads to a good discussion about how counseling works and a good percentage of these people decide to "give it a try."

It could be the case that the counselor has tried to move too fast, taking people into emotional territory they were not expecting to deal with, or did not want to face, or did not see as relevant. This can happen when a Bowen family systems theory counselor attempts to convince counselees that all of their problems are bound up in their family rather than in their current situation. Counselees will correctly question the relevance of this approach. Early on, we ought not to stray far from the presenting concerns of counselees. The Bowen theory is always directly relevant to these presenting issues and it can be a resource to them even if their family of origin is never mentioned.

Counseling relationships are just like any other in that they need a certain "chemistry" for the relationship to take. Sometimes this just does not happen. However, if a high percentage of counselees terminates early in the counseling, or do not return after one or two sessions with a counselor, then very likely there is some difficulty around the counselor's ability to connect with people. This needs to be addressed in supervision.

Ideally, beginning counselors videotape their counseling sessions and these can be discussed with the supervisor. Perhaps a counselor is unable to demonstrate an interest in counselees' difficulties, or is judgmental or too dismissive of their concerns and wants to point them toward what the counselor thinks is important. For counseling "to take," counselors have to be seen as interested, relevant to the presenting issues, and nonjudgmental.

Around 10 to 15 percent of the counselees I work with do not continue with me beyond a few sessions, for whatever reasons. A portion of these people generally cancel their next appointment over the phone and I make a point of calling them back if I have not talked with them already about stopping. If they will return for a concluding session with me before stopping that is best. In either case, I am curious about their reasons for stopping and, regardless of what these are, I do my best to end with them on a positive note and to wish them well in whatever they decide to do about their situation. I never want to send a message that they are somehow a "failure" in counseling for "quitting early." Sometimes they want names of people who work with some other modality, different from mine, and if I know, I give them those names.

Termination in Later Phases of the Work

Another 25 to 30 percent terminate somewhere around the end of first-phase work. The total number of sessions this group has and the length of time I work with them varies. It is generally ten to twenty sessions. Most of this group see some significant change in their symptoms and say they generally feel better. In the final session, I ask them about what seemed most helpful in what we did and in what ways they have improved. I also ask what they wish might have been different in the counseling. We also discuss what sort of personal goals they have, if any, for the future or what sort of issues they need to be on the lookout for. I congratulate them on their accomplishments and say they are always welcome to return if they feel the need.

Another 10 to 15 percent move into the transition phase toward middle phase and think about possibly doing family work but then decide they will stop. Generally, they think they have done more than they expected originally and feel gratified by what they did. In addition to the terminating conversations above, I feel freer to suggest to them some reading in the Bowen theory. Typically, they do not feel strongly motivated to do the family work although they accomplished various levels of understanding how family is a part of their difficulty.

The remaining group go on to do significant family-of-origin work. They make up almost half of my counseling load. George and Martha would be typical of these people. During middle-phase work with this group, we increasingly spread out the appointments. Depending on the couple and the intensity of the work they are doing, I see them every three to four weeks. With some couples, I see them as little as every two to three months. These people can always ask for more frequent sessions if they get into some difficulty or have a particular dilemma they want to discuss.

It is sometimes difficult to say when counseling "terminates" with this group of people. We do have termination sessions and either they or I can initiate them. People report that they have developed the skills they need for living a more satisfying life and their relationships are running in a happier direction. They have goals for their lives, personally and perhaps professionally, that they are motivated to pursue with energy. I cannot say that any of them have "problem-free" lives, but they have better ways of managing their difficulties and they demonstrate a greater mastery over their personal issues. Of course, my door is always open for them to return at some later date if they feel the need.

In terms of marital conflict, this is always reduced significantly and usually the couple stays together. They enjoy living with each other more happily, and their expectations for marriage, or for what their partner would provide for them in marriage, are very different. Their life within their larger family has also changed significantly, as seen with George and Martha.

A few couples still divorce, even after working with them for a couple of years, but they do a good job of it. I may refer them for divorce mediation if necessary in order to work out all of the practicalities of separating in a marriage that has lasted over many years and inevitably requires carefulness in their coming apart. Sometimes I continue to see one or both of these people after divorce.

In all cases, I tell them the door is always open for them to return if they feel a need, and this sometimes happens. Living in a suburb of a large city, with many of my counselees coming from that area, I often have occasion to see them walking on the street, or in a store, or most often grocery shopping. I quite enjoy these brief encounters; we usually chat, and they fill me in on what is happening in their lives now.

Ending with George and Martha

I am aware that I have chosen, as a primary example in this book, a couple who are no longer typical of the average North American marriage in that they were a "traditional" couple, where Martha was a full-time homemaker and they had a good income from George's work. They were not typical even of my own married life. The level of stress on their family was much less than on most contemporary couples where both partners work. Today, couples have to balance and negotiate many more issues (around household management, roles and responsibilities, child care, family budgets, and significant debt loads) than do couples like George and Martha. All of this adds a huge level of stress to modern marriages.

In choosing a traditional marriage couple, I wanted to simplify the number of issues they had to deal with in order to get through the huge amount of material that is involved in issues of marital conflict. The primary emotional challenges are the same for a contemporary couple even though life is more complicated for them. The ability to negotiate the new terrain of marital and family life in today's two-income families, where perhaps the wife is even the primary "breadwinner," remains the key issue. It requires greater emotional maturity for a couple to develop the flexibility required to meet the challenges of modern life. Differentiation of self is still the key to having this flexibility.

Altogether, I worked for about three-and-a-half years with George and Martha. During the middle phase I saw them once a month for a year, and then in the next half-year every two months. After the last counseling session, we agreed to meet in six-months' time just to see how their work was going. We did and they were managing well. They said life was much different from when they first came in. They were functioning differently and gave me examples. They both managed to be less focused on how others were with them, more focused on how self was with others and whether they were being true to their own beliefs and principles, and they reported all of their relationships were "much better," including between Martha and her mother. They were having regular contact and both seemed to appreciate having this important relationship reestablished. Her mother had become much closer to her own sister, Martha's aunt. Their son, Tom, enjoyed getting to know these people as well and liked that he now had "more of a family."

They each affirmed how differently they felt about themselves subjectively. Martha could not put words on it but she said she felt "somehow more solid." She said that "feeling more grown up"—as George described the change for himself—did not quite say what she experienced, but she liked the feeling "a lot."

George and Martha are not an example of my most difficult couples. They were a good example, however, of a heavily conflicted, less well-differentiated couple who were nearing divorce. They did good work and they realized the benefits of doing it. My shortened verbatims do not reflect the challenges of doing the work with them. There was quite a bit of expressed emotionality and reactivity that went on, especially in the first year of counseling. Even at the end of the counseling, they could get back into the old space quickly and easily, but both had learned a lot and they could get out of it on their own almost as quickly. Most importantly, the intensity was not there, and their commitment to each other strengthened.

Rethinking Beliefs and Values

George and Martha had been nominal church members but we never once overtly discussed issues of faith and values. From my point of view, as a pastoral counselor, we were always in that territory but just without using the specific language of faith. At some point early in the counseling, they noticed that I was a pastoral counselor. They admitted that if they had known this when they made the first appointment they probably would not have come in to see me. After that, we had no more specific discussions about faith. It is not that I avoided the topic, but I think I am always dealing with issues of faith in counseling even when we never use the language of faith.

As part of their family work, however, and as they let go of reactivity to family, they began to be clearer about the need for principles around how they wanted to behave—in their life generally and in relationship to others. I asked them questions like, "What do you believe about how you want to be as a person in the world? What is important to you in terms of your values and basic beliefs and how they affect your relationships?" They reexamined their previous assumptions about these things and, on their own, they could see the lack of consistency between the way they lived their life on a daily basis, and what they said they believed.

One day when they came in during the last year I saw them, they started commenting on a sermon their minister gave, and they asked if I knew him. I said I did, and that I thought he worked with some of the same ideas I did (he had been in my clergy-training program), but that I did not realize that they were going to church regularly now. Was that new? They said, "Oh, yes. It seems like we have been thinking about such important things lately that we just wanted to get some more input on it from our church, and that has been valuable. We joined an adult discussion group and that has been very stimulating and thought provoking." In addition, they were developing friends within this group.

Then one day George told me that he had changed jobs and was working for a new company. I asked what that was about and he said that he had become increasingly uncomfortable with his boss's ethics and had not found any way to change this in the company. He said his boss was angry with him but that he (George) remained nonreactive while also being clear with his boss, and his coworkers, about why he was leaving the company. His mother was also angry with him for doing this, saying, "That man is the best person you could ever work for." He remained nonreactive with her; their discussion about his decision went well and she better understood his decision. He reported that he could now think about things like this with his own head, and not have her in his head second-guessing his every move.

As people rethink their basic life goals, principles, beliefs, and values during the middle phase of counseling, a number of them, on their own, have turned to their faith community for help in clarifying these things. Many are not previous church members. They realize that they are developing a new life and they want some solid basis to it. These changes continue beyond their own lifetime in that they affect their parenting. Their children and grandchildren are affected by these solid changes and, as a result, they have a bit more of an edge toward a better level of differentiation.

Because a major part of the Bowen theory is clarifying the principles by which we live our lives, I see these sorts of developments as inevitable. I do not have to "make" people think about the role of their faith. In my neutral stance, I am not an advocate for faith. I only "prepare the way" and watch what people do with that. I find it very rewarding work.

Afterword

On Character

I witnessed Dr. Bowen's last public interview. He gave it just three days before he died, in October of 1990, when he was honored at the annual convention of the American Association for Marriage and Family Therapy. He clearly was not doing well physically. Dr. William Doherty asked him, at the end of the interview, if he had any final words for the audience. Dr. Bowen said, "Yes. You have inherited a lifetime of tribulation. Everybody has inherited it. Take it over, make the most of it. And when you have decided you know the right way, do the best you can with it." I think most of us in the audience felt quite moved, as did Dr. Doherty who responded, "Can I say 'Amen' to that?" Dr. Bowen said, "Yep."

These nearly theological words sum up much of Dr. Bowen's life work. He understood we are all born into families that have difficulties and challenges. We become a part of these difficulties as we develop within our family. It is our job to try to understand them, and do the best we can with them. In doing so, we may be able to pass on a little less tribulation to our children and grandchildren and all those we associate with beyond family.

In the famous passage of Romans 5:3, Paul says that tribulation and suffering produce patience and endurance, and that these produce character and hope. I understand differentiation of self, in part, to be about producing a stronger character in the midst of life's challenges. The more we develop that character, the more hopeful we can be about our families and our society. We will be better able to live the faith that we profess and be better people. This is what I have seen happen in the lives of counselees. They have a more solid character as they face life's challenges.

Character is a forgotten virtue in these "culture of the therapeutic" times that tend to focus on the damage that has been done to people, mostly in their families, and the feelings they have as victims. Before Freud took us into the interior world of motivations and drives, helpers spoke of character as a way to overcome the challenges of life. This was lost as the therapeutic ethic took over our society. The Bowen theory has brought us back to this primary issue and given us a way to relate to counselees that automatically enhances the development of character without being moralistic.

I see people move from being focused on what they think others have done to them to looking at how they behave with others. They see their part in the family drama of tribulation and in the reactivity of others to them. They stop trying to "have it out" with others, either a marital partner or a family member, and start working at being a person of character. They establish more intimate, one-on-one relationships with people they have been at odds with for many years.

In attempting to better differentiate a self within the emotional system of our family, we take strides forward in dealing with the tribulations of life and making life better for everyone with whom we are connected. However, we do not emerge from this work as people who are problem free and for whom life is just perfect. Of course, there will be times when it feels perfect, but the life of tribulation continues to happen and we will be back in it. The difference is that we can bring a new attitude, a new way to think about what is important, and a new level of maturity.

Part of the improvement will simply be because of lowered expectations. We adjust our expectations to reality. The inheritance of tribulation in human society is massive and we, at our best, can only make a very, very small dent in it. When we stop expecting others and ourselves to be perfect within the midst of our "trials and tribulations," life does get better. The effort is worth it, not only for ourselves but also for those with whom we live. I think of those I have worked with who have managed some small degree of improvement in their functional level of differentiation. In their networks of human interaction, they bring gifts that improve those relationships. This is the good we can all do as we work at becoming the best we can be.

Afterword

A good friend and colleague of mine, who does the best he can with the Bowen theory, became the president of his handball association. After about a year of service one of the longtime members said to him, "You are the best president we've ever had. Our meetings were always chaotic and competitive before you came on the scene, and we rarely got things accomplished. You have calmed us down and gotten us on track." This trivial example shows how this way of relating can make a small difference in the larger world.

About two years after concluding the counseling with George and Martha, I ran into her at the supermarket. She told me about being out to lunch with her mother and, without any prompting from Martha, her mother apologized for her "awful" behavior as a mother. All these years she had known she had behaved badly as a mother, but it took this long to say it. I am sure that it was possible because Martha had developed a new way of relating to her mother.

I asked Martha how she responded. She said, "Well, you know, that's the interesting part. There was a time when this would have felt like a great vindication, and a victory. I would have thought it was a necessary apology that was due to me. But I didn't feel any of that. I barely took note of it, actually. I almost missed it. I didn't feel the need to forgive my mother. I was seeing the whole situation so much more clearly. I just said, 'Mom, those were tough days for all of us and we just didn't know how else to handle it. I'm sure I was a difficult daughter to live with.'" Martha told her that she had her own difficulties in life, as her mother knew (she had told her about her marital difficulties and getting counseling), and that she was trying to be more the person she wanted to be in her marriage. Martha had developed a stronger character.

I have noticed that the issue of forgiveness changes in this work. I have no doubt that Martha's mother behaved in ways that would be easy to call "emotionally damaging." But as Martha grew and changed and felt less like a victim in life and more like she was a part of something that everyone in the family struggled with, she felt much less "done in" by it all. She felt less damaged, less need for an apology, and less need to forgive.

Of course, the issues are different when there is actual physical and sexual abuse. The sexual abuse of incest can be highly damaging to a person's psyche. Even here, there is variation in the reactions of the victims, and some women (a few victims are men) have more emotional resilience in dealing with the experience than others. The essential thing for everyone's recovery is the ability to regain a sense of self that they are in charge of. Differentiation of self is what can make the difference, and nurturing that in our work with counselees is what brings that about.

Conflicted couples can present us with such an incredible variety of difficulties and there are so many things that we can take note of and focus on as "the problem." The Bowen theory helps us to navigate through this terrain and to stay focused on what is essential in helping people to make their own way through their own particular tribulations. We do not have to have answers for them. In the way that we relate to them, we help them to develop the thinking and emotional skills they need, and to develop some understanding of how it all works.

I have attempted in this book to demonstrate a different way of caring for people. Unlike what many of us think as the usual, compassionate, pastoral-care stance, the Bowen approach gives an option. Echoing Isaiah 40, it is a way of comforting and "speaking tenderly" to those in tribulation that announces the "warfare is ended, that iniquity is pardoned." This image is central in my thinking about my counseling ministry. However, I enact this announcement behaviorally, from a neutral stance, as I relate to counselees.

I have found this way of working, of being both connected to people in tribulation and neutral around the way they live out their difficulties, to be a way of showing God's grace without condescension or condemning people for their sins. In bringing our best, most objective thinking to those in difficulty and thinking their situation through with them, being neutral within the unhappy and sometimes horrific stories they tell and looking at how they each participate in those difficulties, we are ministering to them in a way that encourages their own strengths and abilities to develop.

Rescuing and being pastoral are not synonymous terms. This is one problem with shepherding images of pastoral care. Sheep are dumb animals. They often need rescuing from the dangers they encounter. Human beings have been given a mind in order to think things through for themselves. They only need an environment in which they can do this.

I am happy to talk about faith issues with counselees to the extent that they want, but often when this happens we discover that these "issues of faith" are really about their experience with family. Images that people have of God and the church are often tied in with their experience of their father and mother, in that order. As people sort out things with their family, their faith, as well as their relationships in their church and with their pastor, are also sorted out in a more mature way.

One aspect of the work of the Holy Spirit is to lead us into new truth and this is part of what is involved in the word *growth*. I have seen the work of the Spirit in people's lives. Another work of the Spirit is to enliven, to give us energy and hope for doing good and building character. I have seen this as well.

Dr. Bowen posted the famous prayer of St. Francis of Assisi on the bulletin board of the Family Center in Georgetown. He said of this prayer, "It would be hard to find a better definition of differentiation of self."

> Lord, make me an instrument of your peace,
> where there is hatred, let me sow love;
> where there is injury, pardon;
> where there is doubt, faith;
> where there is despair, hope;
> where there is darkness, light;
> where there is sadness, joy.
> O Divine Master, grant that I may not so much seek
>   to be consoled as to console;
> to be understood as to understand;
> to be loved as to love.
> For it is in giving that we receive;
> it is in pardoning that we are pardoned;
> and it is in dying that we are born to eternal life.

One part of developing greater maturity is having the wisdom, to paraphrase another famous prayer, to know what we can and cannot change, and to put our energy into the one and not the other. The biblical equivalent to differentiation is wisdom. People feel calmer and develop greater mastery over their lives when they gain this wisdom.

Our work as counselors is a magnificent privilege. I see counselees clarify the principles and values by which they want to live their lives and discover the means needed for differentiating a self. It is always for the good when this happens. I enjoy watching them discover new things about the people with whom they have grown up, changing self in relation to these people, and seeing them develop the strength and skills they need to do the best they can within a life of tribulation. I wish the same for you in your ministry.

Appendix 1

Family Diagram Symbols

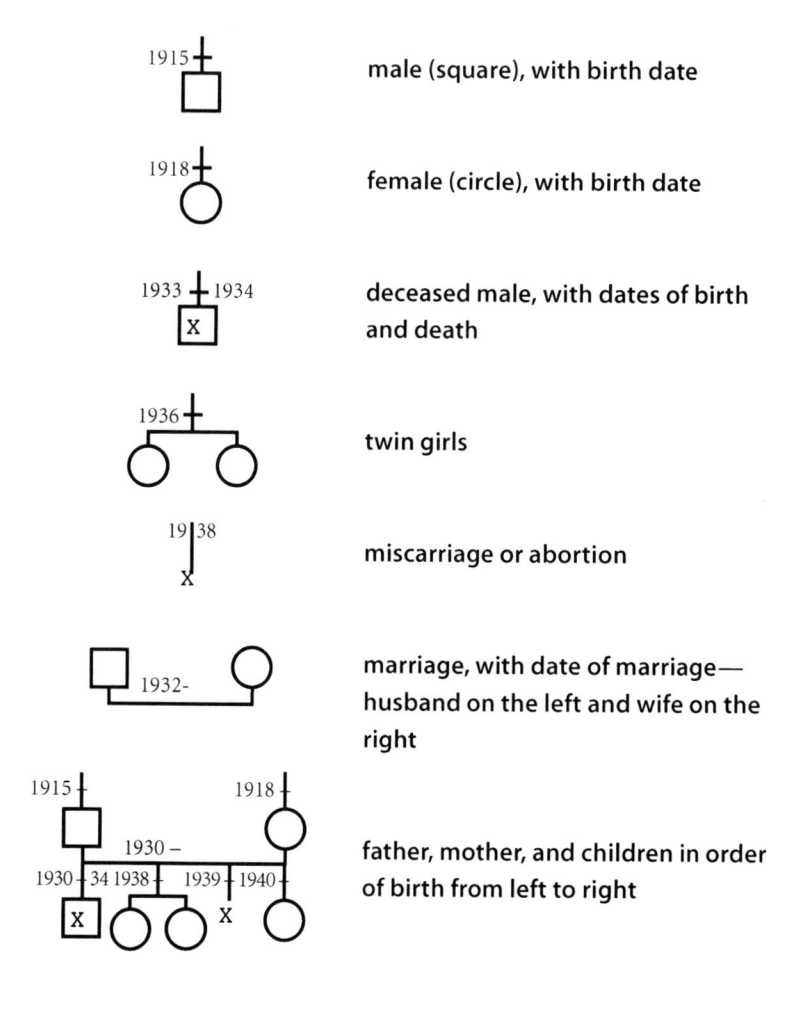

1915 ☐	male (square), with birth date
1918 ○	female (circle), with birth date
1933 ☒ 1934	deceased male, with dates of birth and death
1936 ○○	twin girls
19|38 X	miscarriage or abortion
☐—1932—○	marriage, with date of marriage—husband on the left and wife on the right
1915 ☐ — 1930 — 1918 ○ ; 1930–34 ☒, 1938 ○, 1939 X, 1940 ○	father, mother, and children in order of birth from left to right

237

Appendix 1

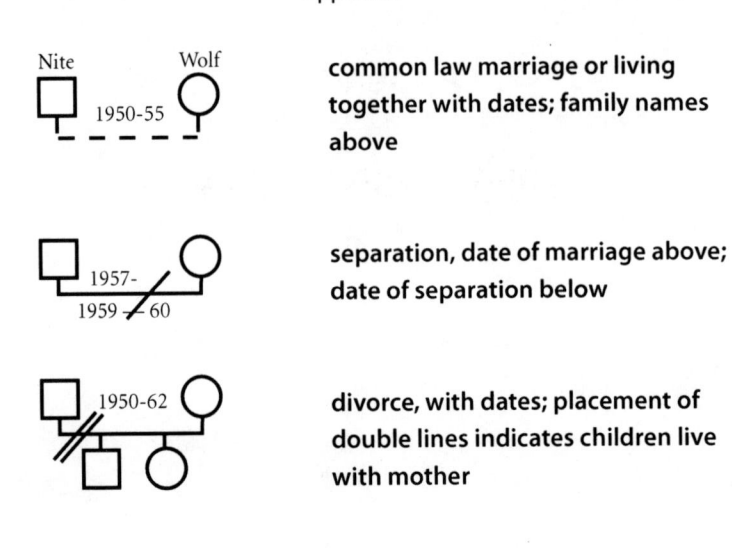

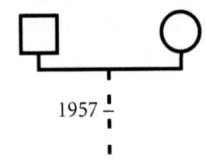

Nite Wolf
□ – – – ○   1950-55

common law marriage or living together with dates; family names above

□ 1957- ╱ ○
    1959 ╱ 60

separation, date of marriage above; date of separation below

□ ╱╱ 1950-62 ○
  □   ○

divorce, with dates; placement of double lines indicates children live with mother

□   ○
  1957 ┊

foster or adopted child, with birth dates below and date of entering family above

Appendix 2

Training Programs in Bowen Family Systems Theory

The Bowen Center for the Study of the Family offers introductory to advanced training opportunities at the Georgetown Family Center in Washington, D.C. For information, go to www.thebowencenter.org.

The programs listed below are directed by persons trained in Bowen Family Systems Theory. For information about learning opportunities offered at these locations, go to the websites provided.

Programs in Bowen Theory
Sonoma County, California
www.programsinbowentheory.org

Living Systems
Vancouver, British Columbia
www.livingsystems.ca

The Center for Family Consultation
Evanston, Illinois
www.thecenterforfamilyconsultation.com

The New England Seminar on Bowen Theory
Dorchester, Massachusetts
http://www.bowentheoryne.org

Princeton Family Center
Princeton, New Jersey
www.princetonfamilycenter.org

Center for the Study of Natural Systems and the Family
Houston, Texas
www.csnsf.org

CSNSF Border Programs
El Paso, Texas/Juarez, Mexico
www.csnsf.org/borderprograms
Please note: This website is available in English and Spanish.

The Prairie Center for Family Studies
Manhattan, Kansas
www.theprairiecenter.com

Southern California Education and Training in Bowen Family Systems Theory
San Diego, California
www.socalbowentheory.com

The Kansas City Center for Family and Organizational Systems
Kansas City, Missouri
www.kcfamilysystems.com

Western Pennsylvania Family Center
Pittsburgh, Pennsylvania
www.wpfc.net

Vermont Center for Family Studies
Essex Junction, Vermont
www.vermontcenterforfamilystudies.org

Source: www.thebowencenter.org/pages/outsideprograms.html
(accessed May 10, 2010)

Selected Bibliography

Bowen, Murray. 1978. *Family Therapy in Clinical Practice.* New York: Jason Aronson.

Friedman, Edwin H. 1985. *Generation to Generation: Family Process in Church and Synagogue.* New York: Guilford.

Guerin, Philip J., Leo Fay, Susan L. Burden, and Judith Gilbert Kautto. 1987. *The Evaluation and Treatment of Marital Conflict: A Four-Stage Approach.* New York: Basic Books.

Hendrix, Harville, *Getting the Love That You Want: A Guide for Couples, Twentieth-Anniversary Edition.* New York: Holt.

Greenberg, Leslie S., and Susan M. Johnson. 2010. *Emotionally Focused Therapy for Couples.* New York and London: Guilford.

Kerr, Michael E., and Murray Bowen. 1988. *Family Evaluation: The Role of Family as an Emotional Unit That Governs Individual Behavior and Development.* New York: Norton.

Papero, Daniel V. 1990. *Bowen Family Systems Theory.* Boston: Allyn and Bacon.

Richardson, Lois, and Ronald W. Richardson. 1990. *Birth Order and You: How Your Sex and Position in the Family Affects Your Personality and Relationships.* Vancouver, B.C.: Self-Counsel.

Richardson, Ronald W. 2005. *Becoming a Healthier Pastor: Family Systems Theory and the Pastor's Own Family.* Creative Pastoral Care and Counseling. Minneapolis: Fortress Press.

———. 2008. *Becoming Your Best: A Self-Help Guide for Thinking People.* Minneapolis: Augsburg Books.

———. 1996. *Creating a Healthier Church: Family Systems Theory, Leadership, and Congregational Life*. Creative Pastoral Care and Counseling. Minneapolis: Fortress Press.

———. 1984. *Family Ties That Bind: A Self-Help Guide to Change through Family of Origin Therapy*. Vancouver, B.C.: Self-Counsel.

Schnarch, David M. 1991. *Constructing the Sexual Crucible: An Integration of Sexual and Marital Therapy*. New York: Norton.

Titelman, Peter. 1998. *Clinical Applications of Bowen Family Systems Theory*. New York: Haworth.

Index

abandonment, fear of, 116
abuse, 74, 107, 233–34
   assessment for, 114–17
Adam and Eve (biblical characters), 9, 12
affairs, 91, 113, 151–55
agency and emotionality, 52
alcohol abuse, 70, 116–17
Allen, Woody, 123
American Association for Marriage and Family Therapy, 231
anxiety, 25–31
   acute, 26, 65, 69
   and alcohol abuse, 70
   and change, 216
   chronic, 25, 26–27, 30, 69, 111, 190
   of counselors, 189
   degree of in individuals, 25
   and family life cycle, 65, 71, 80
   and fusion, 27–29
   and individuality, 21–22, 29–31
   as infectious, 69
   reducing, 119–22
   and rescuing, 10
   signs of, 188
   as threat, 25
   and togetherness, 21–22, 29–31
   and triangles, 45
   and vulnerability, 99, 112
arguing and connection, 49
assessments, 103–4, 108, 109
   for abuse, 114–17
   criteria, 111–14
automatic behavior, 122–23
autonomy, 16, 94

Becoming a Healthier Pastor (Richardson), 211, 215
biofeedback, 25–26
birth order. *See* sibling position
bitterness, 113–14
   example, 178–81
blaming, 79, 115, 152
Bowen, Murray, 5, 235
   on anxiety, 25
   on closeness, 34
   on detriangling, 149
   on differentiation of self, 12–13, 33, 39, 44
   on family systems, 6–7
   on fusion, 28

Bowen, Murray (*continued*)
  interview, 231
  on pseudo-self, 36
  on reciprocity, 74
  on sibling position, 66
  on significant other, 91–92
  on symptoms, 69–70
  on triangles, 45
  on triangular process, 78–79
  on viewing conflict, 124
Bowen family systems theory, 6–7
  on autonomy, 93–94
  characteristics, 15
  on counseling, 86–87
  on emotional latitude, 87–88
  family diagrams, 110, 215, 237–38
  family life cycle, 65–66
  on principles, 229–30
  on stability/instability, 16
  on symptoms, 69–70
  training programs, 239–40
  See also counseling; family-of-origin work

calmness
  and anxiety, 42, 69, 80, 120, 151
  in counseling, 18, 120, 186
  and dyadic interaction, 50
  and togetherness/individuality, 21
  and triangles, 48
causation, 11
change, 15–16, 149–51, 160–61, 216, 218
character, 231–32, 233
children and projection, 15, 69, 77–78, 79–81, 171
closeness
  close/distance dance, 51–53, 136
  defined, 35–36

  and distancing, 48–53
  and fusion, 34
  See also emotional pursuers/distancers
coaching
  concerns in, 218–21
  counseling as, 95–96
  example of, 198–203
  family-of-origin work, 211–23
  and safety, 213–14
  supervisors for, 221
  See also counseling
comfort zones, 48
communication, 124, 155–56
companionate contract, 61
connectedness and arguing, 49
Constructing the Sexual Crucible (Schnarch), 154
counseling, 12–13
  altering emotional climate, 122–23
  assessment for abuse, 114–17
  assessments in, 103–4, 108, 109, 111–14
  and being in charge, 123–26, 132
  as coaching, 95–96
  completion session, 104
  confidentiality in, 108
  counselor anxiety, 121–22
  curiosity in, 219
  and dual relationships, 102–3
  engaging people, 134–35
  expectations of, 224
  and expression of feelings, 94–95
  and family expectations, 137–40
  family history of counselor, 89–90
  fee setting, 106
  first contact, 99–101
  first session, 104–7, 127–32, 225

fourth session, 108–10
goals for, 119–40
inner vs. interactive processes, 126–27, 161, 166
and interruptions, 132
marital, 61–62, 100
middle phase, 195–209, 225, 226
and motivation, 198, 211
and neutrality, 96–97, 99
and openness, 74, 101, 216
premature termination, 223–25
providing, 4
and reciprocity, 74
referrals, 74
on relational process, 126–27, 135–37
relationship, 85–86, 90–91
as representation of God, 92
and safety, 213–14
second/third sessions, 107–8
and secrets, 101–2
and self-focus, 133–34, 157–60, 232
and symptomatic mechanisms, 69–70
termination example, 227–28
termination phase, 223–30
and themes, 221
and transference, 86–87, 95, 219
transition phase, 186–88, 225
triangles in, 45–46, 99, 141–56
See also family-of-origin work
courage, 188
criticism, 157–58
cutoffs, 15, 71, 80, 202, 203–9, 221

Darwin, Charles, 5
David and Bathsheba (biblical characters), 46
detriangling, 58–59, 149, 155, 217
differentiation of self, 12–13, 15, 33–44, 219–20, 234
and anxiety, 27, 29
and closeness/distancing, 71
continuum of, 39–44, 64
defined, 36, 231
degree of in individuals, 25, 133
functional, 65
vs. fusion, 27, 30, 37, 40–41
and individuality, 124
vs. isolation, 30
and leadership, 44
in marriage, 63–64
precursors of, 173–74
and projection to children, 77
and triangles, 216–18
and trust, 135
and wisdom, 235
distancing
and affairs, 154
close/distance dance, 51–53, 136, 157–60
and closeness, 48–53
vs. detriangling, 217
as symptomatic mechanism, 69, 70–71
types, 50–51
See also emotional pursuers/distancers
divorce
after counseling, 226
and bitterness, 114
as change, 15
and death of child, 43
emotional, 71
and family life cycle, 65
as loss, 26
and marital contract, 61
and one-partner counseling, 101
rate, 67
and sex, 112
Doherty, William, 231

domination, 6
drinking. *See* alcohol abuse
dysfunction
  and reciprocity, 74–77
  as symptomatic mechanism, 69
  and triangles, 46–47

EFT. *See* Emotionally Focused Therapy (EFT)
emotional attachment. *See* unresolved emotional attachment
emotional fusion. *See* fusion
Emotionally Focused Therapy (EFT), 94
emotional pursuers/distancers, 22, 48–53, 112, 136, 154, 189, 217–18. *See also* closeness; distancing
emotional systems
  and context for families, 8–11
  and continuum of differentiation, 39–40, 64
  and cutoff, 15
  described, 17–19
  and domination of emotion, 40–41
  and feelings, 20
  and latitude, 87–88
  and life decisions, 37
  nuclear family, 15
  process characteristics, 15
  process in families, 7–8, 166
  societal, 15
  and solid self, 42–43
  triangles in, 45
empathetic listening, 120–21
emptiness, example, 181–83
Eve (biblical character). *See* Adam and Eve (biblical characters)

faith, 64–65, 190, 228–30, 235
families
  anxiety in, 70, 80
  and emotional context, 8–11
  emotional expectations, 137–39, 192, 212
  emotional process in, 7–8
  family contract, 61
  family life cycle, 65–66
  and function, 10, 12
  fusion in, 196
  as group, 8
  and heavy drinking, 70
  interactions, 6
  as primary triangle, 53, 148
  researching, 212–15
  and romantic expectations, 63
  and understanding human functioning, 7
family-of-origin work
  coaching, 211–21
  described, 140
  example, 198–203
  family diagrams, 110, 215, 237–38
  as middle-phase counseling, 195
  preparing for, 197–98
  readiness for, 156, 186
  researching family, 212–15
  and theory/practice, 9
  and unresolved emotional attachment, 63, 111, 137, 184, 191, 195–97, 212
family systems. *See* Bowen family systems theory
Family Ties that Bind (Richardson), 208, 211
fear, 188
feelings
  awareness of, 220
  defined, 20

expression of, 94–95
in transition period, 187–88
finger-temperature machine, 25
Francis of Assisi, St., 235
Freud, Sigmund, 6
fusion
and closeness, 34
defined, 27–28
vs. differentiation of self, 27, 30, 37, 40–41
family, 196
in marriage, 63–64
and reciprocity, 74
and responsibility, 72–73
and triangles, 73–74
and we-ness, 47, 64

galvanic skin response (GSR), 25
goals
for counseling process, 119–40
focus on, 42, 44, 189, 203
God, representation of, 92
Gottman, John, 26
GSR. *See* galvanic skin response (GSR)
Guerin, Philip, 113, 146

Hendrix, Harville, 94
Holy Spirit, 235
humanity doctrine, 12
humor, 123, 143
hurt, example, 174–78

identity
desire for uniqueness, 22
individuality
and anxiety, 21–22, 30
support for, 124
and togetherness, 21–24, 125–26
individuals
degree of anxiety, 25

differentiation of self, 25
and human functioning, 87
and problems, 7
and triangles, 45
intellectual systems, 19–20, 38
intimacy, defined, 35
irreconcilable differences, 62

Johnson, Sue, 94
John the Baptist, 12, 97

leadership and differentiation continuum, 44
loss, 16, 17, 26, 66

marriage
and accommodation, 35
assessment criteria, 111–14
and closeness/distancing, 71
conflict as symptomatic mechanism, 69, 72–74, 81
counseling, 61–62
and differentiation, 66
expectations, 226
and faith, 64–65
fusion in, 31, 69
marital contract, 61–62
and sibling position, 67
and togetherness, 23
and triangles, 46, 81
See also counseling
Midler, Bette, 19
motivation, language of, 10
muddlers, 198

neutrality, 10, 58–60, 96–97, 99, 217. *See also* objectivity

objectivity, 19. *See also* neutrality
observation, 5, 6
openness, 74, 101, 216

passive-agressiveness, 76
passivity, 6
pastoral counseling. *See* counseling
projection process
   and children, 15, 69, 77–78, 79–81, 171
   multigenerational, 15
   and sibling position, 67, 68
   as symptomatic mechanism, 69
pseudo-self, 36, 64

reciprocity, 74–77
reflective listening, 120
relationship systems
   competence in, 44
   and focus, 42
   and relational process, 126–27, 135–37
   and togetherness/individuality, 23–24
relaxation strategies, 187
religious contract, 61
rescuer, role of, 9, 234
resistance, 134
responsibility and fusion, 72–73

sanctification, 12
schizophrenia treatment, 6
Schnarch, David, 154
Scriptures
   Isaiah 40, 234
   Romans 5:3, 231
secrets, 91, 101–2
self-definition, 59–60, 99, 142–44, 151, 200. *See also* differentiation of self
self-focus
   and bitterness, 178
   in counseling, 133–34, 157–60, 232
   example of, 161–71

sex frequency, 112, 154
sibling position, 15, 66–68
significant others, importance of, 91–93
Sontag, Susan, 21
spiritual crises, 188–90
staff groups
   and families of origin, 8
   and use of triangles, 56–57
stress
   chronic, 111
   cluster, 111
   fight or flight, 115
   in modern marriages, 227
   and relapse, 187–88
   and triangles, 141
subjectivity, 19, 125, 160, 170
suicide, 88–89
symptomatic mechanisms, 69–81
   listing of, 69
   and reciprocity, 74
   use in counseling, 104, 197, 219
   See also specific mechanisms, e.g. distancing
systems
   and attachment, 16
   characteristics, 15
   described, 15–16

theological anthropology, 12
theory
   importance of, 4–6
   understanding of, 85
   use of term, 5
   See also Bowen Family Systems Theory
therapeutic relationship. *See* counseling
thinking systems. *See* intellectual systems
threats, anxiety as, 25

togetherness
- in counseling, 124
- and individuality, 21–24, 125–26
- and manipulation, 31
- and marriage, 23

Toman, Walter, 66–67

triangles, 9, 15, 45–60
- affairs as, 151–55
- and change, 149–51
- in counseling, 45–46, 99, 141–56
- defining self in counseling, 142–44
- detriangling, 58–59, 149, 155, 217
- and differentiation, 216–18
- and dysfunction, 46–47
- examples, 46–48, 146–48
- fluid/fixed, 54–58
- and fusion, 73–74
- good friend, 148
- in-law, 146–48
- and labels, 220
- and marital conflict, 76, 81, 113
- and neutrality, 58–60, 217
- primary, 53, 148
- professional, 146
- and stress, 141
- triangular process, 78–81, 145
- working with, 144–45

unresolved emotional attachment, 63, 111, 137, 148, 184, 191, 195–97, 212

values, 228–30
victims, 9
vulnerability, 112, 135, 165, 171, 177, 190, 192

wisdom, 235